# Jung & Film

Jungian film studies is a fast-growing discipline, but this is the first book to bring together the best new writing from both sides of the Atlantic. The essays represent both clinical and academic perspectives, forming an essential bridge between analytical psychology as therapy and Jungian studies as a way of understanding the world. Scholarly thinking and analytic insight come together in focussing on the place of movies in our psychological development – both through seminal films such as *2001: A Space Odyssey, Blade Runner, Pulp Fiction*, and other important movies which exemplify key concepts in gender and typology. The post-Jungian perspective may be summarized as a truly psychological involvement with the imagery and narratives of movies which, through exploration of the emotional relationship between the unconscious and the image on the screen, offers a transformative experience for the audience. Christopher Hauke and Ian Alister have brought together an outstanding array of contributors from Jungian analytic practice and from the field of Film, Media and Cultural Studies.

**Christopher Hauke** is lecturer in Psychoanalytic Studies at Goldsmiths College, University of London, and an IAAP Jungian Analyst in private practice in Kent. He has recently published *Jung and the Postmodern: The Interpretation of Realities* (Routledge, 2000).

**Ian Alister** is a professional member of the Society of Analytical Psychology (SAP), in full-time private practice in Cambridge. He is currently involved in the analytic training and teaching of supervision at the SAP, London.

Ian Alister and Christopher Hauke are co-editors and contributors to *Contemporary Jungian Analysis: Post-Jungian Perspectives from the Society of Analytical Psychology* (Routledge, 1998).

# Jung & Film

## Post-Jungian takes on the moving image

## Christopher Hauke and Ian Alister

BRUNNER-ROUTLEDGE
ALERE FLAMMAM
Taylor & Francis Group

First published 2001
by Brunner-Routledge
27 Church Road, Hove, East Sussex BN3 2FA

Simultaneously published in the USA and Canada
by Taylor & Francis Inc
325 Chestnut Street, Philadelphia PA 19106

*Brunner-Routledge is an imprint of the Taylor & Francis Group*

Reprinted 2002

Typeset in Times by Keystroke, Jacaranda Lodge, Wolverhampton
Printed and bound in Great Britain by TJ International Ltd, Padstow,
Cornwall
Cover design by Terry Foley

*British Library Cataloguing in Publication Data*
A catalogue record for this book is available from the British Library

*Library of Congress Cataloging-in-Publication Data*
Hauke, Christopher, 1953–
     Jung & film : post Jungian takes on the moving image / Christopher
Hauke and Ian Alister.
          p.   cm.
     Includes bibliographical references and index.
     ISBN 1-58391-132-4 — ISBN 1-58391-133-2 (pbk.)
     1. Motion pictures—Psychological aspects. 2. Jung, C. G. (Carl Gustav), 1875–1961.
     I. Title: Jung and film. II. Alister, Ian, 1951– III. Title.

PN1995 .H394 2001
791.43'01'9—dc21                                          2001025532

ISBN 1-58391-132-4 (hbk)
ISBN 1-58391-133-2 (pbk)

# Contents

# Complete list of films

All About My Mother (Almodóvar, 1999)
American History X (McKenna, 1998)
Angels with Dirty Faces (Curtiz, 1938)
Any Given Sunday (Store, 1999)
Apocalypse Now (Coppola, 1979)
L'Avventura (Antonioni, 1960)

Bambi (Disney, 1942)
Basic Instinct (Verhoeven, 1992)
Batman (Burton, 1989)
Being John Malkovich (Jonze, 1999)
The Big Sleep (Hawks, 1946)
Blade Runner (Scott, 1982)
The Blair Witch Project (Myrick and Sanchez, 1999)
The Blue Angel (von Sternberg, 1930)
Blue Velvet (Lynch, 1986)
Boys Don't Cry (Pierce, 1999)
Breaking the Waves (Von Trier, 1996)
Broadcast News (Brooks, 1987)

Cat People (Tourneur, 1942)
Cider House Rules (Hallstrom, 1999)
Citizen Kane (Welles, 1941)
A Clockwork Orange (Kubrick, 1968)
Close Encounters of the Third Kind (Spielberg, 1977)
The Color Purple (Spielberg, 1985)
Crossfire (Dmytryk, 1947)
The Crying Game (Jordan, 1992)

Dark City (Proyas, 1998)
Dark Habits (Almodóvar, 1984)
The Deer Hunter (Cimino, 1978)
Dick Tracy (Beatty, 1990)
Disclosure (Levinson, 1994)
Double Indemnity (Wilder, 1944)
Duel (Spielberg, 1971)

8½ (Fellini, 1963)
The Elephant Man (Lynch, 1980)
Empire of the Sun (Spielberg, 1987)
Eraserhead (Lynch, 1976)
E.T. – The Extra-Terrestrial (Spielberg, 1982)
The Exorcist (Friedkin, 1973)
Eyes Wide Shut (Kubrick, 2000)

Falling Down (Schumacher, 1992)
Farewell My Lovely (Dmytryk, 1944)
Farribique (Rouquier, 1946)
Field of Dreams (Robinson, 1989)
The Flower of My Secret (Almodóvar, 1996)
Forest of Bliss (Gardner, 1985)

Ginger and Fred (Fellini, 1986)
The Godfather (Coppola, 1971)
The Great Ecstasy of the Sculptor Steiner (Herzog, 1973)
The Great Train Robbery (Porter, 1903)

Hamlet (Almereyda, 2000)
Heart of Glass (Herzog, 1976)
High Heels (Almodóvar, 1991)
Hook (Spielberg, 1991)
How to Marry a Millionaire (Negulesco, 1953)

Ikiru (Kurosawa, 1952)
In a Lonely Place (Ray, 1950)
Indiana Jones trilogy (Spielberg, 1981, 1984, 1989)
The Insider (Mann, 1999)

Jaws (Spielberg, 1975)
Juliet of the Spirits (Fellini, 1965)

Jurassic Park (Spielberg, 1993)

Kika (Almodóvar, 1993)

LA Confidential (Hanson, 1997)
Labyrinth of Passion (Almodóvar, 1982)
Laura (Preminger, 1944)
Law of Desire (Almodóvar, 1987)
Live Flesh (Almodóvar, 1997)

The Maltese Falcon (Huston, 1941)
Mask (Bogdanovich, 1985)
Matador (Almodóvar, 1986)
Matrix (Wachowski, 1999)
Mean Streets (Scorsese, 1973)
Mildred Pierce (Curtiz, 1945)
My Own Private Idaho (Van Sant, 1991)

1941 (Speilberg, 1979)
Ninotchka (Lubitsch, 1939)
Notorious (Hitchcock, 1946)

Old Yeller (Stevenson, 1957)

The Paradine Case (Hitchcock, 1948)
Pepi, Luci, Bom . . . (Almodóvar, 1980)
Persona (Bergman, 1966)
The Piano (Campion, 1993)
Pretty Woman (Marshall, 1990)
The Prince and the Showgirl (Olivier, 1957)
Pulp Fiction (Tarantino, 1994)

Raiders of the Lost Ark (Spielberg, 1981)
Reservoir Dogs (Tarantino, 1992)
Roman Holiday (Wyler, 1953)

Saving Private Ryan (Spielberg, 1998)
Schindler's List (Spielberg, 1993)
Song of Ceylon (Wright, 1935)
Stalker (Tarkovsky, 1979)

A Star is Born (Cukor, 1954)
Star Wars (Lucas, 1977)
The Straight Story (Lynch, 1999)
Sugarland Express (Spielberg, 1974)
Summer of Sam (Lee, 1998)
Superman (Donner, 1978)

Tender Mercies (Beresford, 1982)
The Terminator (Cameron, 1984)
Thelma and Louise (Scott, 1991)
Tie Me Up! Tie Me Down! (Almodóvar, 1990)
Timecode (Figgis, 2000)
Trainspotting (Boyle, 1996)
Trip to the Moon (Melies, 1902)
The Truman Show (Weir, 1998)
2001: A Space Odyssey (Kubrick, 1968)

Vertigo (Hitchcock, 1958)

Walkabout (Roeg, 1970)
What Have I Done to Deserve This? (Almodóvar, 1985)
Whistle Down the Wind (Forbes, 1961)
The Woman in the Window (Lang, 1944)
Women on the Verge of a Nervous Breakdown (Almodóvar, 1988)
Wonderland (Winterbottom, 1999)
Workers Leaving the Factory (Lumiere, 1895)

# Notes on contributors

**John Beebe** is currently President of the C.G. Jung Institute of San Francisco. His articles on film have appeared in *The Journal of Film and Popular Culture*, *The Psychoanalytic Review*, The Chiron Clinical Series, *Psychological Perspectives*, and *The San Francisco Jung Institute Library Journal*. In lectures and movie showings throughout the United States and Europe, he has brought an original perspective on Jung's psychological types to the analysis of film. (Dr Beebe's schema of the archetypes carrying the various types is presented in detail in *Living with Paradox*, edited by Anne Singer Harris.) His own book, *Integrity in Depth*, argues the role of the anima and the psychological types in fostering the capacity for moral wholeness. This line of thinking is carried forward in an interview entitled, "Typology in the Development of Integrity," published in the August–September 2000 issue of *In Touch* by The Educational Center in St Louis. John's elegant demonstration of the way the types structure the narrative of the 1939 film *The Wizard of Oz* forms a chapter of *The Vision Thing*, edited by Thomas Singer. John can actually be seen discussing American movies in the 1990 award-winning documentary, *The Wisdom of the Dream*.

**Pat Berry** is a graduate of the C.G. Jung Institute Zurich. She received a master's from St Johns College and a Ph.D. from the University of Dallas. Over the years she has been active in Jungian training, serving as President of both the Inter-Regional Society of Jungian Analysts and then the New England Society of Jungian Analysts. She has taught widely and is currently an adjunct faculty at Pacifica Graduate Institute. She is the author of *Echo's Subtle Body: Contributions to an Archetypal Psychology* and has an analytical practice in Cambridge, Mass. She also rides horses, a mean motorcycle, and is a national-ranked Slam performance poetry champion.

**Mary Dougherty** MFA, ATR, NCPsyA, is a Jungian psychoanalyst and art psychotherapist in private practice in Chicago. She is President of the Chicago Society of Jungian Analysts and is on the faculty of the C.G. Jung Institute in both the Public Program and the Analyst Training Program. She lectures nationally and internationally on the impact of Jung's thought upon creative development and artistic production, as well as on active imagination in the clinical exploration of gender conditioning. As printmaker and performance artist she has exhibited nationally and internationally, including the Museo Contemporaneo, Brazil, the Centre du Film et de la Photographie, Canada, the International Museum of Photography, the Cooper-Hewett Museum, Franklin Furnace, Yale University and the University of Chicago, USA.

Mary lives with her husband, Peter Thompson, documentary filmmaker and Professor of Photography and Film/video at Columbia College Chicago. They have four children and five grandchildren. Besides reading psychoanalytic theory, her interests include designing interiors and gardens and hanging out with her grandkids.

**Don Fredericksen** earned his doctorate in film studies from the University of Iowa. He is an associate professor of film, and the present director of the undergraduate program in film in the Department of Theatre, Film, and Dance at Cornell University, Ithaca, New York. He also serves as a faculty affiliate in the Religious Studies and Visual Studies Programs. He regularly offers a seminar regarding "Jung, film, and the process of self-knowledge." In addition to his Jung-informed scholarship, he has published *The Aesthetic of Isolation in Film Theory: Hugo Munsterberg*, and essays on the modes of film reflexivity, the state of film scholarship, and the analogy of film to music. He is also involved in seeing that some key works in Polish film scholarship are translated into English. At mid-life he earned a graduate degree in counseling psychology, with an emphasis in depth psychology, from the Pacifica Graduate Institute, and now practices part-time as a psychotherapist in the Jungian tradition.

**Luke Hockley** is Head of Department of Media Arts at the University of Luton. He has a Ph.D. in Analytical Psychology as Film Theory, and has published on various aspects of film and television studies, including special effects as spectacle and commodity and science fiction television. His most recent publication is *Cinematic Projections: The Analytical Psychology of C.G. Jung and Film Theory* (University of Luton Press, 2001). A related field of interest concerns new media technologies and their psychological and cultural implications.

**John Hollwitz** is currently Vice-President for Academic Affairs at Fordham University, the Jesuit university of New York City. He holds a doctorate in Psychology from the University of Nebraska and a doctorate in Speech from Northwestern University. He taught communication and film for nineteen years at Creighton University, where he was A.F. Jacobson Professor of Communications, and then served as Dean of the College of Arts and Sciences at Loyola College in Maryland. Dr Hollwitz has written a number of articles in communications and organizational behaviour. With Murray Stein, he was the editor of *Psyche at Work* and *Psyche and Sports* for Chiron Publications.

Dr Hollwitz is married to Therese Boyd Hollwitz, a clinical social worker. They have two children. He has a great love for the movies. However, he has been frustrated in his abiding wish to play middle linebacker for the Green Bay Packers, the renowned American football team. Convinced that age and athletic ineptitude are transient conditions, he pursues an avocation in athletic training.

**John Izod** is Professor of Screen Analysis in the department of Film & Media Studies, University of Stirling, where he has taught since 1978. He was Dean of the Faculty of Arts, 1995–98 and was elected a Fellow of the Royal Society for Arts in 2000. He is the author of several books and numerous articles. They include "Reading the Screen"; "Hollywood and the Box Office"; and a Jungian study, "The Films of Nicolas Roeg." With Richard Kilborn, he wrote *An Introduction to Television Documentary*. His *Myth, Mind and the Screen: Understanding the Heroes of our Times* (forthcoming Cambridge University Press, 2001) adapts Jungian psychoanalytical theory to the analysis of film and television.

**Lydia Lennihan** is a licensed counsellor in private practice in Albuquerque, New Mexico. She is also a painter, writer, and a freelance editor. She has a master's degree in Mythology and Depth Psychology from Pacifica Graduate Institute, as well as a master's degree in Counselling. Her background in the arts and humanities has contributed to a life-long curiosity about mythology, psyche, and culture, and how they are manifested in the arts, especially in contemporary film.

**Jane Ryan** lives in Las Cruces, New Mexico, where she writes about matters Jungian – watched over by the Organ Mountains and visited by mountain lions and foxes. Through the University of Luton, UK,

Jane is working on a doctorate which brings a Jungian analysis to the films of Stanley Kubrick. Besides film, she is also interested in applying Jungian thought to one's choice of vocation and she is researching an article, which may be the basis for a future book, on the airline service industry. Jane has five children and she is raising them with Jungian principles in mind. With some success – so far.

**Don Williams** graduated from the C.G. Jung Institute, Zurich in 1975. Since that time he has practiced as an analyst in Boulder, Colorado, USA, and has been an active member of the Inter-Regional Society of Jungian Analysts. His articles on film are online at the C.G. Jung Page (www.cgjungpage.org). He has been the editor of the Jung Page since its creation in 1995.

**James Wyly** holds doctoral degrees in clinical psychology from the Illinois School of Professional Psychology, and in music from the University of Missouri. His diploma in Analytical Psychology is from the C.G. Jung Institute of Chicago. He is especially interested in the relationship between psychology and the arts, and he has published a number of studies in this area, including a series of papers on the work of Pablo Picasso. In music, he is active as a harpsichordist and organist, specializing in the organ music and baroque organs of Spain and Mexico. He has recently performed in Chicago and in Mexico. His private practice of Jungian analysis is in Chicago.

# Acknowledgments

The editors and publisher gratefully acknowledge permission to publish the present versions of the following chapters which are published here with permission of the authors and previous publishers:

Don Fredericksen's chapter "Jung/sign/symbol/film" is a shortened and revised version of two papers titled "Jung/sign/symbol/film", Part One, *Quarterly Review of Film and Video*, 4:2, Spring, 1979, pp. 167–192, and "Jung/sign/symbol/film", Part Two, *Quarterly Review of Film and Video*, 5:4, Fall, 1980, pp. 459–479.

Lydia Lennihan's chapter "The alchemy of *Pulp Fiction*" is a version of a paper that originally appeared in the *San Francisco Jung Institute Library Journal*, Vol. 16, No. 3, 1997, pp. 65–78, and which also appears as a chapter in *The Soul of Popular Culture*, edited by Mary Ann Kittelson, published by Open Court, 1998.

John Izod's chapter "*2001 – A Space Odyssey*" is a revised version of a paper that first appeared as "Classics Revisited: Accounting for Difference in Two Jungian Readings" – co-written with extra material by Jane Ryan – in the *San Francisco Jung Institute Library Journal*, Vol. 18, No. 4, 2000, pp. 7–31, and which appears in another version in his forthcoming book *Myth, Mind and the Screen: Understanding the Heroes of our Time*, Cambridge University Press, 2001. Reproduced with permission.

John Beebe's chapter "The anima in film" is a revised version of a paper that first appeared in *Gender and Soul in Psychotherapy*, edited by Nathan Schwartz-Salant and Murray Stein, Chiron Publications, 1992, pp. 261–277.

James Wyly's chapter " 'Gay Sensibility', the hermaphrodite, and Pedro Almodóvar's films" is a revised version of a paper that first appeared in the *San Francisco Jung Institute Library Journal*, Vol. 17, No. 4, 1999, pp. 19–35.

# Introduction

This book widens the possibilities for film criticism and appreciation into areas untouched by other film texts. Many of the writers are extending their vision of film and the cinema to include themes that are implicitly or explicitly concerned with transformation and the "alchemy" of our conscious–unconscious processes. Such alchemical transformations can only take place where there is a projection to relate to, and moreover, one which requires a much larger screen than most of us can generate in our personal lives. Jung himself put it this way:

> the psyche is only partly identical with our empirical conscious being; for the rest it is projected and in this state it imagines or realises those greater things which the body cannot grasp, i.e., cannot bring into reality. The "greater things" . . . referring to the world-creating imagination of God; but because these higher things are imagined by God they at once become substantial instead of lingering in a state of potential reality, like the contents of the unconscious.
>
> (Jung, 1944/*CW* 12: para. 399)

We do not refer to God so much in this book – much more to a range of cultural manifestations and projections – but, among several ways of saying the same thing, why *not* think of the film director as the "God with a very big imagination": one that allows us to project our punier ones onto it with a view to transformation and growth. This metaphor grasps the singular importance of cinema as a medium of unprecedented technical capacity in articulating the imagination which, in its power, strikes many as (G)god-like.

Jung was impressed by what cinema offered in terms of the imagery, narratives and the dynamics of film – both photographically and in the human processes depicted. In an era dominated by materialism, where our unconscious processes, our images and our dreams are still only poorly attended to, cinema offers both a means and a space to witness the psyche – almost literally in projection. Cinema films deliver a contemporary experience set apart from "daily life" – collectively experienced with others in a dark place dedicated to this purpose. This experience of psyche-in-projection travels further and differently from that offered by the theatre due to the flexibility involved in the photographic medium – and especially when this is harnessed to computer-generated imagery. Cinema has the possibility of becoming an imaginal space – a *temenos* – and by engaging with films a version of active imagination is stimulated which can then engage the unconscious – potentially in as successful a fashion as our conscious attention to dream imagery and other fantasies.

In addition to this, and similar to the Jungian psychotherapy session, the experience of film offers a special place where psyche can come alive, be experienced and be commented upon. This book aims to support that commentary: ways of looking at the experience that will have a distinctive Jungian tone, just as the comments in a psychotherapy with a Jungian would have – as opposed to those from a different theoretical perspective. Often, the experiences sought and encountered in therapy can be both intense and painful and for this reason they are often defended against and avoided in daily life. Popular cultural forms such as cinema can provide the holding necessary for intense experiences in a similar fashion to therapy, making such experiences more accessible and more bearable. When an intensity of experience is mixed with the less intense, psychological and emotional replenishment and growth may be made more bearable and possible. As in therapy, the raw material offered by cinema is made available in a form that the subject can then work upon psychically.

This book also takes on board the developing area of critique that views Jungian thinking as part of a postmodern understanding of contemporary Western life. In this view, modernist, Enlightenment styles of thinking which tend to privilege only one side of an argument, or to hierarchise "truths", come under fire from the fresh approaches provided by post-Jungian perspectivism and pluralism (cf. Hauke, 2000 and Samuels, 1993 and 2001). Jung is being revalued as the psychologist who observes deficiencies in the specialising tendency of modern consciousness, but in addition notes how contemporary culture in its complementary or compensatory fashion also produces opportunities for the opposite to occur. Cinema – the photographic image that shrinks (!) time to moments and to "surface" imagery typical of postmodernity – is, in the post-Jungian view, the very medium that is able to direct us back towards depth in the psyche of postmodern individuals.

Cinema is a collective experience which involves both an individual response side-by-side with a shared experience in common. The postmodern attitude involves a valuing of subjective experience and small-scale collectives. So while films may be the epitome of a product mass-produced for mass-consumption, cinema represents a rebirth of collective, shared experience with, nowadays, a greater value being placed on the subjective point of view of the individual observer. These writers offer a deeper analysis from this Jungian psychological position which brings together popular (mass) culture and complex thought – not in a reductive fashion, as other psychological approaches have tended to, but in an expansion of the analysis.

This book is structured around different approaches to the Jungian analysis of film. Some chapters deal with the content and form of film along the lines of Jungian psychological theory – either broad sweeps involving the concepts of the collective unconscious and individuation, or, more specifically, concerning a discrete archetype such as the *anima/animus*. Gender themes in general are especially to the fore in several of the chapters, as are concerns around the advance of technology and science which feature in many of the films with stories set in the near future. Further approaches consider how alchemical imagery and the narrative of the search for the Grail enlighten our understanding of movies that, at first glance, appear unconnected from such themes. The writers in this volume bring clear perspectives so we may view these films with fresh eyes and deeper appreciation of the human psychological processes being expressed.

This facet of a post-Jungian analysis of film falls in line with a revitalised interest in Jungian ideas generally which is occurring across a variety of disciplines. One such field is literary theory, where academics in university literature departments are taking a great interest in writers whose work is inspired in the same way; these scholars then use the Jungian frame for the analysis of other literature where a Jungian approach is both justified and enlightening (see Rowland, 1999).

The book is organised so that those who are unfamiliar with Jungian theory may start with three initial chapters we have collected under the heading of "A Jungian Perspective". These chapters may be read in conjunction with the Glossary to orientate readers to the Jungian and post-Jungian approach they will encounter in more detail in subsequent chapters. All of the contributors, half of whom are members of university film studies departments, are very aware of the relationship of Jungian views to others in the field and although these feature throughout the book the specificity of a Jungian approach is the focus of this section. Don Fredericksen begins the collection by considering the contrast between a Freudian *semiotic* approach and the Jungian *symbolic* perspective on the psyche and to film analysis in "Jung/sign/symbol/film". Fredericksen is interested in accounting for the felt power of images in film – an account that requires more than an analysis from a theory of signs. He feels that film studies up till recently have had too narrow a vision and by using a Jungian perspective he wishes to add meaning and, he predicts, wisdom to such an analysis.

In a scholarly survey he introduces us to the semiology of Barthes, Wollen and Armes as well as the work of Christian Metz, Bettettini and the recently translated research of Jurij Lotman. Fredericksen notes how Freudian approaches have used Lacan and he makes the important distinction between the different meanings of "symbolic" in Jung and in Lacan. Don Fredericksen notes how previous complaints against the "old Freud" (as Barbara Leaming refers to them) do not necessarily lead on to a Jungian symbolic perspective. Moving from the tendency to assign fixed meanings to one which involves a multiplicity of meaning still falls short of an expansion into the depth of potential meaning that is entailed by the Jungian symbolic. The "meaning" of the monolith in *2001 – A Space Odyssey*, for example, need not, and should not, be reduced to a singular or fixed interpretation. This example is followed up in John Izod's chapter later in the book. For Jung, the symbol may be defined as "the best possible description or formulation of a relatively unknown fact" – thus an image that represents something is, in this formulation, actually a sign (see the Glossary for more on this). Fredericksen concludes with an extensive analysis of the bird images in *Song of Ceylon* (Basil Wright), and demonstrates how the Jungian symbolic approach adds to our appreciation of, and engagement with, the moving image.

In an extraordinary paper, Lydia Lennihan analyses the story and the imagery of Quentin Tarantino's *Pulp Fiction* in a highly original manner. Although the imagery and symbols of the alchemists are not the exclusive property of a Jungian perspective, Jung studied this ancient and medieval imagery in great depth. In doing so, he noticed a compelling parallel between the imagery and the aims of the alchemists and the phenomena and aims of his own method of analytical psychology. In a nutshell, he found that this early form of chemical experimentation – the oft-repeated objective to "turn base-metal into gold" – also involved the alchemists projecting aspects of the psyche into their work. As in psychotherapy, what they were in fact doing was working on themselves in a psychological fashion. The chemical reactions and the accompanying imagery were, for Jung, an expression of psychological individuation (see Glossary).

Lennihan tracks the alchemical imagery of *Pulp Fiction* and links this with the differing individuation of various characters as the film narrative progresses. The fate of the characters – how some seem to grow in wisdom while others shrink from greater knowledge of themselves – is detailed alongside the alchemical imagery that parallels these developments. The mysterious golden glow from the briefcase is a fine example of what Fredericksen would regard as a numinous symbol that would only be diluted and lost through something other than the present Jungian approach. Lennihan never indicates the degree to which Tarantino may have been aware of the alchemical connections she finds in his imagery, but, whether he was or not, it is fascinating to view the film as an example of the depth of the psyche bursting out in this product of popular culture. Of course, this raises the question of whether such an analysis is being imposed on the film or, conversely, whether such a powerful film cannot help but evoke it for one who has the experience and articulation to present us with her understanding as Lennihan does.

Pat Berry sees the emergence of film as a response to our need to become more aware of organising patterns for psychic activity. The stimulation of the senses within urban industrialisation at the turn of the twentieth century formed part of the conditions which gave rise both to psychoanalysis and the cinema. Cinema's technological power and diversity developed as one way in which subjects cope with the almost exponential increase in stimulation in their external lives, from the Industrial Revolution to the Internet. The bombardment of modernity required a discrete representational space or "digestion zone". Berry makes the point about the extraordinary simplicity of very early movies that the very act of filming transforms what is filmed – in the same way that speaking out loud does – thus creating a parallel to the work in psychotherapy. Berry also presents the idea that as life becomes evermore complex we need to master more and more; but with this thought comes the suggestion that a part of the mastery is accepting one's inability to do so, and instead to learn to dispense with what is unimportant – a theme in *The Straight Story* and several of the other films that she considers. In the films she discusses lies the idea of giving adequate attention to the minutiae of our internal processes, how editing and camera-work, lighting, music, the rejection of cliché, can stimulate and bring into view a second-by-second experience that we are all capable of but seldom attend to. We are running an internal movie all the time and in these complex times we need to be more conscious of it and its meaning than ever before, so as to have a better grip on and comprehension of the complexity of external phenomena.

John Hollwitz approaches his analysis of the film *Field of Dreams* (starring Kevin Costner) from an angle that seems tangential to the film itself. What, he asks, might account for the way in which the setting where the film was made – a cornfield in the Midwest – has been uncommercially preserved and now attracts many hundreds of visitors a year? In this case, a film's popularity and meaning for people has spilled over from the celluloid into an existing geographical space. Unlike the set of the house in *Psycho*, for example, which also draws visitors, this is no "set" but "just" a field near Dyersville, Iowa, USA. Hollwitz then proceeds to answer the question as to what it is that has been stirred by the movie, which then gets further projected onto such a *place*.

Before he proceeds, Hollwitz surveys important recommendations and caveats for the Jungian perspective on cultural phenomena. Particularly valid Jungian methods that he draws our attention to are *amplification* and the *dynamic nature* of symbols that are characterised by the way in which they promote psychological *movement* and are, to an extent, directing towards a *goal*. Above all, as he says, "if you seek psyche, look first for the visionary" (p. 86). Hollwitz points out how the power of the film – and probably the drawing power of the field in which it was made – lies in the way it invokes an archetypal theme: the search for the Grail. He notes the links not only between this myth and male individuation and father–son reconciliation in the movie, but also between the Grail's ability to discriminate between the worthy and the unworthy.

Neither heaven nor earth, "the field makes more sense as a mystical terrain or a geography of dreams" (p. 91) which brings his Jungian analysis alongside new Freudian views on the psychoanalysis of space (Pile, 1998). The Grail confers youth and heals a kind of psychological and spiritual impotence – something that is as relevant to the contemporary audience as it is to the chief character Ray Kinsella (Costner). Hollwitz deepens our understanding even further by linking the film's narrative with the myth of Demeter and Persephone and their connection with corn and the cycle of the seasons. Similar to the myth, *Field of Dreams* involves the loss of innocence and the move from child to parent. Hollwitz demonstrates how a Jungian approach – using largely the work of Marie-Louise von Franz and Emma Jung – enhances our viewing of the film considerably and, indeed, *moves us on* psychologically and spiritually.

It was Jung himself who, in many writings, urged us to be aware of how our hugely differentiated consciousness was leading humans to invent technologies that may then overtake and marginalise aspects of our humanity that we can scarcely live without. He saw a good deal of the pathologies of individuals and of society as arising from our failure to attend to the balance between a sophisticated, conscious rationality and other aspects of the psyche such as the spiritual, historical, communal and fantasy. Don Williams's chapter on the movie *Blade Runner* (Ridley Scott) brings this Jungian theme critically up to date with his phrase summarising the film's theme around, "the quest to determine for ourselves what it means to be human" (p. 111). He does so by focusing on the coming together of the couple in the film – one a human male and the other a non-human female who is the product of human technological ingenuity. In *Blade Runner*, Williams finds the opportunity to explore further the Jungian theme of the *hierosgamos* – "sacred marriage" – which is a way of depicting the integration of the conscious and unconscious by analogising it along gender lines as in alchemical symbolism. However, along the way, Williams covers several themes of modern life such as the postmodern quality of the narrative, the presence and absence of empathy, class and capitalism – connecting all these to a Jungian analysis of the contemporary psyche and its deficiencies. The concept of the "post-human" seems to be our current version of what Jung intuited as the result of our developing a one-sided over-rational consciousness to the neglect of the rest of the psyche. But, like Jung, Williams is not entirely pessimistic about this. Although humans may tend towards the "hyperextension" of these qualities – technology and power – in *Blade Runner* he also finds the hyperextension of love and of consciousness in a more fulfilling and creative direction because, "with consciousness which Jung called the second creation – we can also approach a future that is the best we can imagine and think" (p. 121). *Blade Runner* also offers the vision that technology is our possession and it is up to us humans to limit our ambitions around it. In the film this theme becomes expressed by the relationship between Deckard (Harrison Ford) and Rachel (Sean Young) and the triumph of love over power. Williams reminds us that Jung considered the opposite of power to be *relationship*, not powerlessness, and concludes that, as Jung asserted, humankind is "indispensable for the completion of creation" (p. 127).

Jane Ryan's chapter on the film *Dark City* deals with technology and post-human issues in a different way. The film holds elements of *Blade Runner* and *The Truman Show* set on a *noir Batman* stage, precursing *Matrix*, and is a narrative of individuation under the most extreme conditions. Murdoch is the hero of science fiction/science fantasy who has to descend into the underworld of the Strangers – the aliens who are disrupting the memories and ego-identities of the City's human inhabitants. His task is a classic encounter of a hero with the dreadful Other – and on the psychological level the attempt towards the integration of ego and self (see Glossary).

Ryan stakes a claim for a Jungian perspective being particularly suited to an analysis of *film noir* – a theme which is developed in a later chapter by Luke Hockley. She reminds us of how Jung drew attention to an ongoing imbalance in contemporary culture – one which favours Logos discrimination and cognition over its opposite: the irrational and spiritual. In *Dark City*, as in many *films noirs*, the balance is also missing "just as the sun is missing from the darkened city". Here too, the Strangers' abilities favour science and technology, and the hero's path involves an attempt to restore balance as in Grail legends of the impoverished kingdom that is in need of restoration. The dominance of vertical perspectives, shadows and psychological distancing between individuals equally press for a dynamic in the opposite direction which is then supplied by the hope conveyed by the story-line. All paths of individuation involve periods of darkness and despair, whether imagined as Jonah in the belly of the whale, the night sea journey or the dark night of the soul. For Ryan, *Dark City* grasps this imagery and develops it – through characters as well as film techniques – in a brilliantly dark portrayal of a soul attempting to strive toward the light and toward a degree of psychological and spiritual completion.

One of the most famous films that deal with the near future, technology, and mankind's place in all this must be Stanley Kubrick's *2001 – A Space Odyssey*. In his chapter, John Izod makes the point that man and God – or Ego and Self – are in an interdependent relation to each other. Izod sees the God of Jung's "Answer to Job" as a powerful and determined force – not as omnipotent or omniscient but more as an unsophisticated and primitive "consciousness" for whom essential areas of the psyche are also projected, and one in need of a relational interdependence as Man himself and, moreover, *with* humanity itself. Opposites are a central theme in *2001* – often rendered subtley such as the vastness and slowness of space compared to the vaulting ambitions of man, and the music of the cosmos contrasted to the bland discourse of humans.

What we can and cannot "bear to see" is another thread that runs through Kubrick movies. The computer HAL (interestingly the letters next to IBM in the alphabet) with its single eye represents a primitive part of the psyche, overcome by the humanness of astronaut Dave Bowman who has a binocular view of events. As he goes through the stargate we see his eyes taking in the radical stimulus of the journey. In *A Clockwork*

*Orange* Alex is forced to "see", with callipers preventing his eyes from involuntarily closing. In his last film, *Eyes Wide Shut*, Kubrick embodies the dangers of what we want to look at – and what we will not look at – as well as the counter-impulse to creative imagination suggested in his title.

In his analysis of a sequence of six films by the director Steven Spielberg, Christopher Hauke not only tracks the development of several important themes, but also makes a bridge across to the next section of chapters which concern gender issues. Jungian approaches are particularly enlightening in this field – perhaps more so than in other depth psychological systems. From a Jungian perspective, gender identities are not only regarded as part of a range of human psychological expression which is less prescribed by anatomy than by culture, but the imagery and representation of masculine and feminine are taken more flexibly for the symbolic content they convey rather than the literal man or woman we see represented.

Hauke takes six Spielberg films which span the last thirty years and tracks them for the way in which male characters develop in terms of their relationship with various Others. He points out how a shift from heroic autonomy – found in *Duel* (1972) – gradually involves an increasing integration of other aspects of humanity found in the women, in children and in the wider community as the Spielberg canon develops. The relationship between "belonging" and the outsider, conveyed through images of madness or primitive actions, is set within themes of resistance to hegemonic authorities, conformities and the theme concerning the necessity to leave and to return "home". Suburbia, regarded by some critics as a conformist, legitimising theme in Spielberg, is revised as more a necessary backdrop against which individual transformation has to take place.

Hauke uses some fascinating quotes from Spielberg's televised interviews to amplify the very Jungian theme of how one creative artist's path is expressive of a development in masculinity for the culture as a whole. In doing so Hauke notes the struggle to resist reducing movie narratives and imagery simply to influences from the director's or writer's childhood – an approach which has been ubiquitous throughout the last century and which owes much to the limitations of how many still believe depth psychology should be used. Above all, Hauke makes the case for the serious treatment of so-called escapist or popular commercial movies by pointing out how their very popularity – far from proving a manipulation of the audience – actually demonstrates a resonance with unconscious needs in the collective psyche to which the cinema frequently responds.

Luke Hockley begins with Raymond Chandler's description of Philip Marlowe's office from *The Little Sister* – one Marlowe novel that has not been made into a film. He does this to illustrate how our expectations of certain forms of imagery construct and confirm our conclusions: "perhaps in our haste to put our knowledge of genre to work", he states, "we confuse stereotype with archetype" (p. 177). In doing so we are at risk of failing to notice and appreciate archetypes at work within these genres – a warning that resonates through many other chapters of this book. The originality of Hockley's approach, however, lies in the way he applies a Jungian perspective not so much to specific films but to *a particular form of film analysis itself*.

Hockley offers an invaluable and succinct discourse on genre theory in general terms and links this to aspects of Jungian analysis. For instance, he compares the emphasis on audience involvement with the film as "text" to Jung's emphasis on analytic understanding as "the fruit of joint reflection" and not the result of interpretations imposed by "one who is supposed to know". As in Jungian analysis, "audience-driven morphology", Hockley quotes, "assumes that film-viewers either validate existing mythological forms or require that they undergo revision" (Berry, 1999: 29).

In his survey of the variety of *films noirs*, Hockley points out how such different manifestations may be viewed as varying expressions of archetypes which in themselves remain unconscious and are only known through the images they generate. When getting down to detail, Hockley also brings in an archetypal view of particular signifiers found in *film noir* – the trench-coated detective in all his maleness contrasted with the woman as femme fatale. In this he compares psychoanalytic approaches involving castration fear with the view of male–female complementarity found in Jungian psychology, and post-Jungian approaches to the archetype as a "site of tension between biology and culture" (p. 192). Hockley is far from uncritical of archetypal theory and notes how it may eschew ideology on the one hand and have a determining influence on images on the other. He sees a way forward in the post-Jungian emphasis on deliteralising images as recommended by Andrew Samuels and James Hillman, a move which counters the literalising tendencies of psychoanalytic ideas on, for example, "decoding" the Oedipal desires which they detect in the representation of certain pairs of men and women on screen.

Hockley finishes with an examination of *LA Confidential* (Hanson, DVD 1997), where he shows how the representational aspect of films may be "downplayed in favour of exploring their psychologically expressive qualities" (p. 190) thus making the watching of films, and the reflection this stimulates, a rich and meaningful psychological activity.

Mary Dougherty considers the way in which five popular films can be seen as a reflection of genderising practices, as well as being active agents in the formation of genderised ideas. Dougherty approaches the multiplicity of roles which women on the screen can represent from a feminine perspective, thus offering a range which may be outside the audience's personal experience of images but which innate unconscious preconceptions can, nevertheless, "mate". She notes, in particular, how these very powerful images are carrying the emotional charge of the shadow archetype, "an image that my psyche metabolized at the level of body consciousness that awakened me to unlived aspects of my personality" (pp. 196–197). She points out that these shadow elements in the film undermine as well as reinforce conventional gender roles. In as much as the spectator becomes an illicit participant she is open to being moved by the emotional impact of the experience rather than defending against it in the guise of a critical observer. She quotes Jung's view that powerful images are the natural language of the unconscious, and that emotion is the chief source of consciousness. The ego immersed in the experience of a film can be moved at a level below that of conscious attitudes. Like fairy tales, films deal with universal issues at the level of the imagination.

Dougherty is also interested in the problems of feminist film criticism which can look too much for what is missing – as in Lacanian ideas of "lack" and Freudian notions of penis envy – rather than appreciate the creative value in an apparently "negative" view of the feminine, which always contains an opposite with which the audience can illicitly participate. The spectator does not have to be a victim of the overt political message of the director to achieve psychological enhancement from these film narratives. Dougherty is a practising Jungian analyst and is thus able to offer us clinical illustrations of how movies can act as a therapeutic point of reference where unconscious aspects of the self can be seen in projection, with a particular focus on developmental lacks and neurotic splits that develop along gender lines.

In his classic paper on the *anima* in film, John Beebe understands the auteur director to be akin to the Self in creating a living image of the archetype on screen, an image which in its evocation of "feeling-toned complexes" in the watcher acts as an essential bridge between ego and Self. Beebe emphasises the particular importance of the female image in stimulating emotionally relevant fantasy, and on the singular significance of *anima* as an uncanny and not a naturalistic presence. He underlines the capacity of certain directors – Bogdanovich, Cukor, and Hitchcock,

– to understand that cinema, unlike theatre, is a medium not of actors but of images, and in that sense is more closely linked to the transpersonal. Beebe's paper also takes up the idea that any dramatic production can be read as an opening out into many characters, which derives from the internal working of a single personality. In a film you can observe – and engage in active imagination about – the behaviour of an archetype (*anima*) and how she changes in relation to the characters she affects. This notion connects to Jung's idea of the analyst being fully in the work with his patient, and also changed by it.

In a detailed study of the work of Spanish film-maker Pedro Almodóvar, James Wyly points out further echoes of the singular power of the *anima* in the way that Almodóvar uses his actresses, particularly Carmen Maura, to personify such a wide range of registers. Wyly is drawing a connection between this and Jungian and post-Jungian ideas of the hermaphrodite, and he also notes how Almodóvar's work has grown out of the unusual socio-political context of post-Franco Spain – specifically the way in which the Iberian Peninsula was unique in Western Europe in not passing through the liberal revolutions of the 1960s.

Whilst accepting that anatomy does not dictate masculine or feminine qualities, Wyly differs from Jung in his understanding of the hermaphroditic position. Whereas for Jung gender construction evolves from an undifferentiated and therefore childish hermaphrodite, Wyly sees the hermaphrodite as separate from the male or female pole and as evolving from polarised adult sexuality. In Almodóvar's latest film, *All About My Mother*, the leading characters all appear to occupy this bridging position: there is no apparent need for opposite-gendered partners. Wyly describes how Almodóvar explores this theme in particular by inviting his leading actresses to embody difference, by such a woman playing a male actor playing a transsexual, for example.

If we are to summarise our view – in addition to what we say above and what all the writers convey in the following pages – these chapters say something about the way we see cinema as a psychological art in which, like any other art form, we allow ourselves to engage at a feeling level and release our own associative train of fantasies. Later we may reel them in frame by frame and begin to make sense of our emotionally charged imaginal response. Classical psychoanalysis began with the rule of "free association" – an awareness that we are all the time running an internal movie of associated images and sensations to which we pay scant attention. We can find meaning in this constant stream, but only if we allow our feeling and thinking to be in a more constant relation to these images, and, as importantly, we trust in their purposefulness. *It is not a new interpretation we need but a new attitude to our engagement with these images.* If this book has a specific purpose it is to bring together a series of structural possibilities, based in Jungian and post-Jungian thinking, through which we might – in an increasingly world-wide and cross-cultural context – make fuller sense of the imagery and imagination discovered in the social dreaming that cinema has for a century reflected.

Information on Jung and analytical psychology on the web: www. cgjungpage.org. Email the editors at c.hauke@gold.ac.uk.

Christopher Hauke and Ian Alister, January 2001

## References

Berry, Sarah (1999) "Genre", in Toby Millar and Robert Stam (eds) *A Companion to Film Theory*, Oxford: Blackwell, pp. 25–44.

Hauke, Christopher (2000) *Jung and the Postmodern: The Interpretation of Realities*, London: Routledge.

Jung, C.G. (1944) *Psychology and Alchemy* in *Collected Works*, Vol. 12, London: Routledge.

Pile, Steven (1998) "Freud, dreams and imaginative geographies" in A. Elliott (ed.) *Freud 2000*, Cambridge: Polity, pp. 204–234.

Rowland, Susan (1999) *C.G. Jung and Literary Theory*, London: Macmillan.

Samuels, Andrew (1993) *The Political Psyche*, London: Routledge.

Samuels, Andrew (2001) *Politics on the Couch. Citizenship and the Internal Life*, London: Polity Books.

# Part I

# A Jungian perspective

# Chapter 1

# Jung/sign/symbol/film

*Don Fredericksen*

The more we see the more we must be able to imagine.
Gotthold Ephraim Lessing

## Introduction

I want briefly to discuss meaning – meaning as we behold it in films, and meaning as we attribute it to films. I can as well say that the topic is explanation – what counts as satisfactory explanation, and what we mean when we say we have "dealt with" a film by explaining it. What follows is based upon C.G. Jung's distinctions between sign and symbol, and between a semiotic attitude and a symbolic one. To my mind these distinctions have immediate correspondences in film and film study, and far-reaching implications for the latter.[1]

By this discussion I hope to demonstrate our need and our capacity to be open to meaning – filmic and otherwise – of a kind and in places where semiotic attitudes have not previously found it. This need is not wholly or simply scholarly. Indeed, this essay grew from my own sense of personal and professional inabilities – an inability to account for the felt power of certain images, films, and film-makers (in their person and in their testaments), many of which I cherish; an inability to satisfactorily articulate the meanings of some very meaningful works and statements of purpose – and, out of growing conviction that currently fashionable notions of meaning (both those we have generated within film studies and those we have imported) are too narrow. By this narrowness we are denying ourselves a sense of meaning – and a wisdom – at once very old and very alive in the contemporary world, including the world of film. My thesis is that an understanding of the symbol and the symbolic attitude as defined by Jung significantly aids one in overcoming some of those inabilities and in escaping that narrowness.

## Semiotic and symbolic attitudes in depth psychology

Jung gives an extended definition of sign and symbol in *Psychological Types*, from which the following is selected:

> The concept of a symbol should in my view be strictly distinguished from that of a sign. Symbolic and semiotic meanings are entirely different things . . . A symbol always presupposes that the chosen expression is the best possible description or formulation of a relatively unknown fact, which is nonetheless known to exist or is postulated as existing . . . Every view which interprets the symbolic expression as an analogue or an abbreviated designation for a known thing is semiotic. A view which interprets the symbolic expression as the best possible formulation of a relatively unknown thing, which for that reason cannot be more clearly or characteristically represented, is symbolic . . . The symbol is alive only so long as it is pregnant with meaning. But once its meaning has been born out of it, once that expression is found that formulates the thing sought, expected, or divined even better than the hitherto accepted symbol, then the symbol is dead, i.e., it possesses only an historical significance . . . An expression that stands for a known thing remains a mere sign and is never a symbol. It is, therefore, quite impossible to create a living symbol, i.e., one that is pregnant with meaning, from known associations. For what is thus produced never contains more than was put into it . . . Whether a thing is a symbol or not depends chiefly upon the attitude of the observing consciousness; for instance, on whether it regards a given fact not merely as such but also as an expression, for something unknown . . . There are undoubtedly products whose symbolic character does not depend merely on the attitude of the observing consciousness, but manifests itself spontaneously in the symbolic effect they would have on the observer. Such products are so constituted that they would lack any kind of meaning were not a symbolic one conceded to them.
>
> (Jung, 1971, *CW* 6: paras. 814–818)

Jung is not making merely "academic" distinctions here – quite the contrary. Based upon his clinical experience and research into mythology and comparative religion, he is simultaneously countering a theory that constrains psychological meaning within the limits of the known, and arguing for the personal and cultural importance of the meaning which grows from the relatively unknown. His understood antagonist is Freud. Indeed, Jung's argument with Freud regarding the meaning and value of incest symbolism, published in 1912 and now titled *Symbols of Transformation*, first brought him to the distinction. We must understand that Jung's distinction between sign and symbol ultimately elaborates two distinct modes of apprehending and explaining the psyche and its products – not just two distinct psychologies but two distinct ontologies and philosophies of value.

This point is succinctly illustrated by Jung's and Freud's differing explanations of, and attitudes toward, incest fantasy and symbolism. Freud interpreted the incest fantasy concretely. Since this impulse cannot be maintained by the ego at the conscious level of the psyche, it is repressed into one's unconscious, only to return in disguised or distorted forms in dreams or neurotic symptoms. The psychoanalyst's task is that of making conscious to the patient what the patient once knew. This is accomplished by working back along a causal chain connecting the disguised or distorted wish to its undisguised source – hence Freud's distinction between manifest and latent dream content, the "dreamwork" which connects them by an ensemble of semiotic tactics, and the "dream censor" (see Freud, 1900/1954). Freud labels the distorted or disguised expressions of the incest wish "symbols," incorrectly so according to Jung. For the latter, Freud's "symbols" are in fact signs, standing for the putatively known, albeit repressed, desire of the patient to have physical intimacy with a parent. Their meaning can be completely explained by Freudian analytic procedures that reduce them to their underlying cause. When the explanation is complete, the disguised or distorted expressions *per se* are taken to be empty of meaning, for they have been exposed as mere covers. And the explanation itself brings patient and analyst to a full-stop; there is, as we say, "nothing more to say." Indeed, nothing more can be said, for the explanation has said everything. Or so it might be thought. To his dismay, Freud found incest imagery persisting, and persisting in its fascination, after its concretistic, allegedly semiotic meaning was made again conscious to the patient.[2] Jung's experience led him to conclude that something relatively unknown, neither explained by, nor satisfied by, concretistic interpretation and its attendant semiotic attitude, generates such imagery. That something, Jung claimed, is the psyche's urge toward rebirth – not another physical birth, but a spiritual birth into any one individual's truest "self." What appeared to Freud as mere regression into the infantile was for Jung a necessary step into the "maternal depths" for spiritual unfoldment and psychic wholeness:

Wisdom dwells in the depths, the wisdom of the mother; being one with her means being granted a vision of deeper things, of the primordial images and primitive forces which underlie all life and are its nourishing, sustaining, creative matrix.

(Jung, 1967, *CW* 5: para. 640)

The incest imagery generated by this urge toward renewal is essentially symbolic, linked as it is, simultaneously, to the relatively unknown depths of the psyche and to the psyche's unknown future. Jung's attitude radically revisions the meaning and value of symbolism, including that of incest. The Jungian scholar and analyst Frey-Rohn points out:

The characteristics of the symbol (its transforming and modulating qualities, unifying the opposites) should make it sufficiently clear that the symbolic truth was anything but a compromise formulation, the result of distortion and falsification – as was Freud's contention. In Jung's psychology, the symbol has the function of a creative "transition from one attitude to another."

(Frey-Rohn, 1974: 267)

The contrast between Freud's semiotic attitude and Jung's symbolic one is significant, not only in the depth psychological analysis of individuals but also in our response to the character and functions of humankind's cultural artifacts, including films.

## Matters of definition

Roland Barthes aptly states a warning that must be kept in mind as one works through the various definitions of sign and symbol *vis-à-vis* Jung's:

Now this term, sign, which is found in very different vocabularies (from that of theology to that of medicine), and whose history is very rich (running from the Gospels to cybernetics), is for these reasons very ambiguous . . . According to the arbitrary choice of various authors, the sign is placed in a series of terms which have affinities and dissimilarities with it: signal, index, icon, symbol, allegory, are the chief rivals of sign. Let us first state the element which is common to all these terms: they all necessarily refer us to a relation between two relata. This feature cannot therefore be used to distinguish any of the terms in the series; to find a variation in meaning, we shall have to resort to other features . . . expressed here in the form of an alternative (presence /absence) . . . It must be added that the distribution of the field varies from one author to another, a fact that produces terminological contradictions.[3]

(Barthes, 1967: 35–36)

The point to be gained here is that terms such as "sign," "symbol," "index," and "signal" are to be understood in each instance according to the differentiating criteria used by the author or authors in question and cannot be assigned stable definitions across authors. As we have seen in Jung's typology, the essential differentiating criterion is the presence or absence of a relatively unknown entity for which a known entity stands – presence signals a symbol, absence signals a sign. Like Jung, I want to counter the too-easily-assumed thesis that every case of semiosis in the broad sense is an instance of the sign-process in Jung's narrower definition of sign. That is, *I want to counter the thesis that every time one entity "stands for" another, we have an instance of one known thing "standing for" another known thing.* This inflation of the narrower notion of sign to encompass all semiosis leaves no room for the symbol as Jung defined it and denies legitimacy to his symbolic attitude. To counter that inflation and its underlying attitude in film study is my secondary and polemical goal. The primary aim is to argue for the meaning in, and the meaningfulness of, filmic situations in which a known entity "stands for" a relatively unknown one.

## The semiotic attitude in film study

Within modern American and European film study there are three major semiotic approaches: film semiotics as such, Freudian and Lacanian psychoanalyses, and the various Marxist approaches. In their various guises, they have set the agenda in the field for the last thirty years. My purpose in this section is not to attack these approaches, but rather to note in each case the absence of that which Jung designates the "symbol." That absence in turn signals the absence of what Jung tagged the "symbolic attitude." If there are films partially or wholly symbolic in Jung's sense, for which a symbolic attitude is appropriate, if not compelling, then it follows that the notions of meaning used in semiotic approaches are too narrow and in need of augmentation.

The first of these semiotic approaches is the one which conventionally label as such, instanced by works such as Peter Wollen's sketchy but seminal *Signs and Meaning in the Cinema*, Christian Metz's equally seminal *Film Language: A Semiotics of the Cinema* and *Language and Cinema*, Gianfranco Bettettini's *The Language and Technique of Film*, and Jurij Lotman's *Semiotics of Cinema*. The tasks these authors assign themselves are not identical. Also, with the exception of Wollen's discussion, these studies have moved, under the influence of Saussure and contemporary linguistics, well beyond consideration of the traditionally defined sign (Barthes's "relation between two relata") *in isolation*. The question of meaning has been increasingly moved from what Lotman calls the "semantics" of the film-sign to the sign's place and function within a larger system of signs – in keeping with Saussure's thesis that meaning is essentially generated by differences within a system.

In Metz's work one consequently finds little mention of signs *per se*, the emphasis falling instead upon higher-order concepts such as "message," "code," "text," and "system." (For definitions, consult Heath, 1973: 225.) Jung certainly does not ignore the systemic in dealing with the meanings of signs and symbols, but the criterion by which he differentiates sign from symbol is not placed there. Where the character of semantic ties is not given much attention, concern for differentiating criteria – and for the possible implications of different kinds of ties – will not occur.

Suffice it here to cite three instances where Metz – the most sophisticated and influential of the film semiotics scholars – reveals the absence of the symbolic attitude as it is understood by Jung. First, an example from his discussion of filmic connotation:

> Suffice it to say that cinematographic connotation is always symbolic in nature. The significate [signified] motivates the signifier but goes beyond it. The notion of motivated overtaking may be used to define almost all filmic connotations. Similarly, one says that the cross is the symbol of Christianity because, although Christ died on a cross (the motivation), there are many more things in Christianity than there are in a cross (the "overtaking"). The partial motivation of filmic connotations does not prevent them from giving rise quite often to codifications or to conventions
>
> (Metz, 1974: 109)

Metz's notion of the symbolic here is, to put it bluntly, strikingly mundane. There is indeed more "in" Christianity (its dogma, its 2,000-year history, its rituals, and so on) than there is "in" the figure of the cross, which reminds us of its crucial historical event. But to define the cross as a symbol of Christianity for that reason is, in fact, to define it as a sign, simply because one known thing (the cross) "stands for" another known entity (Christianity) which happens to have *more knowable* aspects to it. The cross, however, serves as a symbol of Christianity, not because Christ died on one and there is more in Christianity than in a reminder of that death by analogy, but because Christ himself symbolizes an urge to psychic wholeness which various cross figures symbolized long before Christianity appeared. The cross is an ancient quaternity form of the mandala which finds only one of its many "homes" in Christianity. Jung and others have demonstrated its appearance in widely scattered times and places as a symbol for a psychic process which goes beyond rational understanding – the coming to psychic wholeness through a union of opposites within oneself. (For Jung's discussion, see Jung, 1959/1968, *CW* 9:II; for an important complementary discussion, see Edinger, 1972: 131–156.)

A second example is drawn from Metz's criticism. Here one finds a similar divergence between semiotic and symbolic attitudes *vis-à-vis* essentially symbolic material by comparing his discussion of the "circle" at the end of Fellini's *8½* with Isabella Conti's Jung-based symbolic reading. Metz:

> Having organized his fantastic dance, Guido, holding his wife by her hand, himself now enters the circle. Is this merely the symbol of that complacent tenderness – Fellini's as well – that ties Guido to his own memories and to his own dreams, and of which he has accused himself (not without some complacency and some tenderness) in earlier sequences? . . . It is now Fellini's film that will commence. No longer is Guido at the center of the magic circle; now it is only the small child dressed in white, and blowing his pipe, the ultimate, the first, inspirer of the whole fantasy – Guido as a child has become the symbol of Fellini as a child.
>
> (Metz, 1974: 233–234)

Conti:

> In the end, Guido gathers the fruits of all his efforts, as the persons of his life, the symbols of his unconscious, the products of his fantasy, all transfigured by the creative act, join hands in a round carousel, a living mandala signifying the birth of the whole man and the reunion of the ego and the self. In fact, Guido too, abandoning with the megaphone his role of director and holding the hand of Luisa, joins the circle. The individuation process is thus completed. From it, a child is born, as only the little Guido remains dancing in a circle

of light at the end of the day. This child, another symbol of the rejuvenated self, is the forebearer of new hopes that will light the way to the man who has finally accepted his maturity.[4]

(Conti, 1972b: 161)

In contrast to Metz, Conti not only conveys the feeling-tone of elation which characteristically accompanies a time of psychic renewal and which constitutes part of its meaningfulness, but is able through symbolic interpretation (e.g., interpreting the child as a symbol of the rejuvenated self) to explain some of the resonances the scene has for viewers. Metz's description and interpretation do not touch the symbolic as Jung understood it, but allow the magic and the meaning to slip away unhonored.

Third, in keeping with the semiotic attitude in general, Metz tries to appropriate the symbolic for the realm of the socially and culturally coded – thereby closing off the question of whether or not the symbol's origins are deeper – from within a psychic realm that predates any such strictly human coding:

In general, if the sum of the effects of meaning we call expressive, or motivated, or symbolic, etc., appears to be "natural" – and is indeed so in a certain way, for example, to a phenomenology or a psychology of meaning – it is mainly because the effects are very deeply rooted in cultures, and because they are rooted at a level that, in these cultures, lies far beyond the various explicit, specialized, and properly informative codes . . . If as a general rule the system-user experiences them not as codes but as effects of natural meaning, that is because he has sufficiently "assimilated" them to the extent that he does not possess them in a separate state. Thus, as a paradoxical consequence, the deepest cultural codifications are experienced as the most natural.

(Metz, 1974: 78)

Under the general influence of semiotics and of Barthes in particular, we have become generally wary of assertions that "natural," uncoded, and "innocent" significations occur – assuming, in keeping with Barthes's claims, that such assertions are part of a vast, aggressive historical process by which the bourgeoisie labels its own world-view "natural" and rejects all others. Jung's discussion of the symbol reopens the question, bringing into play an historical scale much vaster than the one employed by Barthes. Jung did not deny that the psychic products he called symbols receive cultural and conscious elaboration; indeed, within religion, myth, and folklore such elaboration often extends over long periods of time. In the process codification occurs – for example, in the elaboration of religious dogma and of interrelated myths – and relatively fixed meanings are assigned. These so-called "cultural symbols" may appear in the artifacts and dreams of people within a particular culture. Not infrequently the symbol becomes so detached from its original manifestation that it "dies" as a symbol and becomes a mere sign for something known. By this means history and conscious elaboration continually move originally symbolic material into the semiotic arena. "Cultural symbols" do not exhaust the range of symbolic material, however. At another level, symbols tagged "natural" and "living" by Jung manifest themselves *spontaneously* in dreams, artifacts, and visions, with little or no conscious elaboration. They are not confined to any one cultural area or period of time, and they present a wide range of meanings. (See Mattoon, 1978: 99 and Jung, 1959/1969, *CW* 9:I: paras. 11–43. The latter is one of Jung's most powerfully imagistic essays.) Symbols at both levels occur in film; however, given film's social institutional character and mass economic function, cultural symbols dominate, in part because they are psychologically safer and more easily understood.

The second semiotic approach, the psychoanalytic, gained prominence in the 1970s and 1980s, as Metz and his French, English, and American followers expanded semiotic analysis beyond the *enoncer* (roughly, what is uttered) to *enonciation* (the act of uttering). Metz's work is based on the controversial reading of Freud performed by the French psychoanalyst Jacques Lacan, a reading whose essential thesis about the unconscious is that it is structured like language. (For two descriptions and critiques of Lacan's project, see Wollheim, 1979: 36–45, and Borch-Jacobsen, 1991.) Metz states at the beginning of his "The Imaginary Signifier":

> Reduced to its most fundamental approach, any psychoanalytic reflection might be defined in Lacanian terms as an attempt to disengage the cinema object from the Imaginary and to win it for the Symbolic, in the hope of extending the latter by a new province . . . That is to say, in the field of films as in other fields, the psychoanalytic itinerary is from the outset a semiological one, even (above all) if in comparison with the discourse of a more classical semiology it shifts from attention to the enonce to concern for the enonciation.
>
> (Metz, 1975: 14)

As used here, "imaginary" and "symbolic" are technical Lacanian terms, which can be glossed in this manner:

> Lacan distinguishes between the two stages of symbol-acquisition
> . . . whereas in the Imaginary stage the infant is involved in a dyadic
> or two-term relation, in the Symbolic stage it is involved in a triadic
> or three-term relation. The two terms to the Imaginary relation are
> . . . infant and image . . . The three terms are infant, sign – and the
> Other . . . The Other is that preexistent "world of rules" into which
> we are born . . . It is through language that the infant becomes
> constituted as an individual . . . he is therefore bound into an external
> and collective entity – the community – whose values and, above all,
> whose prohibitions he absorbs from its speech.
>
> (Wollheim, 1979: 37–38)

For Lacan, the unconscious is the discourse of the Other. If we can
assume that this "world of rules" is known or knowable, and we have
good reason to so assume within Lacan's framework, it follows that
in Lacan's theory meaning is bounded by, and arises from, the known or
knowable.

The third major semiotic approach is the Marxist one, of which work
*Jump Cut* (US), *Screen* (UK) and *Cahiers du Cinema* (France) – the latter
especially in a period after 1968 – stand as representative samples. I label
Marxist film criticism and theory semiotic because it characteristically
takes films as signs for known or knowable underlying processes which
are material and economic. The thesis upon which this gesture depends
is given in Marx and Engel's *Preface to A Contribution to the Critique
of Political Economy*:

> In the social production of their life, men enter into definite relations
> that are indispensable and independent of their will, relations of
> production which correspond to a definite stage of development
> of their material productive forces. The sum total of these relations
> of production constitutes the economic structure of society, the real
> foundation, on which rises a legal and political superstructure and to
> which correspond definite forms of social consciousness. The mode
> of production of material life conditions the social, political, and
> intellectual life process in general. It is not the consciousness of men
> that determines their being, but on the contrary, their social being that
> determines their consciousness.
>
> (Quoted in Eagleton, 1976: 4)

In what is now generally termed "vulgar" Marxism (by, among others,
Marxists), attempts are made to explain the "superstructure" of society

(its laws, politics, governmental forms, religious, ethical, and aesthetic notions) wholly as the result of a direct and unidirectional causal link from that society's "infrastructure" (its economic structure). Cultural criticism of that kind no longer has much credence. In its place we now see Marxist criticism that maintains the workings of various mediating factors between "infrastructure" and forms of social consciousness such as film. Also, the causal linkage between "infrastructure" and "super-structure" is seen to operate in both directions, although the primacy of the "infrastructure" to "superstructure" vector is still maintained. There is a sense of the relatively autonomous development of forms of social consciousness, and of the need to deal with them in their material complexity.[5] Notwithstanding the growing sophistication of Marxist film criticism and theory – which complicates the notion that the superstructure in some sense "stands for" the infrastructure – the fundamental semiotic gesture remains: regarding the forms of production and the forms of social consciousness, there is no ultimate mystery, and we again find meaning confined within the known or knowable.

## From the semiotic to the symbolic

I do not wish by my remarks to foster the conclusion that semiotic approaches are inherently "wrong" or useless. Only folly would deny that many films, perhaps a majority, are predominantly semiotic in character. (Why this is so is a crucial cultural question needing separate attention.) At times they are indeed disguised or distorted signs for known or putatively known underlying processes. Many appear to be manifestations – displaced or otherwise – of known social codes. (For an incisive critique of semiotic notions and theses, see Harman, 1977: 15–24.) In such cases, there is a felicitous marriage between the film-sign(s) and the semiotic attitude(s). To that one can agree, while remaining critical of the efficacy of any particular semiotic approach or project

However, I do find the semiotic approaches limited, and the semiotic attitude limiting. Semiotic approaches are limited to psychic expressions that are in fact signs, and to that subset of symbolic expressions for which one can attempt semiotic interpretations. Another subset of symbolic expressions is open to the semiotic attitude and its various approaches only by a kind of colonization. Such products of the psyche are, as Jung says, "so constituted that they would lack any kind of meaning were not a symbolic one conceded to them" (Jung, 1971, *CW* 6: para. 818).

The semiotic attitude is ultimately limiting because it either denies the existence of the symbolic realm by definition, or denies its existence in practice by attempting to explain symbolic expressions semiotically. Frequently it does both simultaneously, since the two denials implicate one another. The limiting character of the semiotic attitude involves a clear hubris of – and often a fear by – the rational and the conscious mind toward the irrational and the unconscious mind. Throughout his life Jung warned against this hubris, without ever denying the absolute necessity of reason and consciousness in one's striving for self-realization. For Jung, *the point is not to identify with either the conscious or the unconscious mind, but to forge and keep a living tie between them.* To this end a symbolic attitude is crucial, because symbols rising from the deep layers of the unconscious are precisely that tie made manifest. There are clear indications here of the dangers which attend the semiotic attitude's denial of a separate and autonomous symbolic realm, and which attend the semiotic approaches' attempts to explain symbols as signs. Edward Edinger summarizes these as a "reductive fallacy":

> The reductive fallacy is based on the rationalistic attitude which assumes that it can see behind symbols to their "real" meaning. This approach reduces all symbolic imagery to elementary known factors. It operates on the assumption that no true mystery, no essential unknown transcending the ego's capacity for comprehension, exists . . . The abstract, objective attitude appropriate for an understanding of outer reality is applied to the unconscious psyche in an attempt to manipulate it. This attitude does violence to the autonomous reality of the psyche.[6]
>
> (Edinger, 1972: 111)

Jung's warning regarding the hubris manifested in the reductive fallacy is founded upon a conception of the unconscious profoundly different and more comprehensive than Freud's. The unconscious in Freud's view (and in the view of those who follow him), is essentially constituted by the repressions of the conscious mind; its contents, once conscious and hence knowable, are knowable again. Hence, as well, Freud's semiotic attitude. Jung did not deny the existence of this layer of the unconscious, which constituted part of what he labeled the "personal unconscious"; however, he postulated another, deeper unconscious realm, at first in his writing termed "primordial images," later the "collective unconscious," and finally the "objective psyche." These various labels point to the fact that the unconscious at this level is not constituted by personal repressions of the conscious ego, i.e., by something once known, but by transpersonal factors that predate ego-consciousness itself.

When psychic expressions such as dreams, fantasies, and works of art are in touch with the objective psyche they have fairly universal characteristics: they can exert an extraordinary fascination upon consciousness, but for reasons that transcend strictly personal associations. They are impersonal and frequently nonhuman; often they are abstract, e.g., circular or quadripartite. In the case of dreams and fantasies, they come from within us, but strike us as having a life of their own. (The same impression occurs to artists who "create" symbolic works.) When they occur, they do so spontaneously, outside the powers of the conscious will. They carry large amounts of energy and have an energizing effect. These several qualities of the symbol make our symbolic experiences numinous. And they indicate a psychic reality to which each person potentially has access, but which transcends the bounds of personal history.

Most people are aware that Jung developed his theory of the archetypes in explaining such psychic manifestations, but fewer have a concrete sense of what he meant, or how he came to propose the theory. Some such knowledge is important, however, for an understanding of the symbol and the symbolic attitude in film. By substituting "symbolic" for "religious" in the following from Jung's preface to *Answer to Job*, we can form a quick understanding of his view. (This substitution is in line with the fact that the religious statements and experiences Jung considered in *Answer to Job* are symbolic.):

Religious statements refer without exception to things that cannot be established as physical facts . . . The fact that religious statements frequently conflict with the observed physical phenomena proves that . . . the spirit is autonomous, and that psychic data is to a certain extent independent of physical data. The psyche is an autonomous factor, and religious statements are psychic confessions which in the last resort are based on unconscious . . . processes . . . Whenever we speak of religious contents we move in a world of images that point to something ineffable. We do not know how clear or unclear these images, metaphors, and concepts are in respect to the transcendental object . . . [However], there is no doubt that there is something behind these images that transcends consciousness and operates in such a way that the statements do not vary limitlessly and chaotically, but clearly all relate to a few basic principles or archetypes. These, like the psyche itself, or like matter, are unknowable as such.

(Jung, 1958/1969, *CW* 11: paras. 554–555)

Archetypal imagery is symbolic because it links us with a living, albeit relatively unknown realm. This realm is not unknown to us because we have repressed it; it is unknown because consciousness has not yet or cannot reach that far. Jung for this reason, among others having to do with the therapeutic benefits of the symbolic attitude, found the semiotic attitude toward it inappropriate:

> Contents of an archetypal character are manifestations of processes in the collective unconscious. Hence they do not refer to anything that is or has been conscious, but to something essentially unconscious. In the last analysis, therefore, it is impossible to say what they refer to. Every interpretation necessarily remains "as-if." The ultimate core of meaning can be circumscribed, but not described. Even so, the bare circumspection denotes an essential step forward in our knowledge of the pre-conscious structure of the psyche, which was already in existence when there was as yet no unity of personality . . . and no consciousness at all.
>
> (Jung, 1959/1968, *CW* 9:I: para. 265)

It is crucial to understand that *this situation sets limits on the symbolic approach to meaning via the hermeneutic of amplification – just as surely as the semiotic approaches are limited in their own ways.*

Jung's understanding of the archetype is strongly informed by Kant's claim "that there can be no empirical knowledge that is not already caught and limited by the *a priori* structure of cognition" (Jung, 1959/1968, *CW* 9:I: para. 150). Jung claims, in turn, evidence for such structure deep within the unconscious:

> The concept of the archetype . . . is derived from the repeated observation that, for instance, the myths and fairytales of world literature contain definite motifs which crop up everywhere. We meet these same motifs in the fantasies, deliria, and delusions of individuals living today. These typical images and associations are what I call archetypal ideas. The more vivid they are, the more they will be colored by particularly strong feeling tones . . . They impress, influence, and fascinate us. They have their origin in the archetype, which in itself is an irrepresentable, unconscious, pre-existent form that seems to be part of the inherited structure of the psyche and can therefore manifest itself spontaneously anywhere, at any time.
>
> (Jung, 1964/1975, *CW* 10: para. 847)

Again and again I encounter the mistaken notion that an archetype is determined in regard to its content . . . Archetypes are not determined as regards their content, but only as regards their form and then only to a very limited degree. A primordial image is determined as to its content only when it has become conscious and is therefore filled out with the material of conscious experience.

(Jung, 1959/1968, *CW* 9:I: para. 155)

Having proceeded this far in a description of the symbol and its emergence from the archetypes of the objective psyche, we must now return to film and ask a crucial question.

## The symbolic cinema

Do we have evidence from film-makers for the emergence of symbolic material, with the universal characteristics described above? I think we do. It can be found where we might expect it – among the "visionary" avant-garde film-makers of the United States and Europe. The following from Larry Jordan stands as an example:

Color erupted. Just another of the eruptions which began earlier on the animated flats in black-and-white – the interior world coloring up, starting to dance and sing in a different way. I just followed, like being on a train, looking out the window . . . I prefer that the shots (images) construct themselves. This is not a semantic nicety. If one is patient, and sits there with the ego subdued, the images come to life on their own. I admit that this is not the *modus operandi* in all my films. Sometimes I do resort to construction and invention, usually when I am struggling with a new technical process . . . There is a good deal of trust that goes on in this kind of process. To say where the order or the rightness of the ordered images comes from is an insoluble mystery, leading out of art and into philosophy . . . If intuition is a dubious or feared process to an artist, that artist is in trouble.

(Quoted in Russett and Starr, 1976: 155–158)

Within the narrative commercial cinema we have, among others, the testaments of Bergman and Fellini. Bergman on the meaning of *Persona*: "On many points I am uncertain and at one point I know nothing at all" (Bergman, 1972: 21). In response to a question regarding the repeated appearance of certain images and situations in his films, Fellini replied:

A film takes form outside your will as a constructor; all genuine details come through inspiration. And what do we mean by inspiration? The capacity for making direct contact between your unconscious and your rational mind. When an artist is happy and spontaneous, he is successful because he reaches the unconscious and translates it with a minimum of interference.

(Quoted in Samuels, 1972: 121)

In these statements about the genesis and meanings of their works, or some of their works, Jordan, Bergman, and Fellini bear witness to a kind of cinema profoundly informed by the symbol and the symbolic attitude. In more general terms, James Broughton and Buñuel tell us something about the functions of this cinema. Broughton:

For me cinema is not social phenomenon or cultural questionmark, it is a potential oracle of the imagination . . . I am talking about the life of vision. I am talking about cinema as one way of living the life of a poet. I am talking about film as poetry, as philosophy, as metaphysics, as all else it has not yet dared to become . . . Cinema, like life, is only worth living when it is in the service of something beyond the explicit and the mundane.

(Broughton, 1977: 11–13)

Buñuel:

The essential element in any work of art is mystery, and generally this is lacking in films . . . A film is like an involuntary imitation of a dream . . . On the screen, as within the human being, the nocturnal voyage into the unconscious begins . . . The cinema seems to have been invented to express the life of the subconscious, the roots of which penetrate poetry so deeply. Yet it is almost never used to do this.

(Quoted in Kyrou, 1963: 109–111)

These several testaments point to the fact that the cinema in which we find symbols as Jung defined them, or toward which we can maintain the symbolic attitude, is not confined to one film type, but is evident in commercial narrative, and "experimental" films – and documentary, as we shall see shortly, in greater detail. The following list of film-makers, films, and images further indicates the breadth of what I will henceforth call the "symbolic" cinema. (This list is, of course, grossly incomplete.)

Where a brief naming of the symbolic theme, or material handled symbolically, can be given, I have done so.

In commercial narrative film: Kubrick's *2001* (1968), in particular the monolith and the end of the journey (encounter with the Self and psychic transformation); *8½* (1963) (individuation and encounters with anima figures at mid-life); Fellini's *Juliet of the Spirits* (1965) (individuation and encounters with animus figures at mid-life); *Persona* (1966) (the dialectic between persona and shadow, the work of a trauma complex in the aborting of individuation, and recognition of evil as a principle); Roeg's *Walkabout* (1970) and Herzog's *Heart of Glass* (1976) (societies devoid of a living link with primordial images and their impact upon the urge toward individuation); Welles' "Rosebud" (a symbol of wholeness, numinous but unrealized); Donner's *Superman* (1978) (the hero myth as part of the career of individuation); Friedkin's *The Exorcist* (1973) (the numinous encounter with evil as an autonomous principle); and Spielberg's *Close Encounters of the Third Kind* (1977) (the numinous encounter with projected images of individuation, i.e., mandalas), and Tarkovsky's *Stalker* (1979) (the encounter, via shamanic journeying, with the numinous as a defeat of the ego). These films display varying degrees of conscious elaboration upon the symbolic material and are of varying psychological and aesthetic value.[7]

In documentary film: Wright's *Song of Ceylon* (1935), especially "Part One: The Buddha" (symbolization of the elation which comes from ego-transcendence); Rouquier's *Farribique* (1946) (the meaningfulness of timeless rhythms of birth, death, and regeneration); Herzog's *The Great Ecstasy of the Sculptor Steiner* (1973) (self-imposed physical feats integral to an inner drive for a living link with primordial images) and Robert Gardner's *Forest of Bliss* (1985) (the reciprocity of the mysteries of death and life).

In personal film: sets of works by Jerome Hill, Harry Smith, Jordan Belson, James Whitney, Stan Brakhage, James Broughton, Larry Jordan, Sandra Davis, Bruce Baillie, Barry Gerson, and Leighton Peirce among many others. Here the number of films becomes very large, and graphic manifestation of symbols – for example, the mandala forms which appear in Whitney and Belson's work – has its most forceful filmic appearance. Many of these film-makers not only "create" symbolic works, but refer to Jung in their comments upon their work.[8]

## Dealing with the symbolic cinema: the hermeneutics of amplification

If the film-makers' statements given above, and the brief list just enumerated, offer a strong case for the existence of the "symbolic" cinema, they do not yet indicate how we might deal with it. This is no easy question. However, if the symbolic attitude is to have any credence as an interpretative approach it must be answered.

An appropriate starting point is the witness of the film-makers themselves. What are we to make of the statements by Jordan, Bergman, Fellini, Broughton, and Buñuel? When they speak of the positive character of the unconscious and its role in their work, are they merely attempting to rationalize the workings of repressed, infantile factors? If we believe this to be the case, logic will lead us to conclude that the films produced in such circumstances are themselves essentially cover-ups, and that the appropriate interpretative attitude is the psychoanalytic-semiotic one of causally reducing the manifest text to infantile, personal factors. (This would be an example of what has come to be called the "hermeneutics of suspicion," the semiotic hermeneutic that now dominates interpretative work in the humanities, from the foundation set by Marx, Nietzsche, and Freud.) In several related ways Jung balked at this attitude, which reduces even the most extraordinary cultural artifacts to *nothing but* sublimations of infantile factors. Clinical experience taught him that even neurotic symptoms have a positive, forward-looking vector – a "final cause" – which must be reinforced rather than destroyed:

> It would be unjust to assert that this reduction is wrong in a given case; but exalted to the status of a general explanation of the healthy psyche as well as the sick, a reductive theory by itself is impossible . . . Life has also a tomorrow, and today is understood only when we can add to our knowledge of what was yesterday the beginnings of tomorrow. This is true of all life's psychological expressions, even of pathological symptoms. The symptoms of a neurosis are not simply the effects of long-past causes . . . they are also attempts at a new synthesis of life – unsuccessful attempts, let it be added in the same breath, yet attempts nevertheless, with a core of meaning and value.
>
> (Jung, 1953/1966, *CW* 7: para. 67)

This statement is based upon Jung's belief in the self-regulating and purposive character of the psyche – neurotic symptoms being one way the psyche attempts to reveal a one-sided conscious mode. Symbolic art is another. By intruding themselves upon the ego's awareness, neurotic symptoms and symbolic art draw attention to the fact that a change of conscious standpoint is necessary. They thus perform a positive and healing function – if heeded.

Associated with his belief in the homeostatic, purposive character of the psyche and its products was Jung's denial of the distinction between manifest and latent dream contents, which are linked by all the deceitful, semiotic mechanisms of the "dreamwork" described by Freud's *Interpretation of Dreams*. In Jung's view, dreams and other symbolic expressions are typically inscrutable not because they are disguising their "true" meaning, but simply because we do not yet know how to interpret them: "We have no right to accuse the dream of, so to speak, a deliberate manoeuvre to deceive. Nature is often obscure or impenetrable, but she is not, like man, deceitful" (Jung, 1953/1966, *CW* 7: para. 162). Further: "We do not have to get behind such a text, but must first learn to read it" (Jung, 1954/1966, *CW* 16: para. 319). The symbol, as Jung's definition states, is "the best possible description or formulation of a relatively unknown fact."

So, how do we "read" symbolic texts? In answering this question, Jung takes us directly to the method for interpreting symbolic films:

> an exclusively causal and reductive procedure . . . breaks down at the point where the dream symbols can no longer be reduced to personal reminiscences or aspirations, that is, when the images of the collective unconscious begin to appear . . . [these] kinds of psychic material mean next to nothing if simply broken down, but display a wealth of meaning if . . . that meaning is reinforced and extended by all the conscious means at our disposal – by the so-called method of amplification. The images or symbols of the collective unconscious yield their distinctive values only when subjected to a synthetic mode of treatment . . . The procedure is not exactly simple.
> (Jung, 1953/1966, *CW* 7: para. 122)

One lesson of personal and social pathologies is that we cannot reject or neutralize the archetypes *per se*. We are left instead with interpreting their manifestations anew at each stage where old understandings are no longer alive to us. What recourse have we got in this necessary task? In Jung's view, we have one:

> Not for a moment dare we succumb to the illusion that an archetype can be finally explained or disposed of. Even the best attempts at

explanation are only more or less successful translation into another metaphorical language. (Indeed, language itself is only an image.) The most we can do is dream the myth onwards and give it a modern dress.

(Jung, 1959/1968, *CW* 9:I: para. 271)

What Jung says for myth is true as well for other symbolic imagery. In a very real sense, that imagery is itself dreaming forth some relatively unknown entity. The goal of amplification is to continue the symbol's own activity to that point where it is understandable to us:

[The symbol] attempts to elucidate, by means of analogy, something that still belongs entirely to the domain of the unknown or something that is yet to be. Imagination reveals to us, in the form of a more or less striking analogy, what is in the process of becoming. If we reduce this by analysis to something else universally known, we destroy the authentic value of the symbol; but to attribute hermeneutic significance to it conforms to its value and meaning.

(Jung, 1953: 299)

The hermeneutic act has the following character and function:

The essential character of hermeneutics . . . consists in adding further analogies to the one already supplied by the symbol . . . This procedure widens and enriches the initial symbol, and the final outcome is an infinitely complex and variegated picture . . . Certain lines of psychological development then stand out that are at once individual and collective. There is no science on earth by which these lines can be proved "right." . . . Their validity is proved by their intense value for life.

(Jung, 1953: 299)

(The wording for these two last quotes differs somewhat in the *CW* 7 translation: paras. 492 and 493.)

*Symbols cannot be reduced and remain symbols.* We have no recourse but to accept and value their irreducible complexity as the best possible, spontaneous expression of something relatively unknown or ultimately unknowable. However, since symbolic expressions are characteristically puzzling to us, we have the need to make an interpretative effort if they are to be more than curiosity pieces for us. That interpretative gesture is amplification.

Amplification occurs at two levels: the personal and the transpersonal. In those situations where the person from whom the symbolic imagery came is present, e.g., in personal analysis, one begins by collecting that person's personal associations to that imagery. Jung's method here differs from that of Freud; Freud worked by free associations, which quickly lead away from the symbolic imagery in a dream, for example to the patient's complexes. Freud thought himself justified in this procedure by virtue of the view that symbolic imagery is a disguise (i.e., a sign) for the otherwise inadmissible desires that constitute the unconscious through repression.

Jung did not deny the existence or power of unconscious complexes. On the other hand, he pointed out that if our goal is understanding the complexes, we can begin anywhere: word associations, Rorschach images, fantasies, and, indeed, dreams. But using dreams to get to the complexes ignores the dreams' specific character and function and, of course, it denies the dream imagery any *intrinsic* meaning. Thus Jung used a method of directed associations which, as it were, circles the dreams' symbolic imagery but does not leave it.

Personal associations are not always available, nor is a request for them always appropriate. This is especially the case with regard to public symbolic material, including films. Sometimes the material is so ancient (e.g., myths, fairy tales, and pictorial imagery) that no authorship can be assigned. At other times an author may be known and accessible, but may refuse to provide associations – on the grounds that everything he or she wishes to say, or can say, is in the artwork itself. We should respect that refusal. With some change, amplification can be used in film study as the means of dealing with the symbolic cinema. The relevance of the film-makers' association depends in each case upon the degree to which the symbolic material in the text has been consciously elaborated over time. In principle, the film-makers' personal associations are less telling *vis-à-vis* "cultural" symbols than "natural" ones. In neither case are such personal associations sufficient.

This is so because such imagery is essentially collective, transpersonal, archetypal. Only someone with an inflated self-image could maintain that his personal associations exhaust a symbol's possible associations. Rather, one comes to realize that while symbols come from within us individually, they escape our attempts to enclose them within the wholly or essentially personal, and irrevocably link us to the transpersonal.

For this reason the second level of amplification brings to bear imagery which is analogous to the symbol under consideration, but which comes from other sources. This analogous imagery is found in myths, fairy tales, folklore, religious writings and imagery, alchemical texts, archaeology, and the practices of preliterate people. Given our limited access to the personal associations of film-makers, film scholars amplifying symbolic imagery are by-and-large confined to the second, transpersonal level. In this state of affairs, our role is similar to that of an analyst *vis-à-vis* a patient. By definition, the analyst does not provide his personal associations to the patient's symbolic imagery. Rather, he supplies parallels which fall outside personal history, in such a way that the links between individual and collective, fleeting and enduring, are made meaningful. Likewise, in amplifying a particular film, we reveal its links to a psychic base broader than individual personality (as envisioned by the ego).

The process of gathering parallels operates under two constraints, both of which are tied to the fact that "in the unconscious all archetypes are contaminated with one another." The first constraint is that amplification should proceed only so far as is necessary to understand the imagery at hand. Were amplification to proceed indefinitely, the entire archetypal world in its "contaminated" interwebbing would be brought forth, and we would lose that foothold of intelligibility which is amplification's precise purpose. In discussing this constraint Marie Louise von Franz "likened the amplification process to pulling up a blade of grass in a field where all the grass is connected under the surface of the ground . . . If one insists on pulling hard enough, one gets the whole crop of grass attached to the single blade." (Quoted in Hall, 1977: 131; the point is put somewhat differently, and usefully enlarged, in von Franz, 1970/1975: 7.)

The second constraint is intended to deal with the same problem from a different perspective. Jung summarizes it in the following manner:

> It does not . . . suffice simply to connect a dream about a snake with the mythological occurrence of snakes, for who is to guarantee that the functional meaning of the snake in the dream is the same as in the mythological setting? In order to draw a valid parallel, it is necessary to know the functional meaning of the individual symbol, and then to find out whether the apparently parallel mythological symbol has a similar context and therefore the same functional meaning. Establishing such facts not only requires lengthy and wearisome researches, but is also an ungrateful subject for demonstration . . . One has to launch forth into exhaustive descriptions, personal as well as symbological.
>
> (Jung, 1959/1968, *CW* 9:I: para. 103)

Wearisome as this constraint is, it is absolutely necessary if we are not to find ourselves in the situation where everything becomes everything

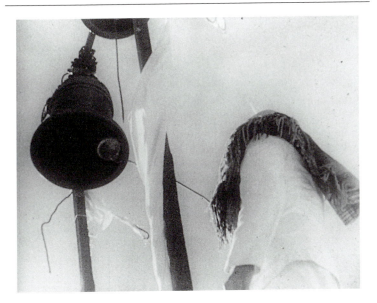

*Figure 1.1*  Man ringing bell at top of Adam's Peak
(Basil Wright's *Song of Ceylon*, 1935)

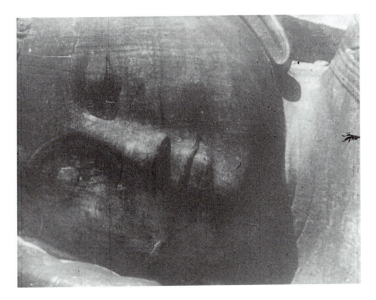

*Figure 1.2*  The Buddha in *parinirvana*
(Basil Wright's *Song of Ceylon*, 1935)

else. Not only would that situation be laughable as a analytic result, it would as well frustrate the specific functions of specific symbolic manifestations. Jung in this regard is explicit:

> The archetype – let us never forget this – is a psychic organ present in all of us. A bad explanation means a correspondingly bad attitude to this organ, which may thus be injured. But the ultimate sufferer is the bad interpreter himself. Hence, the "explanation" should always be such that the functional significance of the archetype remains unimpaired, so that an adequate and meaningful connection between the conscious mind and the archetypes is assured.
>
> (Jung, 1959/1968, *CW* 9:I: para. 271)

The amplification of archetypal imagery should not be seen, therefore, as a "merely academic" activity, as simply one method among others which can be taken up and put down at will. If it is not taken up by a felt necessity, it is better left alone.

## An example of amplification: bird images in *Song of Ceylon*

One of the surprising places in which symbols appear in film is documentary; to mark the significance of that fact I have chosen to amplify imagery from an acknowledged documentary masterpiece, Basil Wright's *Song of Ceylon*. Wright's report of his psychic condition during the making of this film is clear indication that he felt himself to be working in a symbolic situation:

> *Ceylon* was a unique experience in my life. It's the only film I've made that I really loved, and it was in fact a religious experience. I went to Ceylon, as you know, to make four travelogues for the Tea Propaganda Board, and I shot four travelogues; but while I was doing it, I had these extraordinary, inexplicable inner impulses, which made me shoot sequences and things that I couldn't have logically explained. But as soon as I got into the cutting room, they all fell into their places, like the birds flying up, that sort of thing. I had no reason to shoot them; in fact, they were shot at a time when I'd finished shooting for the day and was very tired, but something forced me to shoot a number of shots and the thing built up to a tremendous amount of internal tension, breaking out into expression, coming from one's subconscious very much, I think, and this was all. A sort

Figure 1.3 A bird flying to the left
(Basil Wright's *Song of Ceylon*, 1935)

Figure 1.4 Mountains surrounding Adam's Peak
(Basil Wright's *Song of Ceylon*, 1935)

of magnetic field was created in which we were operating . . . This film grew like a tree growing out of one's navel. Each morning there would be another branch there; you'd have to sort of cut it off or prune it, or keep it as it was, and gradually the film emerged. I still cannot understand it. I walked into an unconscious process, shot the material and turned it into the film it is . . . This was a magical film.[9]

(Quoted in Levin, 1971: 53–54)

The film itself, and the experience it engenders in its viewers, also testifies to the presence of the symbolic. In the space of this essay I cannot attempt to amplify all of the symbolic imagery in *Song of Ceylon* – nor is that my intention. Instead, as a way of showing how one might proceed in amplifying symbols, I will deal with one specific and crucial sequence: the appearance of the birds at the end of "Part One: The Buddha." Most of us, I think, find the appearance of those birds puzzling and moving – a conjunction necessary to an experience of a living symbol. They come as the ending of a reverent and lyric rendering of the annual pilgrimage of Buddhist devotees to "Adam's Peak," from the top of which it is held that the Buddha departed earth. Earlier, during his reported third visit to Ceylon, the Buddha had impressed his two-foot-long footprint upon the mountain's top (Copleston, 1892: 313).

In and of itself, the traditional claim for the Buddha's departure from earth by way of "Adam's Peak" indicates that we are dealing in Part One with a process of transcendence – an indication reinforced by close attention to the progress of Part One, and to the sensation it engenders. (For a discussion of the relationship between mountains and transcendence, see Eliade, 1958: 99–111 and 374–379.) While the Buddha encompasses and permeates this section of *Song of Ceylon*, appearing at the beginning in association with a fawn, in keeping with his peaceful character, and at the end in poses of inward absorption and the *parinirvana*, there is in the interim a distinct progression: close on the heels of the first images of the Buddha full-of-peace, images of historically earlier indigenous "devil" worship drop us into a more primitive and violent state of being. (For a discussion of Sinhalese religious history, see Bechert, 1960: 164–215.) The Buddhist devotees' subsequent climb up "Adam's Peak" is, therefore, not simply or essentially a physical climb. At its core it embodies a spiritual journey up from the "flatlands" of a lesser understanding of man's existence. In keeping with the character of the climb, the dominant feeling manifested in the viewer is a mounting elation, itself "brought to a peak" by the ringing of the bells at the climb's completion. At that point, with that sound, something, we intuit, must *move* – not as cause to effect, but as an image of the celebration and culmination of a numinous process. And thus do we receive a series of shots of single birds, perched for flight, fluttering, soaring, all posed or moving to the left. Part One ends with a leftward tracking shot of hilly landscape; there is no bird visible. Perhaps we have taken the bird's point of view. In any case, literally and symbolically, Part One ends "up in the air."

Any amplification of this sequence must address at least two questions: what does the appearance of the birds mean, and why are they all perched or flying toward the left? Any attempt to explain the birds simply as signs for birds in the area of "Adam's Peak" at the time of the ringing of the bells proves unsatisfactory. We have not seen them prior to their sudden appearance here, and their environment of trees and water does not match the top of the mountain. Moreover, the structure of the sequence contradicts any such semiotic interpretation, since the shots of the birds are intercut with shots of the Buddha in inner absorption and at the *parinirvana*. Clearly, neither the statuary nor the birds are literally present on "Adam's Peak"; nor has the action literally moved from "Adam's Peak" to the locations of the statuary and the birds. The three belong together, however, for in the film they are so: as we leave the images of the pilgrims at the top of the peak, the sound of their bell-ringing continues over the birds and the Buddha. At this point, if not before, we sense that we are in the symbolic realm.

This would undoubtedly be obvious in a culture less literal-minded, less secular, less semiotic – we might also say less "documentary" – than our own, for birds have a long, variegated history as religious, mystic, and alchemical symbols. (They also function as signs, for example, for political entities; but we shall not here cross over into the semiotics of bird imagery.) There are, moreover, other clues that we are, if not wholly then partially, in the symbolic realm. The soundtrack provides no information about Buddhist teaching – no information about enlightenment and the falling away of the transitory's hold upon us which enlightenment effects. Instead, we essentially watch people climb a mountain and ring bells, and we listen to seemingly insignificant selections from Robert Knox's 1681 description of Ceylon's geography, religious practices, and the Buddha's life. The point can be put another way: "Part One: The Buddha" is not in the business of transmitting a wealth of essentially semiotic information about Buddhism; it *is* in the business of allowing us an experience pointedly related to what the Buddha himself experienced, *an experience whose endpoint can only be symbolized*. Using that realization as a starting point, and consulting dictionaries of mythological motifs and of symbols, one quickly sees that Part One is permeated by symbols of rebirth, transformation, transcendence, wholeness: the lotus plant, the "high and vast" mountain, the climb itself, the movement from earth to air, the waters flowing down the mountain in which one pilgrim stands, the descriptions of the Buddha ("from whom is derived the food of life"; his acquaintance with past, present, and future; his levitation, the light which emanates from him), the references to precious stones, and, of course, the birds.[10] A denser locus of symbols probably cannot be found in film – and there it is, sitting squarely in a masterpiece of English "social" documentary. (My speculations as to why this is so constitute the conclusion of this essay.)

In their typical symbolic function, all of these various symbols circle, as I said, around the processes or states of rebirth, transformation, transcendence, and wholeness. Rather than stray away from our attention upon the birds with a lengthy presentation of the evidence for this claim, I refer the interested reader to findings by Eliade, Jung, and Campbell.[11] Regarding the birds, however: how do we proceed?

Let us assume that we realize the symbolic character of some of the visual and aural images preceding the birds, and, further, that we have gained some rough sense of their typical symbolic meanings. When subsequently we go to the usual sources for generating amplifications (dictionaries of mythological motifs, for example), we already have some standard by which to decide whether or not we are in fact in the presence of functional parallels to the bird imagery. By this knowledge we can begin to eliminate as non-parallel certain traditional references to birds: for example, birds as phallic symbols, the mythic instances of birds of prey (which can signify defeat if seen flying from left to right prior to battle), stories in which disgraced women are turned into birds, or those tales in which the soul of a monstrous person resides not in his body, but in a well-guarded bird, the finding and killing of which also causes the death of the monster (de Vries, 1974: 47). (The process of elimination suggested here is primarily one of degree; one could, for example, tease out parallels between the bird as phallic symbol and the birds in *Song of Ceylon*, but they are weaker than the parallels indicated below.)

Other references just as quickly put us on the road leading to the birds in *Song of Ceylon*: for example, the numerous mythic and religious representations of gods as birds, the Hindu depiction of the sun as a giant bird, the bird as a symbol for the transmigration of the soul, and the use of bird imagery in alchemy to symbolize processes of activation such as sublimation, condensation, and distillation. (This last reference becomes particularly useful in light of Jung's seminal thesis that the alchemists' search for the "Philosopher's Stone" was, to a significant degree, a projection upon the material realm of an inner, psychological urge toward wholeness.) Finally, in the ancient Egyptian hieroglyphic system, *Ba* (the soul) was symbolized by a bird with a human head; these birds were "seen" leaving the mouths of the dying.

These references put us in a useful area from which to begin more specific amplifications – those that deal with birds as symbols of spiritual entities or processes in the specific context of ascension and flight. Our work in this particular case is considerably lightened by virtue of the fact that precisely these parallels have been collected and commented upon by Mircea Eliade in his "Symbolisms of Ascension and 'Waking Dreams'" (Eliade, 1960: 99–122). Since Eliade has done the essential inductive work in this instance, we can reverse the normal procedure of amplification by beginning with the interpretative conclusions and then proceeding to one instance from which the conclusions were drawn – an instance especially useful in amplifying *Song of Ceylon*.

Eliade notes that the motif of flight or ascension to Heaven is found at every level of the archaic cultures, and that the mythic-critical theme "bird–soul–ecstatic flight" was probably already extant in the paleolithic epoch (Eliade, 1960: 105). He does not believe any historical causes can be found for this motif, but thinks instead that "very likely, the ecstatic experience . . . is co-existent with the human condition" – a thesis compatible with Jung's thinking about the archetypes (Eliade, 1960: 103). The close tie between the experience of ecstatic flight and spirituality is attested to in the subsequent history of the symbolism of ascension, e.g., by the importance given to symbols of the soul as a bird, to such images as the "wings of the soul," and by the images which mark the spiritual life as an "elevation" and the mystical experience as an "ascension." "Flight" also symbolizes the understanding of secret things and meta-physical truths, as, for example, the Hindu text which states that "he who understands has wings" (Eliade, 1960: 105). Among those who can fly or are described in bird terms are Taoist priests (tagged as "feathered sages"), Chinese and Indian alchemists, Zoroaster, Jesus, yogis, mystics, the shamans of China and Siberia, and Buddhist *arhat* ("illuminated sages"). Shamans in ecstatic trance claim to leave the body and to take flight like a bird, or to ride a bird; the wearing of bird plumage is one sign of their ability to do so. Frequently they enter into ecstatic trance while high in a ceremonial and sacred tree. The shaman's initiation rite involves him in a "death and resurrection," between which his soul flies to both Heaven and Hell. This "death and resurrection" is symbolic of the shaman's passage from one level of existence to another – a fact that brings us directly to Eliade's general conclusion about the meaning of flight and ascension symbolism:

> If we consider the "flight" and all the related symbolisms as a whole, their significance is at once apparent: they all express a break with the universe of everyday existence; and a dual purposiveness is evident in this rupture: both transcendence and . . . freedom are to be obtained through the "flight." . . . One can only interpret all the myths, rites and legends to which we have been referring by a longing to see the human body behaving like a "spirit," to transmute the corporeal modality of man into a spiritual modality . . . It is because they no longer partake of the human condition, and in so far as they are "free," that . . . the yogis, the alchemists, the *arhat*, are able to transport themselves at will, to fly, or to disappear.
>
> (Eliade, 1960: 106–108)

The parallel between the Buddhist *arhat* and the birds in *Song of Ceylon* is especially instructive, because it not only makes intelligible the birds' appearance, but also offers some explanation for the form of editing at that point. "Flight" is so characteristic of the *arhat* that they are linked to the Sinhalese verb signifying "to disappear, to pass instantaneously from one place to another." The *arhat* are, like the yogis, *kamacarin*: beings who can transport themselves at will. Ananda Coomaraswamy comments that *kamacarin* implies "the condition of one who, being in the Spirit, no longer needs to move at all in order to be everywhere" (quoted in Eliade, 1960: 108). This can be seen, I think, to correspond to the character of the cross-cutting between the shots of the Buddha *at rest* and of the birds *in various places* and in various modalities of *flight*. However, I would not claim that this exhausts the meanings in that editing.

There is another relevant aspect of the *arhat*'s flight: their ability to fly, as the Buddhist texts say, "at their own will, break and pass through the roof of the house and rise up into the air" (Eliade, 1960: 109). As Eliade states, "on the metaphysical plane it is a case of the abolition of the conditioned world. For the 'house' stands for the Universe; to 'break the roof of the house' means that the arhat has transcended the world or risen above it" (Eliade, 1960: 109). Now, it is not by chance that such transcending is associated with a mountain, for in Buddhist tradition, among others, creation began from a summit which is simultaneously the "center of the world" and transcendent. ("The creation was effected gradually, thence downward by successive stages" – Eliade, 1960: 113.) To transcend the world is to mount that summit and take flight, because it is at such a "center" that the break occurs between one plane of existence and another. Thus, the significance of the climb up Adam's Peak, which is for the Sinhalese the "*Axis Mundi*," the world center, the place from which the Buddha left the world and entered the "air." This ascent to the summit, the *Axis Mundi*, accomplishes transcendence in two modes: transcendence of space through elevation into Heaven, and transcendence of time by "reentering the primordial instant before the world had yet come into existence" – that atemporal instant preceding the creation whose hold the Buddhist so fervently strives to escape (Eliade, 1960: 115). The crucial point is this: for this state of transcendence there are no signs. The Buddha never said what enlightenment was; he only pointed the Way. For the Way's goal there are only symbols, as Wright intuited in the making of *Song of Ceylon*. And like the state they symbolize, the birds appear instantaneously, without cause, just so.

I believe we have learned now something of the meaning of the appearance of the birds at the conclusion of "Part One: The Buddha." Earlier I noted that the birds are all perched or flying toward the left. Can amplification be an aid in comprehending this additional fact? The individual pieces of an answer lie scattered in the mythology and religious iconography of several different places and times. Let's begin with part of the cosmological legend of the Jicarilla Apache Indians of New Mexico, as described by Joseph Campbell. By the point where the myth is relevant to our question Black Hactcin, the world creator, has already participated in the creation of earth and sky, and is involved in the creation of animals, including birds:

> Then he fashioned a bird from the mud. "Let me see how you are going to use those wings to fly," he said. The mud turned into a bird and flew around. "That's just fine!" said Black Hactcin, who enjoyed seeing the difference between this one and the ones with four legs. "But," he said, "I think you need companions." Then he took the bird and whirled it around rapidly in a clockwise direction. The bird grew dizzy, and, as one does when dizzy, saw many images round about. He saw all kinds of birds there, eagles, hawks, and small birds too, and when he was himself again, there were all those birds, really there.
> (Campbell, 1969: 232–233)

Campbell notes that this image of birds produced in clockwise whirling suggests similar images on Mesopotamian high neolithic pottery where the forms of animals and birds emerge from a whirling swastika (Campbell, 1969: 233). The association of birds and swastikas is very ancient; indeed, the earliest swastika yet found, near Kiev, USSR, appears on the underwing of a bird carved on mammoth ivory (Campbell, 1969: 328). Campbell comments:

> C. von den Steinen, long before the discovery of this site, suggested that the swastika might have been developed from the stylization of a bird in flight, above all of the stork, the enemy of the serpent, and therewith the victorious representative of the principle of light and warmth. And V. A. Gorodcov . . . suggests that in the geometrical motifs of the swastika, rhombus, and zigzag band or meander we may recognize a mythological constellation of bird (specially stork), nest, and serpent.
>
> (Campbell, 1969: 328)

Thus far we have suggested links between birds and swastikas, and have one instance where directionality plays a central role. We are still lacking the crucial link between the Buddha and the swastika. In the Eliade-based discussion above, we established a link between the Buddha and birds; now we seek the functional linkage: birds–the Buddha–swastikas. Campbell himself provides the information about religious iconography which establishes the sought-for link – and in a manner which goes to the heart of the issue of directionality. We return to Black Hactcin:

> The creator whirled the bird in a clockwise direction and the result was an emanation of dreamlike forms. But swastikas, counter-clockwise, appear on many Chinese images of the meditating Buddha; and the Buddha, we know, is removing his consciousness from just this field of dreamlike, created forms reuniting it through yogic exercise with that primordial abyss or "void" from which all springs . . . Now I am not going to suggest that there has been any Buddhist influence on Apache mythology. There has not! . . . What I am suggesting . . . is that in this Apache legend of the creation of the bird we have a remote cognate of the Indian forms, which must have proceeded from the same neolithic stock; and that in both cases the symbol of the swastika represents a process of transformation: the conjuring up (in the case of the Hactcin), or conjuring away (in the case of the Buddha), of a universe that because of the fleeting nature of its forms may indeed be compared to the substance of a mirage, or of a dream.
>
> (Campbell, 1969: 233–234)

I suggest that the leftward movement of the birds in "Part One: The Buddha" is analogous to, and functionally parallel with, the counter-clockwise direction of the swastika associated with the Buddha, i.e., that both have to do with a process of "conjuring away."

On the basis of Eliade's study of "flight" symbolism, we have established a functional parallel between the Buddha and the birds of "Part One: The Buddha." In dealing with the birds' directionality, we have been led to the swastika, which forms, as it were, a mediating "third term." This "third term" appears to carry with it the specific functional parallel of "conjuring away" – a trait much in keeping with the earlier, Eliade-based parallel. These two parallels – "birds–the Buddha" and "birds–swastikas–the Buddha" – bring a deep intelligibility to Wright's editing, whereby leftward-perched-and-flying birds are cross-cut with images of the Buddha far down the path of enlightenment.

## Conclusion: compensation in the symbolic cinema: *Song of Ceylon*

I would like to conclude with some speculations generated by a symbolic attitude toward *Song of Ceylon*, and to return in this manner to Jung's thesis regarding the compensatory function of symbolic art. At the conclusion of one of his rare essays on aesthetics, Jung summarizes the power and function of symbolic art:

> The impact of an archetype . . . stirs us because it summons up a voice . . . stronger than our own. Whoever speaks in primordial images speaks with a thousand voices; he enthralls and overpowers, while at the same time he lifts the idea he is seeking to express out of the occasional and the transitory into the realm of the ever-enduring . . . This is the secret of great art, and of its effect upon us. The creative process, so far as we are able to follow it at all, consists in the unconscious activation of an archetypal image, and in elaborating and shaping the image into the finished work. By giving it shape, the artist translates it into the language of the present, and so makes it possible for us to find our way back to the deepest springs of life. Therein lies the social significance of art: it is constantly at work educating the spirit of the age, conjuring up the forms in which the age is most lacking.
>
> (Jung, 1966, *CW* 15: paras. 129–130)

Insofar as film participates in the symbolic realm – and there is hard evidence that it occasionally does – this compensatory function can be sought out within it.

What might *Song of Ceylon* be compensating? We are familiar with the tenets of the English 1930s documentary film movement, articulated by its leader John Grierson, that citizens be given an information service "on the immediate needs and services of the state," that they be given a "living sense of what is going on," that their sentiments and loyalties be "crystallised in forms which are useful to the people and to the state alike," and that society in general be given "some imaginative leadership in the articulation of a faith" (Hardy, 1966: 275). Central to Grierson's vision of the nature and functions of documentary film is his distinction between the "private" and "public" man, and his privileging of the latter over the needs and demands of the former. He was acutely aware of the mass character of modern democracies, the interdependence of people in highly technological societies, and the role of mass media in forming and directing public opinion. Grierson was suspect toward individual complaints, needs, and compulsions; over them hung, in his mind, the aura of social irresponsibility, "romanticism," and the "yahoo tradition" of individualism:

> You may not be so interested in the individual. You may think that the individual life is no longer capable of cross-sectioning reality. You may believe that its particular belly-aches are of no consequence in a world which complex and impersonal forces command . . . Indeed, you may feel that in individualism is a yahoo tradition largely responsible for our present anarchy.
>
> (Hardy, 1966: 149)

The artist in particular, whom we often conceive as essentially involved in "personal expression" (given the legacy of romanticism), was called upon by Grierson to express the needs of the state, and to accept the notion that the "aesthetic" dimension of his or her work was a felicitous by-product of a well-done social task. In Grierson's perspective there is truth, and the authority that comes from truth. But it is one-sided, because the individual's condition and our categorical need for the individual's standpoint are more complicated than Grierson was willing to allow.

The individual, like humankind in the aggregate, is informed by, and sometimes compelled by "complex and impersonal" *psychic* factors; Jung tagged them archetypal. *These are as compelling and pervasive as the "complex and impersonal" economic and technological forces which commanded Grierson's attention.* Basil Wright found himself in the grips of just such psychic forces in Sri Lanka. In amplifying the images of the birds in "Part One: The Buddha," we have intimated the particular constellation of archetypal factors working in that instance: essentially the urge toward rebirth, spiritual rather than physical. Inherent to such a dynamic is the need to take a symbolic attitude, to apprehend symbolically. Wright did just that.

I suggest that the profoundly symbolic character of *Song of Ceylon* is a compensation for the overwhelmingly semiotic perspective of Griersonian documentary film.[12] It is not a denial; rather, it is a complement, an act redressing a balance. *Song of Ceylon* re-establishes the reality of the mysterious, symbolic, and spiritual within the film form dedicated to demystifying and channeling some of the complex economic and technological forces informing social life. Such compensations as Wright and other symbolic film-makers have performed are the work of the "private" facet of man; they point to the "public" facet's need to listen to that inner space which is at once uniquely individual and transpersonal (archetypal). Without that "inner ear," the public person, whatever the brilliance and triumphs of his or her semiotic investigations, lacks access into deep and essential truths.

## Notes

1   This outline of Jung's distinction between sign and symbol, and semiotic and symbolic attitudes, is a highly abbreviated and significantly reworked version of two essays published in 1979 and 1980, under the same title: Fredericksen (1979: 167–192 and 1980a: 459–479). Grateful acknowledgment is here extended to the *Quarterly Review of Film Studies*, subsequently retitled the *Quarterly Review of Film and Video*. Significant updating of references has also been done. The two full essays and this revision form part of a long-term project to construct from the writings of Jung and Jungians answers to a substantial set of questions in film theory, criticism, and history. Those parts of this project that have been published or presented at conferences are listed in the reference section. Two books are in the works, one on Bergman's *Persona* (1966), another on the liminal cinema as an artistic mode of psychological self-initiation. The sign/symbol distinction was chosen first, because of its logical priority and polemical utility. In my judgment, recent developments in film studies, e.g., "cultural studies" and cognitive film studies, have not altered the validity of the original argument regarding the domination of the field by semiotic approaches and the absence of the symbolic attitude – regardless of any other values these newer approaches bring to the study of film. For an overview of contemporary film theory, see Casetti (1999) and Stam (2000).

2   This occurred in the transference situation, where "incest-toned parental

images were most frequently projected . . . the physician attracting either the father or the motherimage" (Frey-Rohn, 1974: 263). Transference is considered an essential part of most depth psychological analyses, although Jung's attitude toward its importance varied widely within his lifetime.

3  For a general discussion of the use in art theory of the notion of "semiosis" (the process by which one thing "stands for" another), see Beardsley (1966: 342–355). For the ambiguity of "stands for" see Alston (1964: 50–61).

4  I recommend Conti's little-known essay for its insight and high professionalism; she knows Jung's psychology well. "Self" in Jung's psychology can be briefly defined – symbolically – as the psyche in its entirety, conscious and unconscious, and as the agency that strives for wholeness. For definitions of key terms quoted from Jung's writings see Jung (1963: 391–402).

5  An especially valuable contribution is Vazques (1973). I also recommend Morawski (1974) and Baxandall and Morawski (1973). Morawski's long introduction to the 1973 anthology is very much to the point.

6  See Edinger (1972: Ch. 4, "The Search for Meaning") for a concise, lucid discussion of the symbol's character and functions.

7  Jungian analyses of commercial narrative films include the following: Benderson (1974, 1979), Conti (1972a, 1972b), Fredericksen (1995), Izod (1992, 1996), and Izod and Ryan (2000). In addition, the *San Francisco Jung Institute Library Journal* regularly runs brief reviews of current films.

8  Jungian analyses of documentary and personal/experimental films include the following: Fredericksen (1980b, 1981, 1982, 1984, 1988, 1990, 1993, 1996, 1998, 2000a, 2000b).

9  Soon after this essay was first written Wright himself has pointed out the symbolic character of *Song of Ceylon* and his experience in Ceylon; in the same interview he also tagged himself a "Jungian." See Thomas (1979: 480).

10  For dictionaries useful in preliminary work with symbols see Chevalier and Gheerbrant (1969/1994), Cirlot (1962), Cooper (1978), Fox (1916), de Vries (1974), *Herder* (1978/1986), Rosebury (1974), and Walker (1983). Also very helpful is the General Index to the *Collected Works of C.G. Jung* (Jung, 1979, *CW* 20). To all such work one must bring an intuitively informed logic.

11  The following are a sampling from a larger body of relevant work: Eliade (1958), Jung ("Concerning Rebirth" in 1959/1968, *CW* 9:I: paras. 199–258; "The Philosophical Tree" in 1967, *CW* 13: paras. 304–482; "Religious Ideas in Alchemy" in 1953/1968, *CW* 12: paras. 332–554), and Campbell (1968).

12  The compensatory relationship between *Song of Ceylon* and Griersonian documentary film can also be viewed through Jung's categories of "introversion" and "extraversion." See Fredericksen (1980b: 53–57).

## References

Alston, W.P. (1964) *Philosophy of Language*, Englewood Cliffs: Prentice-Hall.

Barthes, R. (1967) *Elements of Semiology*, Boston: Beacon Press.

Baxandall, L. and Morawski, S. (eds) (1973) *Marx and Engels on Literature and Art*, St Louis: Telos.

Beardsley, M. (1966) *Aesthetics from Classical Greece to the Present*, New York: Macmillan.

Bechert, H. (ed.) (1960) *Culture of Ceylon in Mediaeval Times*, Wiesbaden: Otto Harassowitz.

Benderson, A. (1974) *Critical Approaches to Federico Fellini's 8½*, New York: Arno.

—— (1979) "An Archetypal Reading of *Juliet of the Spirits*," *Quarterly Review of Film Studies* 4, 2: 193–206.

Bergman, I. (1972) *Persona and Shame*, New York: Grossman.

Borch-Jacobsen, M. (1991) *Lacan: The Absolute Master*, Stanford: Stanford University Press.

Broughton, J. (1977) *Seeing the Light*, San Francisco: City Lights Books.

Campbell, J. (1968) *The Hero with a Thousand Faces* (2nd edn), Princeton: Princeton University Press.

—— (1969) *The Masks of God: Primitive Mythology*, New York: Penguin.

Casetti, F. (1999) *Theories of Cinema 1945–1995*, Austin: University of Texas Press.

Chevalier, J. and Gheerbrant, A. (1969/1994) *Dictionary of Symbols*, Cambridge, Mass.: Blackwell.

Cirlot, J.E. (1962) *A Dictionary of Symbols*, New York: Philosophical Library.

Conti, I. (1972a) "Fellini's 8½: A Jungian Analysis (Parte Prima)," *Ikon* 80: 43–76.

—— (1972b) "Fellini's 8½: A Jungian Analysis (Parte Seconda)," *Ikon* 82–83: 123–170.

Cooper, J.C. (1978) *An Illustrated Encyclopedia of Traditional Symbols*, New York: Thames and Hudson.

Copleston, R.G. (1892) *Buddhism: Primitive and Present in Magadha and Ceylon*, New York: Longmans, Green.

de Vries, A. (1974) *Dictionary of Symbols and Imagery*, Amsterdam: North-Holland.

Eagleton, T. (1976) *Marxism and Literary Criticism*, Berkeley: University of California Press.

Edinger, E. (1972) *Ego and Archetype*, Baltimore: Penguin.

Eliade, M. (1958) *Patterns in Comparative Religion*, New York: New American Library.

—— (1960) *Myths, Dreams, and Mysteries*, New York: Harper and Row.

Fox, W.S. (1916) *The Mythology of All Races*, Boston: Marshall Jones.

Fredericksen, D. (1979) "Jung/Sign/Symbol/Film, Part One," *Quarterly Review of Film Studies* 4, 2: 167–192.

—— (1980a) "Jung/Sign/Symbol/Film, Part Two," *Quarterly Review of Film Studies* 5, 4: 459–479.

—— (1980b) "Two Aspects of a Jungian Perspective upon Film," *Journal of Film and Video* 32, 1–2: 49–57.

—— (1981) "The Quest for the Imaginal in the American Personal Film Tradition," Unpublished conference lecture series.

—— (1982) "Imaginal Criticism's Aims and Contexts," in *Film Studies: Proceedings from the Purdue University Annual Conference on Film*, Lafayette: Purdue University.

—— (1984) "The Archetype of the Virgin in Nature Documentaries," Unpublished conference paper.

—— (1988) "The Sacred and the Profane in the Ethnographic Fictions of Rouquier," in J. Ruby and M. Taureg (eds) *Visual Explorations of the World*, Aachen: Rader Verlag.

—— (1990) "Bar Yohai," *Visual Anthropology* 3: 119–124.

—— (1993) "The Relationship Between Filmmaking and Dreaming: Larry Jordan's *Patricia Gives Birth in a Doorway*," Unpublished conference paper

—— (1995) "Fellini Gives Birth to a Film in a Doorway: Film and Dream in Liminality," Unpublished conference paper.

—— (1996) "The Liminal Cinema," Unpublished conference paper.

—— (1998) "Finding Adequate Images," Unpublished conference paper.

—— (2000a) In Polish translation: "On the Use of C.G. Jung's Psychology and Victor Turner's Anthropology in Discerning Patterns in Film History," in J. Rek and E. Ostrowska (eds) *Kino ma sto lat. Dekada po dekadzie*, Lodz: University of Lodz.

—— (2000b) "Individuation as Artistic Vocation: Jerome Hill's *Film Portrait*," *Millennium Film Journal* 35/36: 89–106 (forthcoming).

—— (2000c) "Why Should We Take Jungian Screen Studies Seriously?," Unpublished conference paper.

Freud, S. (1900/1954) *The Interpretation of Dreams*, New York: Basic Books.

Frey-Rohn, L. (1974) *From Freud to Jung*, New York: G.P. Putnam's.

Hall, J.A. (1977) *Clinical Uses of Dreams: Jungian Interpretations and Enactments*, New York: Grune and Stratton.

Hardy, F. (ed.) (1966) *Grierson on Documentary* (rev. edn), Berkeley: University of California Press.

Harman, G. (1977) "Semiotics and the Cinema: Metz and Wollen," *Quarterly Review of Film Studies* 2, 1: 15–24.

Heath, S. (1973) "Metz's Semiology: A Short Glossary," *Screen* 14, 1/2: 225.

*Herder Symbol Dictionary* (1978/1986), Wilmette, Ill.: Chiron.

Izod, J. (1992) *Films of Nicholas Roeg: Myth and Mind*, New York: St Martin's.

—— (1996) "*The Piano*, the Animus, and the Colonial Experience," *Journal of Analytical Psychology* 41, 1: 117–136.

Izod, J. and Ryan, J. (2000) "*2001: A Space Odyssey*: Classics Revisited: Accounting for Difference in Two Jungian Readings," *San Francisco Jung Institute Library Journal* 18, 4: 7–56.

Jung, C.G. (1953) *Two Essays in Analytical Psychology*, Cleveland: World.

—— (1961/1965) *Memories, Dreams, Reflections*, New York: Vintage.

Jung, C.G. All other references are by volume and paragraph number to the hardback edition of C.G. Jung, *The Collected Works* (*CW*), edited by Sir Herbert Read, Dr Michael Fordham and Dr Gerhard Adler, and translated in the main by R.F.C. Hull, London: Routledge.

Kyrou, A. (1963) *Luis Buñuel: An Introduction*, New York: Simon and Schuster.

Levin, G.R. (ed.) (1971) *Documentary Explorations*, Garden City: Doubleday.

Mattoon, M.A. (1978) *Applied Dream Analysis: A Jungian Approach*, New York: Halsted John Wiley.

Metz, C. (1974) *Film Language: A Semiotics of the Cinema*, New York: Oxford University Press.

—— (1975) "The Imaginary Signifier," *Screen* 16, 2: 14–77.

Morawski, S. (1974) *Inquiries into the Fundamentals of Aesthetics*, Cambridge, Mass.: MIT Press.

Rosebury, F. (1974) *Symbols: Myth, Magic, Fact, and Fancy*, Natick: Fred Rosebury.

Russett, R. and Starr, C. (eds) (1976) *Experimental Animation: An Illustrated Anthology*, New York: Van Nostrand Reinhold.

Samuels, C.T. (1972) *Encountering Directors*, New York: G.P. Putnam's.

Stam, R. (2000) *Film Theory: An Introduction*, Malder, Mass.: Blackwell.

Thomas, S. (1979) "Basil Wright on Art, Anthropology and the Documentary," *Quarterly Review of Film Studies* 4, 4: 465–481.

Vazques, A.S. (1973) *Art and Society: Essays in Marxist Aesthetics*, New York: Monthly Review Press.

Von Franz, M.L. (1970/1975) *An Introduction to the Psychology of Fairy Tales*, Zurich: Spring.

Walker, B.G. (1983) *The Woman's Encyclopedia of Myths and Secrets*, San Francisco: Harper and Row.

Wollheim, R. (1979) "The Cabinet of Doctor Lacan," *The New York Review of Books* XXV, 21–22: 36–45.

# Chapter 2

# The alchemy of
# *Pulp Fiction*

*Lydia Lennihan*

There's a passage I got memorized. Ezekiel 25:17: "The path of the
righteous man is beset on all sides by the inequities of the selfish and
the tyranny of evil men. Blessed is he who, in the name of charity
and good will, shepherds the weak through the valley of darkness,
for he is truly his brother's keeper and the finder of lost children. And
I will strike down upon thee with great vengeance and furious
anger those who attempt to poison and destroy my brothers. And you
will know my name is the Lord when I lay my vengeance upon you."
I been sayin' that shit for years. And if you ever heard it, it meant
your ass. I never really questioned what it meant. I thought it was
just a cold-blooded thing to say to a motherfucker 'fore you popped
a cap in his ass. But I saw some shit this mornin' made me think
twice. Now I'm thinkin', it could mean you're the evil man. And I'm
the righteous man. And Mr. .45 here, he's the shepherd protecting
my righteous ass in the valley of darkness. Or it could be you're the
righteous man and I'm the shepherd and it's the world that's evil and
selfish. I'd like that. But that shit ain't the truth. The truth is you're
the weak. And I'm the tyranny of evil men. But I'm tryin'. I'm tryin'
real hard to be a shepherd.

(Jules, in Tarantino 1994: 157–58)

## *Pulp Fiction*: projection and redemption of
## the American shadow

*Pulp Fiction* (1994) is a postmodern film directed and co-authored
by Quentin Tarantino. Known for its extreme violence by both viewers
and non-viewers alike, it presents us with our collective shadow in
technicolor, offering us redemption through individuation in that same
violent underworld which we do not want to witness. This film illustrates

culturally as well as individually that our healing lies deep within the very wound which sears us.

The film centers around the lives of several small-time criminals living in the contemporary underworld of Los Angeles. Time is mythical and circular rather than linear as we return to the beginning of the story at the end of the film. The film is divided into three stories, each one a vignette with its own beginning, middle, and end, yet they are all connected and interdependent. Several Jungian principles occur repeatedly throughout the film. The tales themselves are about each character's call to individuation; the call from the collective and the personal unconscious. In addition, there is an alchemical motif woven throughout, in which gold plays an important role both visually and symbolically, and redemption is found in the separation and subsequent conjunction of opposites. And, as in alchemy, which was an *opus* based on rotting *prima materia*, for which a guiding admonition was "It is found in the filth," the spiritual meaning of *Pulp Fiction* is bodily embedded in the rotting materials of pop culture – and in the filthy language and dirty situations that give the screenplay its gamy, but remarkably fertile, texture.

The beauty of *Pulp Fiction* is the redemption of marginal and shadowy figures which represent what has been rejected by the consensus reality of the collective. Collectively, Americans tend to look away, and certainly not pay the price of admission to view acts of violence such as murder, heroin overdoses, and decapitation. Yet these same figures populate our dreams and nightmares at times, and they are asking to be let into our houses, to be heard. They are looking for an epiphany, and like us they are seeking individuation; the life-urge that drives us powers the fiction characters of our collective imagination. Image compels us to follow; film as image defines our mythology. A popular movie can present our greatest moments as a species as well as our darkest impulses. The film's audience would do well to pay close attention to what is being offered.

The film opens with a conversation between African-American Jules (Samuel L. Jackson) and his Caucasian friend Vincent (John Travolta), who are partners working for a black crime boss, Marsellus Wallace (Ving Rhames). They have been sent to retrieve a briefcase which has been used in a drug deal and has been stolen. We are not shown what is in the case as they retrieve it, but, when it is opened, a brilliant golden glow emanates from within, like the mysterious Grail. In the process of retrieving the case, a miracle occurs. A man who has been hiding in the bathroom of the apartment bursts out unexpectedly and unloads his gun directly at Vincent and Jules. Miraculously, not one bullet finds its mark, and they survive this onslaught, which has outraged them. Jules recognizes this as an act of God, but Vincent is cynical and denies that anything besides a freak accident has occurred.

By the end of the film, Jules has decided to quit his life of crime and to wander the earth "like Cain in *Kung Fu*," waiting to see where God sends him. In the moral logic of the film, Vincent ends up getting killed as a result of his refusal to heed what amounts to the call of the unconscious to individuate. The ramifications of this tale as a myth for contemporary American society are fascinating, especially since we seem to be collectively obsessed with fighting crime characters like Jules and Vincent, who hold our nation's projections and shadow, but rarely look within to see what they are saying about us. Jung wrote about this type of collective pathology and how dangerous it is as it manifests in our society, where our projections are played out in the political arena as well as in our most intimate lives. The idea is intriguing that our collective shadow is symbolized by underworld criminals having a spiritual awakening, for this suggests an unsuspected spiritual energy in the shadow.

The crime boss/kingpin Marsellus Wallace is fascinating and has his own drama in the film. The mysteriously glowing golden case is being retrieved for him, and like the Fisher King of the Grail legend, he is also centrally wounded when he is sodomized by extremely evil men, darker even than Marsellus. Wounded not only in eros, this ruler of contemporary darkness is also wounded in logos and consciousness, for there is an unexplained band-aid at the base of Marsellus's skull. Like King Arthur, Marsellus cannot successfully or completely hold onto his beautiful Caucasian wife Mia (Uma Thurman), and unwisely has his lieutenants attending to her while he is out of town. His fate is to be rescued from his attackers by Butch (Bruce Willis), the prize fighter "palooka" who has betrayed and stolen money from him. As Marsellus's savior, Butch is also linked with him in terms of golden imagery, which symbolically brings the two together in the story. This theme of the union of opposites is at play throughout the film; the redemption of good through evil, of healing through the wound, and the discovery of the alchemical gold in the discarded refuse; all are motifs which occur repeatedly.

Three Jungian themes are particularly woven into the texture of the film. These are (1) individuation, which is suggested by the alchemical motifs in the imagery of the film, (2) personified aspects of consciousness and the unconscious in the individual characters, and (3) the union of psychic opposites, particularly those of good and evil.

## The opus

Jung's conception of individuation involves the relationship between the ego and the Self, between the conscious and the unconscious. Jung believed that individuation was the ego's attempt to integrate the collective unconscious, as "parts of the self" (Jung 1978: para. 43). The ego's job in individuation is to assimilate the unconscious contents, and the more numerous these contents are, the closer the ego is able to move toward the Self (ibid.: para. 44). Then the individual nature can more authentically express itself and broaden its experience of the outer world and the inner psyche, enriching life immeasurably.

This theme of individuation is hinted at in the structure of the film, which is a trinity of stories. Edinger discusses the triune as being a symbol for creativity, growth, and stages of development in the individuation process, versus stagnation or completion already achieved (Edinger 1992: 182). Edinger's postulate is that alienation and inflation are prerequisites for individuation (ibid.: 7). The ego's eagerness to identify with the divine (and thus become inflated) is the urge to identify with the Self (ibid.: 80). Jules, who is already alienated from the rest of society as an underworld criminal, is inflated in the sense that he feels completely justified in taking people's lives as an act of retaliation for perceived wrongs. He behaves as if he is God in this regard. In terms of individuation, then, he is ripe for a come-uppance that could shift his world-view.

The character of Jules is being called to develop beyond the boundaries of his ego, to deepen and incorporate aspects of the collective unconscious. His nearly fatal experience is numinous for him; we see that his "self, in its efforts at self-realization, reaches out beyond the ego-personality on all sides" confronting him "with problems which [he] would like to avoid" (Jung 1978: para. 778). Jung observed that even with a small amount of understanding, an experience of wholeness can be achieved (ibid.: para. 777). This nascent experience for Jules is the beginning of a spiritual awakening, which he describes to Vincent when he says: "I had what alcoholics refer to as a 'moment of clarity'" (Tarantino 1994: 148). Emma Jung writes in *The Grail Legend* (Jung and von Franz 1970) that the experience of the numinous is "usually accompanied by a profound emotion which the ego senses as an epiphany of the divine. For this reason it is practically impossible to differentiate between an experience of God and an experience of the Self" (pp. 98–99). Jules illustrates this when he says to Vincent: "What is significant is I felt God's touch. God got involved" (Tarantino 1994: 146).

When Jules is being robbed in the restaurant at the end of the film, his behavior tells us that he is a changed man. Normally, he would think nothing of killing someone who was attempting to rob him of the mysterious golden briefcase. He was in fact doing just that when he had his numinous experience earlier that day. The Self now presents him with the same task again, but this time he changes his behavior. He really has assimilated a portion of the unconscious into his ego. Realizing that what the world is asking of him has profoundly changed, he meets the challenge and responds differently. Instead of killing the would-be robber (Tim Roth), he gives the punk the contents of his own wallet and lets him go, without the briefcase, which still needs to be turned over to Marsellus. Jules feels that he has bought this man's life. Jules's task is not complete, but his process has begun. Like Jung, the film invites us to apply the metaphor of alchemy to Jules's psychic growth.

Jung discovered in mid-career that alchemy was a valuable tool for describing the process of individuation. Alchemical language and illustrations gave him images with which he could symbolize the work (Jung 1970: para. 792). Jung tells us that the rich symbolic content of alchemy is comparable to an *opus divinum* (ibid.: para. 790). This *opus* starts with the *prima materia*, or raw material of the imperfect individual, and then through several processes becomes the "Philosopher's Stone," or gold, the incorruptible substance (ibid.: paras. 355–356). What is essential in understanding Jules's experience alchemically is that the *prima materia*, or starting place of the work, is black like the shadow, that portion of ourselves that is cast out as despicable (Edinger 1985: 12). Jules, whose "blackness" is emphasized in analogy to black-exploitation films, represents the shadow of our culture and of the individual; our most murderous and violent urges which repulse us emotionally. Yet the alchemical transformation requires that we begin with raw material, usually with what has been refused and rejected as contemptible.

Edinger reminds us that there are three stages in the alchemical *opus* (Edinger 1985: 47). The first of these is the *mortificatio* or *nigredo* stage, also known as the *massa confusa*, which enmeshes the soul and the body before separation between the two can take place (Jung 1970: para. 696). The *magnum opus* begins in this black and confused state. The *mortificatio* period is associated with the color black, death, putrefaction, defeat and disintegration (Edinger 1985: 148). In terms of Jules's individuation, it is crucial to know that unlike the other alchemical stages with their chemical processes, *mortificatio* literally means death and killing (ibid.: 147). Jules not only kills people who cross him or his boss, he is also surrounded by death and by the imagery of the *nigredo* phase of individuation.

At one point, Vincent accidentally shoots the head off the black student in the back seat of the car he and Jules are travelling in, literally decapitating him. This violent image is important in light of what Edinger points out, that "the skull as *memento* mori is an emblem for the operation of *mortificado*" (Edinger 1985: 168). Jung discusses the idea of the skull in relation to alchemical processes. In alchemy, the black raven's head represents the darkness of the human soul, but it also represents the beginning of the work of individuation and the dark incubation period that is required for the process (Jung 1970: paras. 727, 729). The *caput corvi* (raven's head) is the symbol for the *nigredo* phase, and is linked with the *caput mortuum* or head of the black Osiris or Ethiopian, the "Moor" (ibid.: para. 730). The severed head of the black king is boiled and turns to gold in Rosencreutz's *Chymical Wedding*. Vincent's action of accidentally beheading the man in the car is symbolic for the necessary separation of logos from eros, which is essential before the final process of union can take place, and the inferior is transformed into gold, and thereby integrated into consciousness (ibid.: para. 730).

*Figure 2.1  Pulp Fiction.* Vincent (John Travolta) and Jules (Samuel L. Jackson) (Mirimax/Buena Vista, Courtesy Kobal)

## Characters as psychic opposites

In the context of alchemy and individuation, therefore, it is significant that the character in the film who begins the process of individuation is the man with the black skin, and that the character who is decapitated is also black. Emma Jung notes that the solar hero (who in our story is the sunny Caucasian Vincent, who has just returned from Europe) does not fare as well in the underworld; it is not really his terrain. She observes that in the underworld the sun hero's role is often repressed and reversed with that of the dark and earthly mortal hero, who now represents altruistic principles (Jung and von Franz 1970: 214). This is exactly what happens. As Jules responds to the call, Vincent is oblivious, continually going into various bathrooms throughout the film, his ego disastrously immersed in the plumbing of the unconscious self, emerging only to find chaos breaking out all around him and finally his own death confronting him.

The human who is given a chance at individuation is called to bring the gold of the spirit to the king of whatever world he or she serves, or to find whom the Grail itself serves. These are ancient issues related to the redemption motif (Jung and von Franz 1970: 295). Disaster strikes if we are called but are not prepared, if we do not know what king we serve, or if the call for self-knowledge is refused; the result may even be literal death. This is what happens to Vincent, as he remains unconscious and refuses to investigate the clues and warnings his unconscious leaves for him throughout the film. As Jung observed, the unconscious is easily able to end a meaningless life very quickly (Jung 1970: para. 675). Vincent's ignorance about his participation in his own life leads us to the second Jungian theme in the film: that of the unconscious and consciousness.

Jung divided the unconscious into two parts, the collective or transpersonal, and the personal (Jung 1978: para. 103). The personal unconscious holds repressed items from the conscious, and contains personal memories, images, and symbols. The collective holds "primordial images" and "thought-forms" which are universal and ancient, which in a sense are inherited by the individual, and "lead their own independent life rather in the manner of part-souls." Jung, of course, referred to these images and forms as archetypes (Jung 1978: para. 104). Archetypes are extremely powerful in the sense that they are numinous; they are containers for images which carry powerful energy. When they appear in dreams, fantasy, or waking life, they compel us to action (ibid.: para. 109). What happens to Jules is numinous: it triggers the archetype of the great Self, or God, and he is compelled to change his life; he has had a spiritual awakening.

Jung cautioned that there is potential danger with the archetypes of the collective unconscious when they are not approached carefully and with respect. There is the chance that the ego may be swallowed by the unconscious, resulting in psychosis. When personal change is called for, "consciousness is confronted by the objective fact of the unconscious, often enough an avenging deluge," as is illustrated by Jules's harrowing experience (Jung 1970: para. 364). This descent into the unconscious is one which can renew the consciousness of the individual, who feels an epiphany. For the one who meets this challenge successfully, rich symbols and numinous energy will appear in the form of archetypes. If, however, the confrontation with the unconscious is not approached within some sort of sacred container, then literalization of the energy is realized, often resulting in death. As Vincent's story suggests, the energy of the arche- types is often fatal if not contained, e.g., by religion (as in Jules's case), therapy, or an initiation ritual, etc.

Vincent's character does not respond to the call of the unconscious as Jules's does. He and Jules argue about what they have both witnessed and survived. Jules has had a powerful, religious experience and he knows it. Vincent is dubious, and the unconscious continues to confront him in the film in ever more negative forms: eventually it swallows him. The viewer is being offered two possible outcomes of the encounter between the ego and the Self (or the unconscious). When the ego's adaptation is disturbed, there is always the potential for great beauty or huge disaster.

Vincent's ego confrontations usually take place after he visits the bathroom, which appears to symbolize the unconscious plumbing of the psyche. The first time he descends he emerges to discover that Marsellus's wife, his charge for the evening and a signifier for his stuck anima, has overdosed on heroin and is dying. Another time he ventures to the rest room, and when he comes out, Jules is in the midst of being robbed. The man who surprises Jules and Vincent in the apartment and nearly kills them both is hiding in the bathroom. Vincent is finally undone, though, when he emerges from the bathroom obliviously one last time: Butch kills him.

Vincent, a heroin addict, is spiritually bereft and cynical. He continues on his way, fumbling through his life, oblivious to the call of the Self. Like Parsifal in the legend of the Grail, he forgets "to ask the vital question because he was not aware of his own participation in the action" (Jung 1970: para. 753). Jules tells Vincent in their debate about their experience: "If you find my answers frightening, Vincent, you should cease askin' scary questions" (Tarantino 1994: 148).

Vincent's fear, I think, is really about his own ego's participation in what the unconscious is presenting to him. Jung observed that the individual must recognize its own involvement in the process, or the potential for change remains in the images only; the psyche stays the same (Jung 1970: para. 753). When one consciously realizes one's involvement, as Jules does, the unconscious elements which are being offered as jewels can be integrated and assimilated, and offer the individual deep and personal meaning in life which then manifests in the outer world as new life.

This integration is what Jung (1970) (following the sixteenth-century alchemist Gerhard Dorn) called the *unio mentalis*, or insight. In alchemy, *unio mentalis* (literally, the mental coming together) is associated with the *albedo* or whitening, the second stage (following the dark *nigredo*) of the three-stage alchemical opus. Jung believed that this kind of spiritual insight was the beginning of actual individuation, which is accompanied by symbols of totality and the Self. The process of becoming conscious involves the individual's confrontation by the outer world as well as confrontation by the inner world, or the unconscious. The process is not complete without both the objective and the subjective states being integrated, and the movement between the two becoming facile. This totality of union cannot be achieved without first gaining total separation of the confused opposites, which is illustrated beautifully in the interpenetration of good and evil in the film.

*Pulp Fiction* can be seen on one level as being simply a film about good and evil, but it is also about the redemption of good out of evil, about transformation, about the individual being called to action and being held accountable for participation in life and its outcomes. The film acknowledges that there is a dynamic cycle of opposites at work in the world, and that nothing can exist without its shadow. Campbell (1972) observes that the "legends of the redeemer describe the period of desolation as caused by a moral fault on the part of man" (1972: 352). Perhaps it is not a moral fault that we have produced, but like Vincent it is our inability to confront our shadow which has created such cultural desolation. The contemporary setting of the film illustrates very well the "wasteland" we live in today. Campbell, who makes a crucial point about the dark times we are experiencing, in terms of humankind's history and mythology, saw that "The golden age, the reign of the world emperor, alternates, in the pulse of every moment of life, with the waste land, the reign of the tyrant. The god who is creator becomes the destroyer in the end" (ibid.).

We see this same cycle occurring in the individual. Jung realized that for evolution of consciousness to occur, there must be tension to induce movement, and that the shadow provides this energy. He observed that the contrast between opposites is essential for psychic energy to become available to the individual (Jung 1970: para. 707). Jung knew that the ego has to come to terms with its shadow. He felt that this is the relationship that is symbolized in the *unio mentalis*, for the alchemists the integration of spirit and soul which created the first stage of the mysterious joining of opposites they called the *coniunctio* (ibid.).

## Coniunctio *as consciousness*

Tarantino (1994) illustrates the interplay of opposites throughout the film. The characters of Butch and Marsellus and their relationship are a good example of the tension, separation, eventual conjunction and subsequent redemption of opposites. Butch, the white boxer hero, has been paid a large sum of money by Marsellus, the black Mafia kingpin, to take a dive in a fight. Butch ends up killing his opponent with a fatal punch and wins the fight. He plans to run off with Marsellus's payoff, and the money he has won in many lucrative bets from the fixed fight. Butch has inadvertently left his great-grandfather's gold watch (which is loaded with symbolism in the context of the film) in his apartment. He decides to risk his life returning to retrieve the magical gold watch. Of course, Vincent and Marsellus are waiting for him to return, so that they can kill Butch for double-crossing them. When Butch and Marsellus have their run-in, they end up trapped together in a very dark situation where Marsellus gets raped. Butch frees himself, and there is a pivotal moment where he almost leaves the raging, wounded, and helpless kingpin to his fate, but instead he returns with a Samurai sword to kill the attackers, thus saving Marsellus.

The aspect of the wounded and helpless king is very important in the process of individuation and the emergence of consciousness. The king "constantly needs the renewal that begins with a descent into his own darkness, an immersion into his own depths, and a reminder that he is related by blood to his adversary" (Jung 1970: para. 471). In our naturally shifting state between opposite poles, we need constant compensation to keep us from becoming stuck in an extreme attitude. In this aspect, we are indeed our own blood adversary. As a symbol, the king stands for consciousness, and originally has the "ability to unite the polarity of all existence in a symbol" (ibid.). Over time, with the increasing emergence of clarity, certain attitudes or ideas gain a "monarchic content" in which the ego can ultimately become tyrannical. The unconscious then has to compensate, and the king/ego has to descend into the underworld to become balanced again (ibid.).

This cyclical state of affairs is what the conjunction of opposites is about. First the separation has to occur of black and white, upper and underworld, conscious and unconscious. Only after this separation can the union and integration take place. Jules has to see his own tyranny before he can behave differently. Butch and Marsellus have to be dragged into the underworld and violated in order for their relation to be anything other than extremely simplistic and oppositional. Then a dignity occurs for both the characters:

> a dignity which makes it morally possible for a man to stand by his soul, and be convinced that it is worth his while to persevere with it. Only then will he realize that the conflict is *in him*, that the discord and tribulation are his riches, which should not be squandered by attacking others . . .
>
> (Jung 1970: para. 511)

These two who are sworn enemies have now gone through a profound experience together. Clearly, they are opposites. One is black, one is white. Once Marsellus was the king and held the power, but Butch holds his life in the balance in the underworld. Butch does not have to save Marsellus; in fact, it is against his nature. Like Jules, he does the opposite of what he would normally do. He had been trying desperately to kill Marsellus right before they got kidnapped. Yet we see that this is what the conjunction of opposites produces: "if a union is to take place between opposites like spirit and matter, conscious and unconscious, . . . it will happen in a third thing, which represents not a compromise but something new" (Jung 1970: para. 765). Now their heroic roles are reversed, yet Butch and Marsellus are connected to each other by the gold imagery; one has the golden time of his ancestors, the other the Grail briefcase that glows with a golden light. They are shadow and light, two aspects of the one, shifting roles and changing. A third, spiritual, thing is now produced from the union of these two opposites; a kind of intimacy arises out of the behavior that has been up to this point alien to Butch. Through his rescue of Marsellus, a different relationship is created between them. It is neither that of sworn enemy nor friends, but something else which their intimate union has produced. Such strange conjunctions create a no-man's land, a liminal territory where creation may exist, and the third option is produced. The situation then is no longer "black and white," but many shades of gray, with peculiar nuances which demand our attention and response, not blind reactions from thoughtless habit and one-sidedness.

The possibilities become endless with the conjunction of opposites because of the creative potential involved and the numinous and liminal space produced. When Butch takes leave of Marsellus, it is to ride off on his attacker's motorcycle named "Grace" to Knoxville, Tennessee, where our nation's gold is stored under the earth.

Another interesting conjunction of opposites involves Jules's quoting Ezekiel from the Old Testament. Jung (1970) notes that Ezekiel's vision of God came from the north, which in Hebrew mythology is the origin of evil. Jung goes on to observe that in a holistic and primitive notion of God, the conjunction of opposites such as God coming from the place of evil is normal; the shadow is part of the godhead. Once conscious reflection begins to develop, however, the concept of opposites becomes an issue, and collectively and individually we do everything to avoid evil (Jung 1969: para. 191). The fact that Jules is quoting Ezekiel is fascinating in the light of these observations. What is happening to Jules is also happening to us as we view the film. Slowly the simplistic, primitive, and one-sided content of Jules's original way of thinking differentiates as he becomes a complex creature, both good and evil, darkness and golden, a union of sublime complexities which we all relate to on a deep level. Like Jules, we are all "tryin' real hard to be a shepherd" because we have all recognized with fear and horror the "tyranny of evil men" in ourselves (Tarantino 1994: 157–58). The feeling this final scene releases is that perhaps, after all, we can be redeemed as well. The characters in this film tell us, as Jung has, that this cannot be achieved without acknowledging our collective and individual shadow.

*Pulp Fiction*'s characters and action provide an excellent opportunity to see several of Jung's guiding principles of individuation illustrated, although this review has addressed only three. The film serves as a reminder of where Americans are as a society, psychologically. We have collectively come to an extreme place of separation which Jung warned about. We have lost sight of the creative elements of the shadow, both as a nation and individually. As Jung predicted, when this happens:

> the result is one-sidedness, which is then compensated from the unconscious without our help. The counterbalancing is even done against our will, which in consequence must become more and more fanatical until it brings about a catastrophic enantiodromia. Wisdom never forgets that all things have two sides, and it would also know how to avoid such calamities if ever it had any power. But power is never found in the seat of wisdom; it is always the focus of mass

interests and is therefore inevitably associated with the illimitable folly of the mass man.

(Jung 1970: para. 470)

As Robert Romanyshyn has observed, "film portrays the mythology of an age. It is a shared myth, a cultural daydream" (Romanyshyn 1989: 19). *Pulp Fiction* serves as a mythical reminder to us of what our potential is, both positively and catastrophically, both individually and as a culture. To avoid Vincent's fate, Americans need to participate in their own awakening and process. The elements of individuation that come alive in this film are the very ones we need to become conscious. Without awareness of the whole cycle, we see only one part, and thus never attain our full potential as human beings. Moreover, the creative energy which is a result of the tension produced by the shadow's interaction with the ego is missing if we negate the underworld. The numinous third option of the transcendent function is missing if the king/ego is given unlimited power. The underworld characters which haunt our dreams and populate the pulp fictions that the world devalues but devours need to be seen for the spiritual strivings that they are: we need to know what they are asking of us, and what they have come to tell us about ourselves. Without their essential darkness, we will become lost in the one-sidedness of the daylight world.

An earlier version of this essay, which appeared in *Projections, The Journal of the Forum for the Psychoanalytic Study of Film*, vol. 10, no. 2 (1996), appears in revised form in *The Soul of Popular Culture: Looking at Contemporary Heroes, Myths, and Monsters*, edited by Mary Lynn Kittleson, Open Court Publishing, 1998.

## References

Campbell, J. (1972) *The Hero with a Thousand Faces*, Princeton: Princeton University Press.

Edinger, E. (1985) *Anatomy of the Psyche: Alchemical Symbolism in Psychotherapy*, La Salle, Ill.: Open Court.

—— (1992) *Ego and Archetype*, Boston: Shambhala.

Jung, C.G. (1969) *Aion: Researches into the Phenomenology of the Self*, trans. R.F.C. Hull, Princeton: Princeton University Press.

—— (1970) *Mysterium Coniunctionis: An Inquiry into the Separation and Synthesis of Psychic Opposites in Alchemy*, trans. R.F.C. Hull, Princeton: Princeton University Press.

—— (1978) *Two Essays on Analytical Psychology*, trans. R.F.C. Hull, Princeton: Princeton University Press.

Jung, E. and von Franz, M.-L. (1970) *The Grail Legend*, trans. A. Dykes, Boston: Sigo.

Romanyshyn, R. (1989) *Technology as Symptom and Dream*, New York: Routledge.

Tarantino, Q. (1994) *Pulp Fiction*, New York: Hyperion.

# Chapter 3

# Image in motion

*Pat Berry*

Film began at the same time as depth psychology, at the end of the nineteenth century. This period is generally thought of as the beginning of so called "modernity." The telegraph had been invented; so had the telephone and photograph. Railroads were at their peak in this time of exploding industrial capitalism and consumerism. People were moving to cities in droves, making street life more complex and chaotic than ever. In cities, people found traffic, noises, storefronts, windows, bodies, glances, things to look at, in, and out for.

The crowd, the notion of a mass audience, had become an entity. Posters proliferated to attract these crowds. A journalist at the time described the poster:

> Triumphant, exultant, brushed down, pasted, torn in a few hours and continually sapping the heart and soul with its vibrant futility, the poster is indeed the art . . . of this age of fever and laughter, of violence, ruin, electricity, and oblivion.

> (Talmeyr, 1896: 216)

And that is just a poster.

With the world suddenly so in motion, not surprisingly impressionism sought to capture moments of it. Photography froze it; museums waxed it still. Folk museums fed on the longing for simpler, bygone days. At the same time, amusement parks, those Coney Islands of the senses, let folks relax and stroll along the midway, then tumbled, snapped, and whirled them in frenzied tempos at break-neck speeds, recreating the very stimulation they were trying to rest from. I see an "addictive" cycle here at the end of the last century. When the psyche moves into revolution, as at the turn of these two centuries, we find the same sorts of frenetic phenomena.

Sociologists wrote about the disturbing increase in nervous stimulation and bodily peril (Singer, 1995: 74), the increase in crime, the loss of traditional values and morality. Psychopathology was "rampant": neurasthenia (last century's "chronic fatigue syndrome"?), hysteria, and what we might call "post-traumatic stress disorder" resulting from train travel. "Railway spine" and "railway brain" were serious diagnoses, medical conditions.

In fact, taking a railway journey is rather like watching a movie. We sit in a seat and watch moving visuals through a frame – the window (Charney and Schwartz, 1995: 6). Movies were lurking in the shadow behind the eye, just waiting for the technology to open them into being.

So, no surprise, film arrived with modernity. Film, born of modern consciousness, represents it. Film is modern consciousness. Further, as film developed and changed, at various periods throughout the twentieth century, it corresponded with changes in the collective psyche. The reverse was also true, of course: As the psyche changed during the century, these changes were reflected in film. The result was the surprisingly liberated films of the 1920s, the screwball comedies of the depression/Hollywood Code era, *film noir* in the disillusionment of the Second World War, the personalistic psychology of the 1950s and 1960s.

One of the first films projected on a screen for people to watch together as an audience was Louis Lumière's 50-second *Workers Leaving the Factory*, made in 1895. By 1896, just a year later, more than two thousand people per day were flocking to the basement of Paris's Grand Café, which Lumière had rented to show his films.

What was going on here? Most Lumière films simply recorded an event: a boat leaving a harbor, a wall being torn down, a baby being fed, workers leaving the factory. Why not just go *watch* the workers leaving the factory? The reality would be more vivid; it has color, sound, and it is free. I think the answer is that the transformation that occurs in the act of filming creates or perhaps releases the "psyche" of the subject. The scene is no longer simply nature, but art. We experience this transformation from nature to art, and are magnetized by it. The transposition into art creates a spark. Of course there is also a loss. The life water, flesh, here-and-now tangibility of the actual event is sacrificed, creating perhaps a vacuum, an emptiness, in the event itself. But in return for this loss, the transformation into art provides form and an aesthetic level of excitement: pleasure. With film, this transformation occurs as the event is framed in the camera's eye. Essentially film is a series of such frames sped through a camera and projected onto a screen.

Perhaps transformation into art is one way of dealing with the overstimulation of modern life. Art binds chaotic impressions into form.

Once bound, the impressions can then become pleasurable. Perhaps film emerged when it did because it was just the therapy people needed to bind into manageable form the chaos of modern overstimulation.

Film taught us as well. How the mind works, associates, pays attention – those were topics of current interest. Jung, for example, was trying in his association experiments to determine what interfered with attention, for indeed the overstimulation of modernity required that attention become sharper, quicker, clearer, more flexible. Consciousness needed to master more because so much more was happening.

Of course entertainment is a paradox: it not only binds but also stimulates. Those 2,000 people a day trooping into the Grand Café were not going there to relax. They were going because witnessing events projected on a screen was exciting, stimulating. Something of life was being transformed, just by passing through a camera and being projected onto a screen. To participate in this experience as a spectator was to be changed, for better and for worse.

For the better because we need to be threatened a bit, overstimulated in order to generate creative processes, individually and culturally. Of course the threat of modernity and post-modernity has spawned pathological offspring: mental illness, violence, crime. But the pressures and displacements of modernity have also challenged us to create forms that spring from, yet transform and bind, the very energies that threaten us.

Things fall apart, the center does not hold, Yeats told us. When we find ourselves on the edge of breakdown, the most creative response to that dis-order, dis-ease, is to make something with it. We cannot put things back the way they were. But we can get in step with the new by creating, using the alignments/materials of the new disorder/order.

In film at the turn of the last century, several women and men were poised to do just that. I will focus on two. The first, George Melies, was an illusionist, a stage magician with a penchant for spectacle. In 1902 Melies made a ten-minute film, *Trip to the Moon*, which was probably the longest, certainly the most innovative, film up to that time. He drew upon elements from Jules Verne's novel *From the Earth to the Moon* (1865) and H.G. Wells's *The First Men in the Moon* (1901).

Melies' film opens with a society of astronomers (the head astronomer and narrator being Melies himself) discussing the possibility of going to the moon. Five are chosen. Assisted by bare-legged assistants in fetching sailor costumes, the scientists change into "traveling clothes," then clamber into the rocketship, and shoot to the moon. Upon landing, weary from the trip, they fall asleep and dream vividly of angry stars. When they awaken, snow has fallen as punishment for their intrusion. They then descend into the interior of a crater, where they come upon moon people, with whom some conflict evolves. To escape, they leap into their space-craft, though one moon person clings to the outside, and plunge into the ocean. This film is of technical and historical interest, and also delightful to watch.

The second pioneer is Edwin Porter, a studio chief for Edison in America. Porter filmed mostly reenacted news events, comic strips, and political cartoons. He is recognized for his canny sense of popular taste. *The Great Train Robbery* (1903) initiated the Western genre in film. As it opens, a group of outlaws are seizing a train station by knocking out and tying up the station master. The villains then mount a train, enter the baggage car, shoot the guard, blow up the safe, rob the passengers, shoot a man attempting escape, wrestle a guard on the roof, knock him out, and toss him off the moving train. Escaping from train to horse, the bad guys gallop off to a spot in the woods where they dismount to divide up the spoil. Just in the nick of time a posse arrives to foil the plan.

Both films are technologically and imaginatively innovative. Both are narratives, but with distinctively different styles. Were we to look at these films ontologically, we might say Melies' *Trip to the Moon* assumes a primacy of imagination, whereas Porter's train robbery mimics a more sensate, realistic world. Jung, judging from his essay "Psychology and Literature" (*CW* 15), would categorize Melies' work as "visionary," thus deeper, more profound, archetypal; he would consider Porter's more mundane or "personalistic," since Porter tells of events from a seemingly more literal, realistic, or conscious level.

However, in film *everything* is a constructed reality. Viewed simply as films, *Trip to the Moon* and *The Great Train Robbery* differ merely in genre: one is science fiction, the other realistic. But these categories are simply forms, ways of imagining. Working with imagination does not mean the setting has to be on the moon. The setting might be the top of a moving train, or indeed the moon. But whatever the location, one can do the work from a basis in imagination.

Put another way, if we begin with the assumption that imagination/ image is primary, then everything we look at will be one or another form of imagining/imaging. Actually the eye, the way of seeing, is what is truly imaginative. But an imaginative way of seeing is imaginative not because it proceeds from a realm or a category designated imagination, or "visionary," but because imagining is how this seeing sees. Thus, imagination exists insofar as the engaged eye is seeing imaginatively. So too, the product of that seeing is a product of imagination, whatever the genre or form.

The camera is a kind of eye. In the first films the camera was simply planted in front of the Lumière factory door and cranked. So the camera was a stationary "perceiver" framing whatever happened in front of it: perceiver here, object/action there. Soon, however, an added wheel or two allowed the camera to move. It could rotate its head, horizontally and vertically. Now not only was the action moving out in front; the perceiver moved as well. And the way the perceiver moved – fast, slow, fluid, jerky – influenced the whole. In film the perceiver (camera) and the object perceived are always interacting. This interaction can be quite complex: the camera might pan 360 degrees, say, while the subject moves vertically. The film we see is the result of this interaction. Thus the camera interacts with the world for and with us, mimicking human perception, thinking for us.

How does film think? Certainly in a way that attempts to parallel, yet also challenge, human perception. Film thinks in many ways, as it reflects and creates human experience. Thus film thinks perspectively – from a perspective. Is the camera low, looking up, so the subject towers, like Kane did so famously, in *Citizen Kane* (1941)? More currently and complexly, in *Hamlet* (2000), Gertrude (Diane Venora), Claudius (Kyle MacLachlan), and Hamlet (Ethan Hawke) sweep along the Manhattan sidewalk and loom larger than life, as they must. The form is tragedy, in which the hero, Hamlet, virtually by definition, must be larger than life. The camera obliges.

If the camera takes the opposite perspective – higher, looking down – what is filmed becomes – not appears but becomes – diminished. The camera creates that reality. Does the camera push up close to accuse, scrutinize, intrude? Consider the ultra closeups of Jeffery Wigand (Russell Crowe) in *The Insider* (1999): a man caught, intruded upon by TV's *60 Minutes*, by his conscience, by the defiant blemishes of his character. We study him in these closeups. We stare at his jaw, the pores of his skin. Or perhaps, as in *Any Given Sunday* (1999), the camera brings us right onto the field, knee-to-knee on the scrimmage line as hunks of Titanic body parts clash and crash around us. Perhaps the camera backs off, allowing relief, context, overview. It may even grant the grace of dissociation as crane shots sweep high above an orchard, branches occluding the acknowledgement of father/daughter incest, in *Cider House Rules* (1999). Perspective creates emotional reality in film.

Film also thinks symbolically, for example east to west. The journey of the pioneers in American Westerns was typically shot right to left (Huss and Silverstein, 1968: 63), toward the setting sun, *naturam*, the way of nature. This directionality works at an unconscious, symbolic level.

Perhaps right to left as east to west is archetypal. Perhaps it is a metaphor for the way map-makers imagined maps. To film's way of thinking, it doesn't matter. What matters is how this direction "works" aesthetically – here, now in this shot, in this film.

Film also thinks elliptically. Shortcuts are key to the medium. Imagine your hand passing all the way across your field of vision. Now cut out the whole middle section of that motion, so all that remains is your hand starting to move, and just finishing. Put these two ends together and you have an abbreviation of the motion. Our perceptual imagination understands this abbreviation immediately. Film is, generally speaking, composed of these abbreviations or "cuts."

Cuts can also connect perspectives. Melies, in his *Trip to the Moon*, shows the landing on the moon from two different perspectives. To perceive physically from two different perspectives we would have to be physically in one place for the first perception, then physically in a different place for the second. That would require a lot of walking around. But our imagination – and the camera – can do it in a flash. Film tutors this increasingly quick and multiple imagining.

Film also loves to experiment, testing the limits of what is possible. "Fast cutting," a spin-off of MTV, is all the rage. Since the number of cuts quickens the pace, current film frequently uses multiple cuts so that films race right along. *The Blair Witch Project* (1999), *Breaking the Waves* (1996), *Wonderland* (1999), to name a few, experiment with hand-held cameras, giving a grainy, intimate, or documentary feel. *Timecode* (2000) is presented on a screen divided into four areas, each a different perspective on the story, each filmed in one long take by video. On the Internet one can now interact with a 360-degree film by pointing and clicking in any direction.

Digital technology has added revolutionary power and ease to exploration in a field already rich in possibilities. When these explorations or experiments work, they change perception, and alter awareness. One of the primary ways awareness changes is through the breaking of clichés.

One example is *The Straight Story* (1999). This film could have been over-the-top schmaltz – it is about family values, after all – were it not in the hands of iconoclast David Lynch (*Eraserhead*, 1976; *Elephant Man*, 1980; *Blue Velvet*, 1986, etc.) and his able cameraman, 81-year-old Freddy Francis.

The film opens with an aerial shot ranging over Iowa cornfields. From this distance, the ground appears abstract, perhaps more like nubby straw matting than fields of corn. Panning down behind a threshing machine, the camera emphasizes by its position the ruler-straight edge of the mowing pattern (straight Iowa?, straight values?, Straight Story?). A dissolve (the standard transition in this part of the film) takes us to the threshing machine, finished for the day, driving down Main Street through late-afternoon, heavily demarcated shadows. The town is empty except for a few dogs wandering in contrary directions. Another dissolve takes us high above a residential yard, dollie left to note someone leaving, back and stop. This is the first time the camera has stopped, though it is still high, impersonal, and somewhat disinterested. Now it tracks down slightly as a woman in pink, sitting in a lounge chair, takes off her sun reflector, gets up, and goes around behind the house. The camera looks to the back area, heavy with demarcated shadows. The camera moves slowly, chilling, almost menacingly, through the shadows, then swoops alongside the house and suddenly stops at a window. We hear a thump within, but the camera remains fixed outside the window.

This stop at the window breaks a cinematographic cliché. We expect the camera to take us through the window into the house, which a camera normally does when it stops at a window – particularly with a thump inside. Here, by *not* going through the window, the camera awakens us. A little angel jumps out at that moment.

Stopping here is also meaningful on thematic levels. One is death. Already in what has preceded we have seen enough metaphors to realize where the story resides on the life/death cycle: end of the season, heavy shadows, harvest, end of the day, the grim reaper (the threshing machine). Even the dissolves (one image gradually fading out as another emerges into focus) bespeak the life cycle. The camera is like death's inevitability: it is as near as death is near, yet impersonal, high, uncaring, then predatory. The camera is not friendly in these opening shots.

The camera sends another message: this is a "closed house," "self-enclosed," "shut in." That is why we do not go through the window. Later old Alvin will leave this "shut in" space where he has been subsisting with his daughter. Heroically he will set off on his lawnmower toward Wisconsin to mend a feud with his failing brother before it is too late. *The Straight Story* is an archetypal journey, a Pilgrim's Progress along the way, a Cain and Abel sin of pride and envy between brothers, a reconnection and completion on the portal of death, and an odyssey as old as Homer. And this is not an exceptional film, really. Many films contain this level of myth.

The window that the camera did *not* go through made these mythemes or archetypes possible by creating them anew. To my mind, myth is not real unless it is cracked open, unless it is fresh. Otherwise, an archetype is simply a cliché, or "type." For an aesthetic experience, like most experience, to be real, clichés must be broken – which is also why I chose "image in motion" as the title of this chapter. I do allude to motion as in motion pictures, but more significantly also to motion as the change necessary for recreating experience to make it vital.

Of course we cannot repeat this shot of the camera stopping at the window. It would quickly become a cliché. We can watch even the most extraordinary older film and experience some moment, gesture, bit of dialogue as obvious to our current sensibility. Film has taught us well over the century. It has trained our perception to be so quick, our understanding to be so adroit. Give us just a hint cinematographically – a gesture, a tone, a look in the eye – and we get it.

How do movies think? Nowadays movies also think COOL. Not cool as the word once meant in the days of beatniks and cool jazz: gentle and progressive. In the late 1960s *cool* meant marijuana mellow, calm, detached. Now cool means anything from novel, to "with it," to simply attractive. Cool is *not* disinterested and not calm. Cool can be brains splattered all over the inside of a car – *Pulp Fiction* (1994) cool. Cool keeps its cool so long as it is ironic, self-conscious. Cool looks at itself; cool rarely takes itself seriously or at face value. Cool is a step removed; cool is a camera looking. With cool, film is, like, "in."

*Being John Malkovich* (1999) is a cool movie. At one moment, in the ultimate point-of-view shot, the camera takes us inside the head of John Malkovich. We peer out through a portal, hear sounds as echoed inside the chamber of his head. This absurd fantasy "works" somehow. Indeed, within the movie it works so well that people line up, stooping under the midget-high ceiling of floor "seven-and-a-half", and pay $200 for 15 minutes of the experience. The joke (and everything in this film is a joke, or at least ironic – which is why it is a cool movie) is about the desperate desire to be someone else, particularly if that someone is a vessel for projection as an actor, a John Malkovich, presumably is.

To want to be somebody else might imply, as it does in this movie, that you dislike being who you are. In the trade we might call that lack of self-esteem, insecurity, poor sense of identity. Indeed identity confusion is said to be symptomatic of our times. With cool you may be so self-reflexive, so self-conscious that you lose the experience of self.

Earlier I maintained that the creative arts need pathology. Here I would add that pathology is, alchemically speaking, the *prima materia*, the base stuff from which any creation takes place. Art requires and responds to pathology. Identity disorder? Film responds to identity disorder by exploring identities. Film is fascinated with dissociated identity, point of view, subjectivity – which it explores by plunging into sometimes the most extreme states.

Current film ushers us into subjectivities we would not have dreamt of entering a few years ago. Spike Lee places us in the shoes of serial killer David Berkowitz. We hear ourselves walking, breathing, we break out in goose bumps, as we prowl the Bronx neighborhood of *Summer of Sam* (1998). Or we turn neo-Nazi in *American History X* (1998), an extraordinary film for understanding from the inside how racist identity is formed. Or we become a girl longing to be a boy (*Boys Don't Cry*, 1999), a boy longing to be a girl (*The Crying Game*, 1992; *All About My Mother*, 1999). Peering through the narcoleptic eyes of River Phoenix (*My Own Private Idaho*, 1991), we nod off. Then we jolt awake with the high-speed, fast-cutting, repetitive, senseless lifestyle of addiction in *Trainspotting* (1996).

We can get into these pathological experiences precisely because our identities are loose, dissociable. Because we are less centered we can be more multiple. We do not know our point of view surely, how we think, so we take pleasure seeing life through others' eyes, thinking others' thoughts. We learn to know ourselves through being someone else.

Such psychopathology is not necessarily bad – or good. But making something with the pathology is a fitting response – certainly it is film's response – to the quandary of our times. Film uses disorder to create order of another sort, uses the lack of singular identity to explore multiple identities, uses the loss of sure-footed reality to explore other kinds of reality, other modes. Film responds to psychopathology by going into it, crafting it.

So too the answer to our postmodern dilemma lies not in merely turning our backs on technological advancement, or in longing nostalgically for simpler, less frenetic times. Film's response to modernity a century ago was to bind its chaos into form by crafting it. Our response a century later is identical. Like film, we create reality by framing life's events, focusing on its particulars. Our angles, values, interactions construct the world in which we live. We are making film all the time. We discover reality as we reframe, as we change focus, angles, directions, rhythms, as we open clichés, and watch angels leap out of closed windows. We are in motion, our world a moving image. Here at the start of the twenty-first century, that is terrifically exciting.

# References

Charney, L. and Schwartz, V. (eds) (1995) *Cinema and the Invention of Modern Life*, Berkeley: University of California Press.

Huss, R. and Silverstein, N. (1968) *The Film Experience*, New York: Dell.

Jung, C.G., References are to the *Collected Works* (*CW*) by volume and paragraph.

Singer, B. (1995) "Modernity, Hyperstimulus, and the Rise of Popular Sensationalism," *Cinema and the Invention of Modern Life*, eds Charney, L. and Schwartz, V., Berkeley: University of California Press.

Talmeyr, M. (1896) "L'Age de l'affiche," *La Revue des deux mondes*.

# Part II

# Four films and a director

# Chapter 4

# The Grail quest and
# *Field of Dreams*

*John Hollwitz*

During the 1990s, thousands of people each summer traveled to Dyersville, a small farm town in the northeast corner of Iowa in the middle of the United States. They came to visit the site on which Phil Alden Robinson had filmed *Field of Dreams*, a 1989 movie starring Kevin Costner. The site was owned by two farmers whose property line ran through a cornfield. The cornfield had been made into a baseball field for the film. The field remained after the shooting because one of the farmers decided not to plant over a part of the field around which the movie's plot was based. The site was not a commercial venture in any sense that Hollywood recognizes. It was unadvertised, undeveloped for visitors, free. At first, the site did not even appear on local maps. Yet thousands of people came each year to see it. They walked quietly around the field, played pickup baseball games, left personal reflections in a series of bound journals which the farmer left on a stand behind home plate.

It is difficult to account in conventional critical terms for such behavior. The movie somehow touched the soul. Understanding the movie may require a critical perspective which takes the soul seriously. I would like to discuss such a perspective based on Jung's psychology. The film uses the archetypal mythologems of the Grail and of Demeter to present a story of masculine wounding and recovery.

Medical psychology shares a common inspiration with literary and film analysis. Important moments in psychological development can be described in something like literary terms because we often experience them in narrative or lyric forms. Psychodynamic literary criticism is almost as old as psychoanalysis itself. Few psychoanalytic theorists have had as strong an interest as Jung's in the narrative construction of psyche. Jung described the unconscious as an author, or at least as a very compelling Muse. In analytical psychology, much of what we think we know about ourselves and the world is based on complex emotional reactions, responses to metaphors; psychological development is an interaction between a creative source and the moderating influence of conscious, rational perspective.

This theme runs through the fifty years of Jung's work. However, he explicitly addressed literature in only a few essays. Others have adapted his psychodynamic model to film and literary criticism. In general, two types of critical perspectives have emerged from his psychology.

The first is a straightforward adaptation of analytical constructs to literary processes. This is perhaps the most conservative Jungian critical method, since Jung used it himself, most notably in his comments on Rider Haggard's *She*. (Except for Jung's fondness for Goethe, of whom he convinced himself he was a descendant, Jung's literary preferences were pedestrian. Freud liked Shakespeare; Jung liked pulp fiction.) This approach to literary criticism examines shadow figures, anima and animus, sometimes archetypal images, occasionally alchemical symbols. In a more general form (such as Northrop Frye, Mircea Eliade, or the young Joseph Campbell) this method became a search for a monomyth.

Although this approach has been very popular, it is severely limited in three important respects. First, it is inevitably reductive, peculiar given Jungians' claims to be less reductive than the Freudians. This Jungian approach adds nothing to psychoanalytic criticism. Certainly Iago can be seen as shadow, or Circe as an anima figure, just as Hamlet, Moses, and Michelangelo had Oedipal problems. But our experience of *Othello* or Homer is not much enriched as a result.

In addition, this approach quickly hits a psychological dead end which reflects a second important limitation of traditional Jungian criticism. Knowing that Hedda Gabler may have an animus problem or that Obi Wan Kenobe is a version of the Wise Old Man leaves us asking "OK, *now* what?" – or, more pointedly, "OK, *so* what?" It is not difficult to use Jungian theory eloquently to show that anything can mean anything else, without actually producing a conclusion for lived psychological experience. Used in this fashion, Jungian psychology becomes yet another form of fashionable postmodern relativism. The problem is conspicuous among some "archetypal" psychologists who denounce a reductive approach in favor of engaging the terrain of archetypal associations to symbolic products. This form of archetypal criticism maintains movement, but it is movement in circles.

A third limitation of Jungian criticism, and of Freud's as well, is that it is often inconsistent with empirical psychological fact. The personality constructs which Jung described were as much products of his time as they were of the human soul. Perhaps Jung would have agreed, but many of his followers do not. Typology, which represents the extent of many people's knowledge of Jung in the United States, is a case in point. Critical traditions based on Jung's *Psychological Types* use constructs like extraversion, introversion, thinking–feeling–sensation–intuition, as keys to character, clinical assessment, or critical understanding. This approach warrants great caution. For one thing, it was not very important to Jung, who hardly mentioned it after the 1920s. Above all, empirical psychology raises serious questions about the validity and utility of Jungian typology.

I propose that an effective critical alternative to these methods should have the following characteristics. First, psychodynamic criticism should be dynamic. By this I mean that it should begin with the principle that symbolic products move psychological life forward, that they are in some sense goal-directed. There are two such goals, those of a director or author and those of the public. Both are suitable for psychodynamic criticism, but I believe that the relationship between symbolic products and the collective is more critically accessible and potentially more interesting.

Second, and following from this, psychodynamic criticism cannot be psychologically reductive. A symbolic product provokes an affective response that cannot by definition be provoked in any other way. The best critical perspective is the one which enlarges that affective response and shows the direction in which it moves. Psychological criticism which does not articulate a *telos* is too often aestheticization, preciosity, and self-indulgence.

Finally, psychodynamic criticism must be empirically defensible. The use of outdated or inaccurate psychological constructs will mean outdated or inaccurate psychological criticism. Further, it is intellectually dishonest and psychologically irresponsible to create film criticism from a patchwork of critical constructs known or strongly suspected to be scientifically untenable. This is precisely the criticism that Jung the physician leveled at the psychoanalysts of Vienna. Unfortunately, this characteristic now requires that many of the constructs of Jungian theory be used cautiously if at all in the light of empirically defined medical and psychological facts.

I would like to describe a psychodynamic critical method which meets these requirements. This method comes from a suggestion of Jung's and the elaboration of that suggestion in Marie-Louise von Franz's method-ology for the understanding of fairy tales. The approach is conceptually conservative, since it uses a technique that Jung applied very early in his work and practiced consistently until his retirement. Second, this approach attempts to be objective. More precisely, it attempts to be consistent with accepted empirical processes for scientific understanding – not perhaps the same kind of understanding that you would expect from a chemistry lab, but the understanding that Karl Kerenyi or Robert Graves sought when they tried to define comparative mythology as a science.

The method uses two approaches. Jung described the first of them as *amplification*, an adaptation of comparative linguistics for dream and cultural analysis. Amplification is a linguistic technique of multiplying parallel or analogous word forms, symbols, or icons (Jung, 1977: 173).

The second approach is von Franz's. As I mentioned earlier, she believed that critical comparisons were meaningless outside a developmental context. Psychodynamic criticism is meaningless if it is not predominately dynamic. If Jung and Freud were right, symbolic materials are supposed to *move* somewhere. In a series of important books on the oral tradition of fairy tales, von Franz sees stories almost as a succession of still photographs. Look where the story begins and then look where it ends. Differences in the settings and in the number or identity of characters are a roadmap to the story's dynamics and underlying meaning (von Franz, 1966).

When Jung described visionary narratives, he meant stories which were touched by the numinous, which seemed to have a kind of special glow that set them apart from other stories. This glow is not aesthetic, or at least not primarily aesthetic. A work may be a substantial piece of literature without being visionary. Similarly, a visionary work may not be a very good piece of literature. Jung's frequent references to Rider Haggard and his dubious opinion of contemporary fiction show his priorities in this regard: if you seek psyche, look first for the visionary.

*Field of Dreams* (1989), directed by Phil Alden Robinson, is a film of this type. The movie features Kevin Costner, Ray Liotta, James Earl Jones, and Burt Lancaster. The film is a fantasy, telling the story of Ray Kinsella, played by Costner. Kinsella, an Iowa corn farmer, follows the instructions of a mysterious voice to build a baseball diamond in his fields for the use of deceased players, including Shoeless Joe Jackson (Liotta), to locate a reclusive writer, Terrence Mann (Jones), and to locate an elderly doctor, Archie "Moonlight" Graham (Lancaster) who in his youth had played one inning of major league baseball without ever coming to bat. During Kinsella's (Costner's) quest, we learn that he had been estranged from his father, John, and had not reconciled when John died. Kinsella's actions heal significant wounds for each of the major characters. Shoeless Joe (Liotta), banned from baseball for his involvement in the 1919 Black Sox scandal, returns to the field of play; Mann (Jones) rediscovers hope and passion; Archie (Lancaster) gets his chance at bat. Finally, Ray meets his father in the form of one of the ghostly players on his field.

In aesthetic terms, *Field of Dreams* (1989) is a good movie, maybe even a very good movie. It is probably not a great movie, at least by the conventional standards of film aesthetics. Why did the film and the field become so popular? Was it the sport itself? The film makes much of the innocence of baseball, describing the game with a rhetoric of sentimentality about its place in American culture. In an important passage in the film, Terrence Mann (Jones) pleads with Ray (Costner) not to sell the farm despite the threat of imminent foreclosure. Mann urges Ray to believe his young daughter that "People will come" to save the field. The one constant in American life, he says, has been baseball, symbol of all that was once good, innocent, and fresh. People will come to touch that innocence. In the end they do. As the film closes, Ray plays catch with his reborn father; the camera tracks back to reveal miles of rural Iowa roads, filled with cars queuing on their way to the farm to see the field. The scene was prescient. Traffic jams on the roads to the site are not unusual, especially in late summer when the corn is tall.

A rhetoric of innocence has characterized many films about American sports. This tradition may have accounted for the substantial commercial success of the movie during initial release, but it does not fully explain the events in that cornfield in the past ten years. Dyersville, Iowa, seems an unlikely center for the preservation of baseball as an icon of American life. Baseball had its roots in the immigrant culture of the urban northeast. Until the advent of national television broadcasts, it had a primarily urban regional appeal. It retained its status as America's national pastime through the 1970s and into the 1980s, when professional American football began assuming progressively larger proportions of television revenue and merchandise sales, only to be overtaken in its turn by basketball, which once again invokes the feel of the city.

Further, baseball has lost much of its innocent glow. A players' strike and owners' lockout in 1995 initially reduced ticket sales, merchandising, and media contracts, even before the effects of the escalating economies of basketball and American football. And yet they keep coming by the carload and vanload, week after week, summer after summer.

The film is visionary in Jung's sense. It contains archetypal images, which is to say images that provoke similar emotional reactions at a level deep enough to be considered numinous. Experiencing these archetypal images is like being touched a little by the gods. The key to the movie's ongoing popularity most likely resides in those images.

Looking at overall shifts in locale and characters (von Franz's technique) suggests that *Field of Dreams* (1989) conjoins two distinct archetypal themes with striking similarities to the mythological tradition of Demeter and Kore (Persephone) and the medieval traditions of the Grail.

The movie's beginning parallels the end. The film starts with Ray Kinsella's (Costner's) voice-over narration of his relationship to his father, accompanied visually by snapshot photographs of him as a child (the first of which is in a cornfield) and of his father, or of his father's world, including the urban settings of Comiskey Field, Ebbets Field, and the Brooklyn Navy Yards, where his father worked. The two are seen in separate pictures, many of which are about baseball. We learn of the deep alienation between them. By the film's end, that alienation has been healed. Baseball again provides the overall context for the father–son relationship. The last scene contains Kinsella and his father, together, playing catch on the diamond. Kinsella is no longer a child and his father no longer an "old man" (Ray's description of him). Ray is older, his father younger, but they meet finally as equals, connected by the game.

Von Franz (1966) suggests that we examine the patterns of relationships which mark the movement from the earliest events to the last. In *Field of Dreams* (1989), the reconciliation is the fourth significant moment of healing in the film. In each of them, Ray (Costner) encounters male figures who were either historically important to his alienation from his father or central to his role as father himself. Terrence Mann (Jones) points out that Ray is doing penance for cruelty to his father. This penance is to provide these older male figures with a life moment that completes each person's individuation, that heals their most significant wounds.

Each of these male figures was central to one phase of Kinsella's life, and he meets them sequentially in the film. Shoeless Joe (Liotta), the first, was important to his childhood and provided the occasion for an adolescent rebellion against his father which was never reconciled. Joe Jackson (Liotta) had been John Kinsella's contemporary and hero. Ray's (Costner's) alienation from his father began with an insult centered on Shoeless Joe, who had been banned for life from the sport. Ray had told his father that he could "never respect a man whose hero was a criminal"; his father died before he could apologize. The field permits Joe to play again.

Terrence Mann (Jones) is the second important male figure, an icon of the 1960s, Kinsella's college years ("Mostly I majored in the '60s," he tells us). Mann has become cynical, disenchanted, misanthropic, until his soul is reawakened by joining Ray's quest and by the opportunity to step off the field into the world from which the ghostly ball players come.

Finally, Ray encounters Archie "Moonlight" Graham (Lancaster), offering him the moment of which he had dreamed since he abandoned baseball to practice medicine – a chance to face a big league pitcher just once. Doc Graham seems the most complex of these masculine figures. He is well adapted, content with his life, a healer and exemplar of the individuated masculine. He easily abandons the game to heal Ray's daughter, who nearly chokes to death during the film's climax.

Von Franz suggests that the progression of such encounters in a story maps the hero's personal transformation. In *Field of Dreams* (1989), this progression is a chronological reminiscence, a précis of Ray's life culminating in the reconciliation which closes the film. The father is missing when the film opens, or present only in reminiscence and guilt. The field and the game serve as a medium in which a succession of male figures connected to the father recovers something lost, connected to an earlier age of personal innocence. In the end, the game heals Ray's wounds, too, bringing his father back to life in a moment of restored innocence.

Well and good. But no matter how much the movie may romanticize the sport, the plot by itself seems insufficient to explain the strong appeal of this film. To do that, we need to understand how the movie works on an archetypal level.

The quest for the parent is an important archetypal motif. The movie explores this quest motif through symbolism reminiscent of Grail tradition and the mythologies of the mother goddess, the goddess of the earth, in Greece represented by Demeter.

The Grail legends represent one of the central myths of western culture. With strong precedents in Irish, Welsh, and possibly Scottish oral traditions, these stories emerged as written texts in a flurry of epics (chiefly prose poems) in the late twelfth century and the early thirteenth. The two most important Grail texts are the unfinished *Le Conte del Graal* by the French poet Chrétien de Troyes, probably the earliest of the Grail writers, and *Parzival*, by Wolfram von Eschenbach. Chrétien's poem was followed by four "continuations." In addition, a half dozen other prose poems of the period retold the story or extended it into Arthurian legend.

Though the stories vary greatly in overall plot and in important details, they share several elements in common. They are all about the quest for the Grail; the quest requires the transformation of a male hero; the Grail inhabits a magical space on the border between normal reality and the eternal; success in the quest heals the keeper of the Grail, a father figure; in most of the stories (though not in Chrétien's) this healing renews the wasteland into which the world had fallen as a result of the Grail-keeper's distress.

Popular tradition holds that the Grail is the cup that contained Christ's blood at the Last Supper. This is only one version of the story. In *Le Conte del Graal*, Chrétien does not specify what the Grail is, saying only that it is holy and that it shines with an unnatural light. In Wolfram's *Parzival*, the Grail is a stone. Other stories present it as a cornucopia, a self-moving source of food, an oracle, an object of precious metals, a reliquary, a patten, or a receptacle to hold Christ's blood. A cup or chalice is only one of its many possible forms, and not the most frequently mentioned.

More important are the Grail's functions. Emma Jung summarized the Grail as a source of food, of spiritual sustenance, of youth and health, of messages from God (Jung and von Franz, 1970: 155). The field of dreams has several Grail-like functions. As a place of pure sport, it suggests innocence, childhood, delight, the lost Eden before the ruptures of adolescence and the seriousness of adulthood. Like the Grail, the field heals people of their wounds. The second voice commands Ray to "Ease his pain." In the end, Ray realizes that this command was actually about himself. Still, encountering the field healed each of the principal figures in the film – Shoeless Joe (Liotta), Terrence Mann (Jones), Ray's father, Doc Graham (Lancaster), even Ray's obstinate brother-in-law, who is trying to buy the farm.

One of the Grail's properties in the early texts was its ability to dispense idiosyncratic remedies. Each person encountering the Grail receives what he or she desires or uniquely needs. The same is true in *Field of Dreams* (1989). Everyone who touches the field, or is touched by it, receives a different gift. Finally, the field retains characteristics of the Grail or of the Grail castle. In the Irish and Welsh oral traditions before Chrétien, the Grail castle restores youth and cures disease, though only for people capable of seeing it. In the written stories, the Grail restores youth eternally to the old, but only to those who are capable of seeing it when it is before them. One of the Grail's most important attributes is its ability to discriminate the worthy from the unworthy. In the movie, the ability actually to see the players is reserved for those with the gift to see beyond the superficial or the mundane. The gift is not given to everyone. Ray's brother-in-law is a greedy skeptic who insists that the field be plowed over and ultimately acquires the mortgage. Only the near tragedy of a choking accident and "Moonlight" Graham's (Lancaster's) emergence from the field open him to the vision that the others already share. In this and in other respects, the Grail story has close relationships to the symbolic iconography of medieval alchemy. The Philosophers' Stone (in popular, though inaccurate, legend that which turned lead into gold) was the healing substance. Like the Grail, the exact nature of the

Stone is unspecified; like the Grail, the Stone is for the elect; like the Grail, the Stone brings only the relief that was needed. Like baseball, the Stone was said to be so commonplace that most fail to notice it.

Some of those who experience the baseball diamond in the film believe that they are in heaven. Shoeless Joe (Liotta) and John Kinsella, Ray's father, both ask about this. (A popular bumper sticker in Midwestern America reads "'Is this heaven?' 'No, it's Iowa.'") The field is neither paradise nor earth. Ray's father, one of those who thinks he might be in heaven, is very clear that heaven does exist. Yet the field is not quite earth, either.

On one level – the level that the film itself invites – the field's heavenly quality comes from the nature of baseball in collective experience, from the appeal of the sacred time of youth to which Terrence Mann (Jones) refers in the critical speech that persuades Kinsella not to sell the farm. Baseball may be the repository of collective and individual memories of idealized innocence and Eden lost, but nothing in sentimentalized memory produces visions or gives youth to long-dead athletes. The field makes more sense as a mystical terrain or a geography of dreams. Again, comparison with the Grail seems appropriate. The Grail castle was traditionally a setting for mystical visions and experiences. In *Parzival* Wolfram describes the Grail as a source of joy equivalent to heaven. Those who visit the castle or meet the Grail King commonly believe that they have been transported beyond earth to Paradise or to a peculiar *demi-monde* which is part heaven and part earth.

In addition, one of the Grail's most important attributes was its ability to confer or restore youth and vigor. The Grail renews the soul and body, banishing age and infirmity, conferring the ability to remain eternally young – at least so long as you remain in its environs. The players cannot step beyond the field except to vanish in the corn stalks bordering the outfield. When Archie Graham (Lancaster) walks beyond the field to save Ray's daughter, he again becomes an elderly man and cannot return to play.

The Grail tradition demands that the hero (Percival, Galahad, or sometimes Lancelot) must find the Grail castle and ask the appropriate questions of the Grail King. Asking these questions produces two results in the later Grail stories. First, the questions heal the Grail King, whose afflictions are variously described in the stories as a wound in the groin, rendering him impotent, or in the feet. Jung, Emma Jung, von Franz, and others interpret the groin wound to suggest a lack of generativity, a state of psychological or spiritual impotence. Sometimes the wound is in the lower legs or feet. Stories of Bran the Blessed, also wounded in the foot, contained many Grail motifs. It may be too great a stretch to note that

Shoeless Joe Jackson got his name as a result of sore feet. However, were this a dream, such a detail could be very significant.

Whether wounded in the groin or in the feet, the Grail King is afflicted with something that causes sterility. But so is the Grail hero, usually through naivety or some unfinished business related to maturity. Ray feels stuck. We learn that he never much liked farming. He fears a life like his father's, a life of numbing routine. Grail authors after Chrétien portrayed a world which had been crippled by the Grail King's affliction. The first continuation of Chrétien's unfinished work credits the Grail hero with restoring fertility to a country which has become desolate and barren. The wasteland motif recurs throughout Grail stories and Arthurian legend, suggesting spiritual desolation or unauthentic life. Those Grail stories which treat the wasteland also describe its cure, the healing of the King's wound, which simultaneously brings the questing hero to maturity. At the end of the film, Ray learns that the mysterious voices which set him on the quest were actually his own.

In discussing the wasteland motif in Grail tradition, A.E. Waite connected the stories to pre-Christian vegetation mysteries surrounding the cycle of the seasons. (We might remember that the annual rhetoric of baseball does the same thing, arriving with the flowers of spring and departing with the fall.) In particular, Waite calls attention to the mythologem of Demeter and Persephone and the archetypal tradition of which they were a part (Waite, 1961).

Demeter was the Greek equivalent of the goddess of agriculture, the archetypal mother. By prior agreement with Zeus, Hades (the lord of the underworld) abducted her daughter, Persephone, to be his queen. Distraught, Demeter withdrew her blessing from the earth, which became barren. Ultimately Zeus arranged a compromise whereby Persephone rejoined her mother for most of the year but spent one season at Hades' side.

Demeter was particularly the goddess of corn. In legend, she introduced corn agriculture and provided the seeds for the first crops. Corn mills were consecrated to her (or to the figure equivalent to her) throughout ancient Europe. She is also related to Hecate, one of the so-called "dark" goddesses, associated like Artemis with the moon and a protector of hidden knowledge and magic. Among other things, Hecate brings her the news of Persephone and serves as a confidante. The archetypal image of Demeter is associated with nurturance, motherhood, abundance, and its opposite.

In the film, the "field of dreams" was originally a cornfield. The players appear in the corn and return to it at the end of each day of play. Apart from whatever symbolic value the cornfield may have, the archetypal feminine has very little explicit role in the film. Annie (Amy Madigan), Ray's wife, comes to share his visions in a critical sequence in which they have a common nighttime dream. And the film has no literal equivalent to Persephone.

The dramatic problem of the movie is Ray's sense of the increasing sterility of his life, the possibility that he occupies a wasteland in the midst of plenty. As I argued earlier, his quest serves as a kind of salvation for significant male figures, each of whom steps from a different and progressively more complex stage of his life, until his final meeting with his father as an equal. In ancient Greece, the Eleusinian Mysteries were sacred to Demeter and Persephone (under the name "Kore"). Relatively little is known of these Mysteries, but oral tradition and surviving iconography give us an idea of what probably went on. The Mysteries were an adolescent rite of passage especially for young women, a symbolic abduction to the underworld by Hades. Accomplishing this initiation prepared the girl for womanhood and motherhood, accomplished by ritualistically wrenching the girl from the childhood world of innocence and a preparation for the roles of adulthood, including the inevitability of death. The Persephone story, and apparently the Eleusinian rites, had something of the "fortunate fall" of later Christian tradition. Her abduction by Hades was cruel and heartless, but it was also necessary because it ultimately impelled her to growth and to an acquaintance with death as queen of the underworld.

Percival's Grail quest has often been described in similar terms, particularly in versions of the Grail story which emphasize the sterility of the land that came from the Grail King's wounding. As we have seen, *Field of Dreams* (1989) makes much of the idealized innocence of baseball and the loss of innocence in the transition to adulthood. This is very much an experience within the constellation of Demeter. The film goes a little further. Ray and Terrence Mann travel to Chisholm, Minnesota to find Archie Graham, unaware that he had died sixteen years earlier (in 1972). When they learn of his death, the film presents one of the few moments when it behaves like a conventional ghost story. Leaving their hotel room for a walk, Ray finds himself in 1972, a fact he realizes from a movie marquee proclaiming *The Godfather* as one of the year's best films. *The Godfather* is about the underworld. He then meets Doc Graham, intending to bring him back to Iowa to realize his deepest dream: the chance to bat against big-league pitching. Doc asks, "And is there enough magic in the moonlight, Ray Kinsella, to make this wish come true?" Magic in the moonlight is the province of Hecate, guardian of Persephone, friend of Demeter, facilitator of the transition from innocence to adulthood, from child to parent. Doc does eventually join Ray Kinsella and Terrence Mann, though in a dramatically different guise as a man returned to youth, for his chance at bat. He abandons his new youth and resumes his elderly persona to save Ray's daughter from choking. It is worth noting too that Demeter was the goddess invoked for choking.

In short, an archetypal reading of the movie offers a way to enrich our experience of this film and possibly to understand why it has subsequently compelled the attention that it has. On one level, the film is about baseball, the innocence of childhood, and the importance of restoring that innocence from a mature perspective. Structurally, the film says much more. The similarities to the far older traditions of the Grail quest or of Demeter and Persephone are more dynamic and much darker than a view of baseball as a romanticized Eden lost. The archetypal structures of the film suggest individuation motivated by guilt and regret. Though potentially life-giving, the masculine is deeply wounded. Failing to heal the wound threatens barrenness, sterility, failure of further development. Healing the wound restores the world and marks the transition to a new psychological condition based on accepting the loss of innocence. Such transitions are not easy. The film is not about regaining innocence, in baseball or in anything else. It is about recognizing the loss of innocence, mourning the loss, celebrating it, and moving on in the world anyway.

## References

Jung, C.G. (1977) *The Symbolic Life*, trans. R.F.C. Hull, *Collected Works*, Vol. 18, Princeton: Princeton University Press.

Jung, E. and von Franz, M.L. (1970) *The Grail Legend*, New York: Putnam's Sons.

Von Franz, M.L. (1966) *The Interpretation of Fairy Tales*, New York: Random House.

Waite, A.E. (1961) *The Holy Grail*, Chicago: University of Chicago Press.

# Chapter 5

# *Dark City*

## Jane Ryan

*Dark City* (directed by Alex Proyas, 1998) is a science fiction film, containing elements of *Blade Runner* and *The Truman Show*, set on a *Batman* stage and precursing *Matrix*. At one level, it tells the story of the human inhabitants of a city built by "Strangers", alien beings who have borrowed the bodies of dead humans. Each midnight, the Strangers, with the help of the mortal but mysterious Dr Shreber (Kiefer Sutherland), change the memories of a group of the city's inhabitants. This disruption of memory is called "tuning" and is performed by the aliens in an attempt to locate the human soul, thought by them to reside in the mind. In Jungian thought, memories are contained in the personal unconscious, that which "contains lost memories, painful ideas that are repressed, subliminal perceptions, by which are meant sense perceptions, that were not strong enough to reach consciousness, and finally contents that are not yet ripe for consciousness" (Jung, 1953, *CW* 7: para. 103). Without awareness of one's personal unconscious, that which the Strangers steal from the humans, the journey of individuation, so necessary to a fulfilled life, becomes impossible. Individuation, Jung wrote, is "a process of psychological differentiation, having for its goal the development of the individual personality" (Sharp, 1991: 67) and "the development of the psychological individual as a being distinct from the general, collective psychology" (ibid.). The Strangers, by being able to reproduce this "soul" within themselves, hope to avoid a foretold extinction. Using a Jungian methodology, this film may be analysed as the journey of the hero, his goal being that of individuation, of psychic wholeness and healing.

John Murdoch (Rufus Sewell) is the hero, initially confused and lost, who awakens, naked and terrified, in a bathtub of cold and dark water. His terror is caused by his loss of memory, his loss of access to his personal unconscious. He has no persona, no identity. Jung wrote of the persona being "that which in reality one is not, but which oneself

*Figure 5.1  Dark City.*
The Strangers.
(1997, New Line,
Courtesy Kobal)

*Figure 5.2  Dark City*
(1997, New Line, Courtesy Kobal)

as well as others think one is" (Jung, 1959, *CW* 9i: para. 221), and of one's identity as "denoting an unconscious conformity between subject and object, oneself and others" (Sharp, 1991: 62).The absence of these in Murdoch's psychology thrust him brutally onto the path towards individuation. His subsequent encounters with the Strangers, his wife, Dr Schreber and the police may be seen as aspects of this eternal struggle, the development of a true Self. The Self is "not only the center, but also the whole circumference which embraces both the conscious and unconscious, it is the center of this totality, just as the ego is the center of consciousness" (Sharp, 1991: 119). From existing solely in the world of consciousness, Murdoch must descend into the underworld of the Strangers in order to accomplish his heroic mission, to integrate the personal and collective unconscious.

The style of *Dark City*, its mise-en-scène, is that of *film noir*. This involves several distinctive characteristics: the majority of scenes take place at night, oblique and vertical lines are preferred to horizontal ones, the actors and the setting are given equal emphasis, compositional tension is largely preferred to physical action, the setting is generally urban and seedy and, finally, images of water are emphasized. In this film, *noir* and a Jungian sensibility are complementary. A brief overview will provide some insight as to how Jungian thought may find satisfactory expression in *film noir* and, conversely, how Jungian analysis may be the most effective methodology for elucidating the underlying meanings of this style of film.

*Dark City* takes place almost entirely at night, in an urban setting which borrows much from futurists' visions from the 1940s. Jung warned of humankind's preoccupation, since the Enlightenment, with science and technology, with the Logos becoming dominant. The "discrimination and cognition associated with Logos", which finds physical expression in the evolution of the modern city, must be balanced by the irrational and the spiritual. As in most *noir* films, this balance is missing, just as the sun is missing from the darkened city. Science and technology are ascendant, represented by the Strangers' abilities to manipulate humankind: the lack of a natural balance is metaphorically and figuratively shown by the absence of the sun. Similarly, the vertical lines of the buildings show a distancing from the natural world. The horizontal lines of nature are replaced by, as Paul Shrader notes (Grant, 1995), vertical and oblique ones, which seem to trap the viewer in a world of absence. One's eye is drawn upwards by the vertical lines, just as with the architecture of a Gothic cathedral. Whereas the Gothic lines indicated a higher reality, the presence of an immanent God, in *Dark City* the lines lead to images of absence, a black sky which promises no redemption. Oblique angles lend a harshness and sense of disorientation to many scenes: the eye is directed to darkened corners. Again, the emphasis in these scenes is on an absence, an absence which John Murdoch must cure. As will be analysed more fully elsewhere in this chapter, nature, as representative of the irrational and spiritual (the feminine Eros, the principle of relatedness), is absent, her place usurped by a masculine Logos. In Jungian psychology, there must exist a balance between these two principles in order for psychological wholeness: the restoration of this balance is John Murdoch's Grail.

The actors and the setting are indeed given equal emphasis: the very existence of the dark city is a mystery to be solved by Murdoch. The buildings change shape each midnight, just as the personal unconscious of the citizens is manipulated as a result of the Strangers' tuning: Gothic gives way to post-modern, small buildings grow upwards toward the dark sky, the actions of the buildings themselves dominating many scenes. Jung wrote that there is a "connection between psyche and matter" (Sharp, 1991: 108), the psychoid unconscious. This concept is nicely delineated in the scenes of tuning, when the psychological power of the Strangers is such that it causes new buildings to "grow".

While there is much physical action in this film, compositional tension is indeed of equal importance. The tension is achieved largely through the use of shadow and darkness, creating an atmosphere of oppression, sinister and frightening. This is analogous, in Jungian terms, to the psychological "shadow", the dark aspects of one's being, those which one keeps hidden. Confrontation of the shadow must occur in order for psychological growth, just as Murdoch must confront the mystery of the darkened city. It is necessary, in Jungian terms, to confront the unconscious, to integrate its power into one's conscious life. It is this tension which John Murdoch attempts to resolve throughout the film.

Images of water abound. The initial scene shows not only Murdoch's awakening in the bath, but also a goldfish swimming in a small glass bowl. Murdoch accidentally shatters the glass, but rescues the fish. This animal is one of the few images from the "natural" world to be found in the film, but it is nature controlled and surrounded. Jung wrote that images of water indicated often an imminent eruption of the unconscious into one's conscious mind: for John Murdoch, his awakening and his saving of the fish represent the first hesitant steps towards individuation. Murdoch's future quest is foreshadowed in his saving of the fish. This prefigures a later occurrence: it is in an amusement hall called Neptune's Kingdom, in which he is surrounded by aquaria, that John has the visionary experience which shows him how the minds around him are being manipulated. Again, these aquaria contain sad vestiges of the natural world, fish confined in glass tanks, removed from their natural environments, controlled by a man in the same way that the Strangers control the humans. The fish exist in a netherworld much as do the inhabitants of *Dark City*.

Likewise, images of Shell Beach form a *leitmotif* throughout *Dark City*: this imaginary ocean is pictured on postcards and novelties throughout the film. Again, these cartoon images are not of a natural ocean, but Disneyfied simulacra, renderings of a dimly remembered past, a nature again controlled, this time by the absence of the artists' imagination. The beach represents the Grail of Murdoch's quest however: the archetypal image of a remembered paradise. The falsity of this image is shown as the penultimate step in Murdoch's quest: Shell Beach is an invention of the Strangers. After confronting this desecration of his archetypal image, Murdoch creates his own Shell Beach. These images may be interpreted in several ways, using the Jungian techniques of both amplification and active imagination, as will be shown later in this chapter.

The themes of *film noir* are generally those of anomie, of a psychological distancing between individuals, leading to film endings which leave little room for hope. John Murdoch's awakening and his subsequent panic do indeed conform to this characterization. However, pessimism and a sense of futility are incompatible with Jungian thought, except where they exist in dynamic equilibrium with optimism and hope. Within this film, the anomie so central to *film noir* exists only so long as John Murdoch allows it to. The depression and neurosis which so characterize him in the opening scenes are overcome when he begins his heroic journey into the netherworld of the unconscious. *Film noir* does not allow for the type of triumph with which Murdoch attains the goal of his quest. It is at this point in the film where the director seamlessly and skilfully abandons *noir* in favour of a *mise-en-scène* reminiscent of a Technicolor masterpiece from the 1950s. The ocean and beach which Murdoch creates through his command of his psychological powers is vividly portrayed, the greys and blacks of the former dark city now lush and voluptuously coloured. The power of the psyche which has attained the dynamic equilibrium of individuation is dramatically shown. By adapting *noir* stylistics to a science fiction film, Proyas creates a film which is elegant and restrained in its Jungian themes. The subtlety with which the director manipulates this style is most evident when he abandons it in favour of the overtly emotional and exultant ending. Discarding *noir*, he nonetheless preserves a cohesive whole in which a Jungian analysis continues to be effective: the universal theme of the journey of the hero. The resolution for Murdoch is represented by integration within his own psyche of his consciousness with his personal and collective unconsciousness

The concept of individuation is central to analytical psychology. The opening scenes of *Dark City* show an entire population in the grip of the collective unconscious, metaphorically expressed in the way the Strangers control the personal unconscious of each individual by their nightly manipulation of memories. The process of individuation is one in which Murdoch comes to not only recognize the power of the Strangers, but also to harness their archetypal strength within his own psyche. John Murdoch quickly learns that he has a higher insight into the unconscious than other humans, demonstrated by his ability to "tune", to change the shape of objects around him and even to create objects *de novo*. Murdoch is, in the words of Dr Shreber, "more highly evolved than most humans". Both conscious and unconscious are vital to the development of the individual. Murdoch's battles are those which must be attempted by each individual: the development of an integration of ego and Self. The images associated with Murdoch and the Strangers' tuning are vivid: doors appear where previously there were high and impenetrable walls, paths are created where once were enclosed and claustrophobic spaces. This may be taken metaphorically also: the opening of the mind which occurs when the unconscious is accessed by the conscious mind.

That the Strangers are symbolic of the collective unconscious is mentioned overtly by Dr Schreber in a voice-over, when he says that they "have one mind" and "are as old as time itself". Later, to John Murdoch, he states "it is our capacity for individuality, our souls, that makes us different from them". Jung described the collective unconscious in terms such as Schreber uses. The very name "Strangers" indicates that they are as unknown to humans as is the collective unconscious itself. Murdoch's embryonic ability to tune indicates that he has somehow gained access to the world of the Strangers, the collective unconscious, an important aspect of one's journey of individuation.

Though an initial viewing ascribes to the Strangers the role of evil interlopers in the human mind, a Jungian reading avoids such premature conclusions. The Strangers' dark powers may be seen within the narrative as metaphorically arising from the primordial archetypes from which erupt all our archetypal images. As such, they are as necessary to psychic wholeness as is one's conscious mind. Jung wrote "it is possible for man to become whole, only with the cooperation of the spirit of darkness, that the latter is actually a *causa instrumentalis* of redemption and individuation" (Jung, 1959: para. 453). The archetypal images are those memories which the Strangers concoct and inject into the minds of the humans each night.

Aiding the Strangers in their task is Dr Daniel Shreber, a Hermes-like figure, a Trickster who also assists John Murdoch in his quest. Shreber refers to himself as "a traitor". While this may be seen, at best, to be a case of divided loyalties, it is rather more effectively seen as an attempt to unify the psyche. Dr Shreber, alone of all the characters, is able to move between the worlds of the conscious and the unconscious. The Trickster is society's attempt to come to terms with its preconscious past. A Trickster figure can only exist within a culture which has at least nascent self-awareness, represented here by Murdoch's initially fumbling and misguided attempts to comprehend his existence. Jung wrote: "the trickster is a collective shadow figure, a summation of all the inferior traits of character in individuals" (Jung, 1959: para. 484). Shreber is indeed disloyal to his fellow humans, a traitor of sorts, but it is through his machinations, his injection of altered memories into John Murdoch's mind, that Murdoch is able to solve the great puzzle of his existence. Only a society which has developed some awareness of its own history (i.e. has begun the process of individuation) can reflect upon its past and its future. This is most appropriate for the Dark City where almost an entire population is unaware of its origins. Schreber's contact with Murdoch will save the city from its own ignorance. The Trickster is a shape-shifter, able to appear in different guises at different times and to different people. Shreber is traitor, doctor, shaman, historian of the humans, philosopher and psychopompos. Joseph Campbell describes the shamanic figure as "interpreter and intermediary between man and the powers behind the veil of nature" (Campbell, 1968: 291). The memories with which Shreber injects Murdoch are ones in which Shreber appears in numerous roles and guises, most appropriate for a shape-shifting Mercurius figure such as he.

Shreber moves between the narrative and the audience. He is immune to the Strangers' manipulations and yet can avail himself of the doors and paths they create by tuning. He is an omniscient narrator, but is he reliable? His identity is unclear, a most satisfactory performance for a psychopompos.

Detective Walenski (Colin Friels) is the only other human who demonstrates some immunity to the Strangers' machinations. Unlike Murdoch, whose ability to tune indicates a further awareness of the unconscious, Walenski is faced with unbearable images from the unconscious which he is powerless to control or interpret. Though possessed of many of the same fears confronting both Murdoch and Shreber, he is unwilling or unable to begin the process of individuation He has been attempting to solve the apparent murders of a number of prostitutes, whose bodies are found mutilated, circles and spirals and other mandala-like symbols cut into their flesh. Walenski undergoes a psychotic breakdown, scrawling mandalas over every surface in his office and his home. He seems to believe that these symbols have a power which will protect him or in some way indicate the truth of his existence. He has some embryonic sense of an existence more meaningful than that allowed him by the Strangers, but the power of the unconscious overwhelms his wretched consciousness. Withdrawing from the world, from the Dark City as he does, is also a withdrawal from the possibility of individuation however. His terror and confusion are parallel to those experienced by John Murdoch, but for Walenski, the sudden eruption of unconscious contents into his conscious psyche causes a fear so profound that he succumbs and commits suicide. Walenski surrenders. In the process of individuation, it is the confrontation with fear of the unknown which gives strength. There is a tacit comparison made within the narrative between Murdoch and Walenski: both are given hints as to the mystery surrounding their strange existence. Walenski says "riding in circles, thinking in circles. There's no way out." Walenski lacks the strength to confront the evil he senses. Overwhelmed by his unconscious, he retreats to dark and stifling places: his claustrophobic office and finally the subterranean station where he kills himself. The circularity of the train map shown on the station wall is ironic: even in killing himself, Walenski cannot escape the symbolism of the mandala. This symbol is usually seen as one of psychic healing and wholeness: "[u]ltimate wisdom is at the hub of the mandala's wheel, the stillpoint at which one is in total balance" (Gold, 1994: 144). It is this promise of balance which so seduces Walenski into madness. Though the outcome of Walenski's attempts to integrate his irrupting unconscious is disastrous, it is clear that he himself comprehends something of the significance of the images that he feels compelled to re-create. Walenski senses the evil inherent in the Strangers' power, as does Murdoch. However, Walenski does not apprehend the concomitant creative possibilities inherent in this power. Marie-Louise von Franz referred to experiences such as Walenski's as "threshold phenomena", irruptions from the unconscious into consciousness, which have both creative and destructive potential. Von Franz wrote that these phenomena come across the threshold in altered form from that which existed in the unconscious: "[w]hen impoverished contents come across the threshold of consciousness, we have to amplify (enrich!) them again in order to understand them" (von Franz, 1972: 87). Murdoch's discovery of his own embryonic tuning abilities represents the first step towards taming the power of the unconscious. Walenski's comprehension of the unconscious as monolithically evil is incorrect: it is necessary for psychological wholeness. Viewed from the level of ego-consciousness, the unconscious is "other" and therefore often feared. Walenski is unable to amplify or enrich the images thrown up by his unconscious which, as von Franz reminds us, is so necessary to our individuation.

Just as Walenski and Murdoch are tacitly compared within the narrative, so too are Walenski and his former partner Detective Bumstead. Dr Shreber describes him as "fastidious, driven, consumed with details, rather lonely". Unlike Walenski, who is overwhelmed by the unconscious, Bumstead is rather Logos-dominated: he values the mores and rules of police procedure and seems incapable of attending to his intuition. In conversation, he seems obsessed with gathering factual information. With Emma, Murdoch's wife, he seems disinterested, distant from his past, unemotional when discussing, however briefly, his mother's death. At no time does any glimpse of the irrational penetrate his consciousness. Bumstead is killed in his encounter with the Strangers, the personification of the collective unconscious. He is thrown off the roof of the world, into the abyss. By denying or being unaware of the power of the unconscious, Bumstead precludes the possibility of individuation and dies both physically and psychologically.

The names of the two detectives may also be analysed from a Jungian perspective. By only knowing their surnames, we are led to view them as representative of a group identity, and not as specific individuals. We see them more as types, even archetypes perhaps. The name "Walenski" is of Polish-Catholic origin. This religion is imbued with ritual and ceremony, replete with symbols which serve to give meaning to existence. It is therefore most fitting that Walenski becomes entranced and entrapped by the symbol of the mandala. Though found predominantly in Eastern religions, the mandala has also a strong presence in Catholic symbolism (e.g. the landscape architecture of convent gardens, constructed to represent a pilgrim's journey). The dogmatism of Catholicism is seen also in his repetitious renderings of the symbol: like a litany from the Tridentine Mass, which in being repeated continually gains meaning. However, like a ritual chant being misunderstood and misused by a novice, the meaning of the symbol becomes obscured and its purpose distorted. Jung's criticism of Christianity in the twentieth century was that the symbols incorporated within the religion had become meaningless. The rituals and rubrics were no longer aids to religious (and hence psychological) development, but had become ends in themselves. It is this inability to comprehend the meaning of the mandala that finally leads Walenski to despair.

Conversely, Bumstead's name, on first hearing, would seem to indicate a meaning diametrically opposed to the character of the Logos-dominated detective. It is a name drawn from American popular culture, a character in a newspaper comic strip whose bumbling misjudgments cause havoc around him. Hardly a description of *Dark City*'s detective. However, it is his misjudgments, though they are not comical, which result in mayhem. Unlike the original Bumstead, who ignored logic, Detective Bumstead ignores instead the influence of the irrational and the existence of the unconscious. His pursuit of the linear solution to the mystery of the murdered prostitutes diverts him from allowing in a larger vision. This blunder results in his death. It is an extension of Bumstead's logical curiosity that inspires him to accompany Murdoch on his journey towards Shell Beach. Murdoch is searching for the meaning of his life. Bumstead wants to solve the murders. Unlike Murdoch, Bumstead does not allow for the irrational. His obduracy is as profound as is the silliness of his comic predecessor.

Walenski's obsession with the aforementioned mandalas is not the only use of geometric symbolism within the film. Both circles and spheres are present in many scenes as well. John Murdoch is initially seen through a small circular window. Several key scenes take place in circular rooms: Dr Shreber is seen swimming in a circular pool which is enclosed by a circular room; his office is likewise circular. The Strangers' abode is a spherical chamber underground. Clocks, which have so important a function, all have circular faces. The map of the city in the Strangers' cavern is circular, as is the maze in Shreber's office. When, finally, the city is seen from above, it is revealed to be an island in space, circular in shape. The symbol of the circle is ascribed the highest significance in Jungian thought. In early civilizations, a circle of stones divided the temples' sacred space from the profane space outside the circle. The first image of John Murdoch would indicate that the circular window separates him from the rest of the city – that he is indeed separate. This is shown to be true: Murdoch begins the sacred journey towards the Self, the sacred. The other inhabitants of his world cannot attempt this. Shreber's swimming pool performs a similar function, protecting him from the incursions of the Strangers. They circumambulate the pool, but cannot cross the barrier. In his role as psychopompos, Shreber is able to move freely between the conscious and the unconscious, to cross this barrier. The Strangers' cavern is spherical, enclosing them in the dimly lit underground. In their symbolic role as the collective unconscious, this is most apt. Except when the collective unconscious irrupts into the conscious, it is contained.

These and the other images of circles have meanings within the particular scenes in which they occur. Their highest significance, however, is in the indication they give towards some other, deeper meaning. Jung wrote, of their functional significance, that mandalas are "instruments of meditation, concentration and self-immersion, for the purpose of realizing inner experience" (Jung, 1959: 383). Jung took mandalas to be indicative of the journey towards the Self, "the traditional antidote for chaotic states of mind" (ibid.: 10). Thus, within this film, all early images of the circle, perhaps especially Walenski's tortured renderings, prefigure the image of the Dark City as seen from above, the city a circular island in space. This island was constructed by the Strangers, created *de novo*. It is a "marriage" of science and technology alone. Unlike a human city it did not evolve and grow slowly, maintaining its connections, however tenuously, to the natural environment. It is the connection with nature, so inextricably linked with the feminine, that John Murdoch must re-establish. It is this that is the material manifestation of the spiritual goal of his journey towards individuation.

Murdoch's quest begins initially when he awakens from what may be interpreted by the viewer as a terrifying dream. A mutilated female body lies naked in the room. Murdoch has no memories. He lacks even the knowledge of his own name. As mentioned previously, his personal unconscious has been taken. He has no knowledge, as yet, of the collective unconscious. This void in his psyche results in fright and panic; he flees the hotel room, assuming that it was he who killed the woman. Thus begins his odyssey, his search for his identity.

The ominous figures of the Strangers, clothed in grey and black, their faces angular and drained of colour, follow Murdoch through the city, attempting, for reasons which he does not yet comprehend, to stop him. This may be seen as the attempt of the collective unconscious to control the conscious mind, to overwhelm Mudoch's tenuous grasp on his own psyche. Several archetypal figures aid Murdoch. Among them are Dr Shreber, a nameless prostitute, Murdoch's wife Emma (Jennifer Connelly) and the figure of the Stranger child. Each of these characters transcends the particular (as has been shown already in the analysis of Shreber's character) and may be seen, in classical Jungian manner, to represent the general, the archetypal and thus the eternal. Interpreting symbols in a Jungian manner must not be done reductively; symbols are complex and cannot be assigned a linear correspondence to any particular meaning. Context must be respected, but primary to Jungian analysis is the process of amplification, which enables more obscure possibilities of meaning to emerge.

Both the prostitute and Murdoch's putative wife (given the tuning of the Strangers, she may simply be responding to the personal unconscious assigned to her by them) represent aspects of his *anima*, the feminine aspect of his psyche. In Jungian analysis, confrontation with one's *anima*, for a man, or *animus*, for a woman, is an essential step towards individuation. The significance of these women in the film is signalled dramatically by the use of vivid colours. Hitherto, the scenes have been dimly lit, grey and black predominating, all the human characters sharing a shabby insignificance. The prostitute, who saves Murdoch from arrest by the police, is a striking blonde, dressed in a luxurious red gown. The contrast to the monotone colours of the other inhabitants is striking and indicates the significance of the woman. Using Ann Ulanov's typology of women, which she developed using Jungian principles, the prostitute may be seen as both Amazon and Hetaira. She is powerful and controlling of the men around her, as seen when she tricks the police into believing that Murdoch is a client of hers, rather than a complete stranger to her. In Ulanov's theory, the Hetaira is a soul mate or companion, one who stays away from emotional commitment or entanglement. This would seem to be true of the prostitute, who intuitively understands that Murdoch is not a murderer, that he is simply lost, both literally and psychologically.

Like the prostitute, Emma is clothed in striking colours. She is first seen on stage in a nightclub where she is a singer. Her dress is emerald green and her lips are painted crimson. Additionally, she is lit directly by a spotlight, indicating the significance she bears. Using Ulanov's typology again, Emma may be seen to represent both the Mother and Medium. As mother, she loves and cares for Murdoch, believing him to be her husband, but disbelieving the accusations of murder against him. She attempts to enlist the help of Bumstead, but is rebuffed. Her irrational, and intuitive knowledge that Murdoch is incapable of murder seems irrational to the Logos-ridden detective. It is this capacity for irrationality which characterizes Emma as a Medium. For Ulanov, a Medium is a woman who is aware of the collective unconscious. Whilst Emma's knowledge of the unconscious may be fragile, what capacity she has enables her to protect Murdoch. Thus one of the first encounters in individuation is here symbolized by the two women with whom Murdoch comes into contact. Having confronted his *anima*, Murdoch is psychologically stronger and more able to continue his journey.

The symbol of the child was thought by Jung to be one of primary importance and that the appearance of such a figure in dreams was an indication of coming change. The child who accompanies the Strangers is a malevolent figure, one whose most memorable utterance is "kill him". Appearing as he does at the beginning of John Murdoch's quest, the child is indeed a figure indicating imminent change, but his appearance may also have other meanings. Jung wrote also of the child symbolizing "the preconscious aspect of the collective psyche" (Jung, 1959: para. 273). As such, the Stranger child fulfils the role of pure unconscious, unmitigated by any rational thought. In this image, one may see the essence of all Jung's writings on the necessity for beginning the process of individuation. The child is the quintessential unconscious, attempting to overwhelm Murdoch's psyche. It is only through Murdoch's pursuit of his goal that the evil becomes controlled. Likewise, Jung wrote that occasionally a child could indicate that one has become severed from one's roots or origins, "unchildlike and artificial" (ibid.: para. 274), as is the case with Murdoch, who lacks any memory of his previous life and hence his own psyche. Thus the murderous child may be interpreted in manifold ways, each of them reflecting a different aspect of Murdoch's psyche, each giving some clue as to his ultimate goal.

The goal of his quest, the Grail for which Murdoch is ostensibly searching, is the omnipresent Shell Beach. Like the city itself, the imaginary paradise so dimly remembered by the inhabitants of Dark City is an artificial construct, as unreal as the memories with which the Strangers inject their human subjects. Murdoch seizes upon this image; the lack of a personal unconscious causes him to attach significance to what is an illusory fantasy, an image used by the Strangers to control the minds of the humans. That the beach is nonexistent implies that Murdoch's goal is a false one and therefore that this process of individuation cannot be successful, founded as it is on fallacy. However, Murdoch, after many attempts on his life by the Strangers, comes upon a huge billboard with the same comic-like representation of Shell Beach, complete with a female figure whose head nods mechanically and metronomically. Tearing aside the paper of the billboard and destroying the false icon, Murdoch then destroys the brick wall behind the advertisement. It is at this moment that Murdoch achieves some measure of individuation: the destructive power of the unconscious is harnessed by his psyche. He defeats the unconscious in its attempts to overwhelm his conscious mind: the Strangers appear as Murdoch breaks through the wall. Beyond this, there is the void of space, limitless. It is however real. In the ensuing melee, Bumstead and several of the Strangers are thrown into the abyss. Murdoch has triumphed, but only partially. The final stage in Murdoch's odyssey is to use the power of the collective unconscious in creating a new world. This incorporation of the limitless possibilities of the unconscious represents the *summum bonum*, the approach towards the Self which Jung saw as the goal of each human being.

Murdoch fittingly creates Shell Beach, a lush and vivid scene in which the ocean is formed from waters until now harnessed in the Strangers' city. The sun appears and the technological marvel that is the city seems to fade into insignificance. The natural, so lacking from the film until now, is restored to its rightful place. The dynamic equilibrium, which Jungian thought sees as the goal of each individual, is now restored. It is important to note that the dark powers of the Strangers have not been diminished in any manner, rather they have been usurped for good and creative use.

The denouement takes place on Murdoch's Shell Beach, where he meets Emma, now called Anna. For her, this is a first meeting. She does not recognize Murdoch as her husband, in a literal sense, because her mind has been subject to tuning by the Strangers, but also, metaphorically, perhaps because John Murdoch, having achieved such difficult goals, is not now the person she originally knew. The film ends hopefully, but not without the inference that there is much left to be accomplished. Jung wrote that individuation could not, for most people, be attained within a lifetime, and it is this continuing journey which faces Murdoch.

*Dark City* is a simple and eloquent modern retelling of the journey of the hero. Using a Jungian methodology, the narrative is seen to be one in which the specific story of John Murdoch has universal themes, ones which recur throughout the myths that humans have always created. These myths give meaning to our lives. Though the medium of expression of these stories has changed from religion to a more secular form of expression, the myth remains, the universally understood story of the heroic quest. John Murdoch encounters the Strangers, escapes from them, struggles to reach the Grail of Shell Beach, conquers the demons and creates a true and real world. In so doing, he recreates the voyage of Odysseus, the wanderings of the knights searching for the Holy Grail, and other mythical heroes. Jungian analysis sees in all myths not only the stories which explain the meaning of our lives, but also that each individual must recapitulate these myths: the journey of individuation is universal and most necessary.

# References

Campbell, Joseph (1968) *The Masks of God: Primitive Mythologies*, New York: Arkana.

Gold, Peter (1994) *Navajo and Tibetan Sacred Wisdom: the Circle of the Spirit*, Rochester, Vt.: Inner Traditions.

Grant, Barry Keith (1995) *A Film Genre Reader*, Austin, Tex.: University of Texas Press.

Jung, Carl Gustav (1959) *The Archetypes and the Collective Unconscious*, trans. R.F.C. Hull, Princeton: Princeton University Press.

Sharp, Daryl (1991) *C.G. Jung Lexicon: A Primer of Terms and Concepts*, Toronto: Inner City Books.

von Franz, Marie Louise (1972) *Creation Myths*, New York: Shambhala Publications.

# Chapter 6

# "If you could see what I've seen with your eyes . . . "

## Post-human psychology and *Blade Runner*

*Don Williams*

As the eye of the camera passes over a dark Los Angeles, year 2019, shrouded from the sun by perpetual blue-gray pollution, these words scroll up the screen:

> *Replicants* were used Off-world as slave labor . . . After a bloody mutiny by a Nexus 6 combat team in an Off-world colony, *Replicants* were declared illegal on earth – under penalty of death. Several police squads – Blade Runner units – had orders to shoot to kill, upon detection, any trespassing *Replicant*. This was not called execution. It was called retirement.[1]

*Blade Runner* (1982) is a postmodern film pointing toward a post-human future. The edge of the post-human condition is reached by genetically engineered humans – *replicants* in *Blade Runner* – created with more-than-human intelligence and strength. The Tyrell Corporation reached this border with the creation of "Nexus 6" replicants who are "more human than human." Dr Eldon Tyrell (Joe Turkel), to avoid crossing the post-human boundary and being surpassed, encoded a four-year lifespan in the Nexus 6 model – they die young. The replicants, however, understand their vulnerability. They hijack a ship and return to earth to demand or engineer more life. Their success would mark the moment of transition to a post-human condition. The principal Blade Runner, Deckard (Harrison Ford), is forced to accept the mission to "retire" the four remaining replicants.

Perhaps the crossover moment is not so far away as 2019. The success of the Human Genome Project has just been announced: over 3 billion biochemical characters of human DNA are now decoded, giving us the potential to change the biochemical instructions for being human. In the meantime, computer technology continues to evolve at breakneck speed, doubling every 18 months as predicted by Moore's Law. In our new technological century computer networks may "wake up," and genetic engineers may produce humans with greater than human intelligence. Either way, we approach a transition to a post-human era where "human nature" is not "handed down" but continuously revised, extended, and refined in a process of ongoing creation.

The union and flight of Deckard and Rachael (Sean Young) – a human Adam and a genetically engineered Eve – at the end of *Blade Runner* anticipates the approaching post-human era. *Blade Runner* shows us a failed human experiment – Los Angeles 2019 – but offers up the image of new "first parents" who distinguish themselves with "the miracle of reflecting consciousness" (Jung 1965: 339). Deckard and Rachael escape to seek a new vision of human experience – they are not cast out of Eden and shackled with guilt as were Adam and Eve. Perhaps, as many people argue, Deckard is a replicant like Rachael; if so, then the movie carries us across the post-human boundary, but it changes nothing about the quest we share with them – the quest to determine for ourselves what it means to be human.

*Blade Runner* is populated by human characters whose consciousness is impoverished. Tyrell, Holden (Morgan Paull), Bryant (M. Emmet Walsh), Chew (James Hong), and Sebastian (William Sanderson) fail to

*Figure 6.1 Blade Runner.* Rachael (Sean Young) and Deckard (Harrison Ford). (Ladd Company/Warner Bros, Courtesy Kobal)

be human. Only the Nexus 6 replicants experience attachment and grief, reflect on their experience, and long to explore being human. The reflective and valuing acts of Roy Batty (Rutger Hauer) in particular inspire us. Deckard, alone among his human companions, does not disappoint us. From the film's perspective we have failed to create and offer up to others a respectful and respectable human era.

Our hope, therefore, is in the symbolic union of Deckard and Rachael where human nature, conscious reflection, and self-creation are mixed together. The way out of our failure is to approach the post-human condition consciously, to outgrow our historically "accepted-as-human-condition." We failed the human experiment. We will not go back to correct our failures but hopefully will go forward responsively to a better union. For a new era we need a psychology to map our participation in the continuing creation of the world and of ourselves. The union of Deckard and Rachael symbolizes an actively conscious relationship to others, ourselves, the world, and the future. We cannot know ourselves without knowing another – the sacred marriage – or without being responsive, over time, to what we make, to the world that holds us, and to who we become.

## Postmodern conditions

As a postmodern film *Blade Runner* lacks a reliable narrator, clear directions, and fixed anchors. Everyone, for instance, has a story but no one's story has authority. Diffuse identities and boundaries – like the diffuse lines of authority – are another postmodern feature. Is Deckard a replicant or human? Is Gaff (Edward James Olmos), the detective shadowing Deckard, a cop, a Blade Runner, Deckard's final enemy, or his friend? Were there originally five replicants or six? We don't know the answers to these questions.

The characters are surrounded by genetically engineered animals – fakes. Only the pigeons scattered by Roy's pursuit of Deckard at the end of the film are authentic. Roy delivers his soliloquy as he sits holding a pigeon in his hands – so different from Tyrell's well-engineered observing owl. When Roy dies, his hands relax, the pigeon is released, and if we let the metaphor wash over us, Roy's soul is liberated.

True to its postmodern roots, *Blade Runner* never lets us know where we are. We see humans act inhumanly and replicants act more intelligently and empathically than humans. Reality in *Blade Runner* is socially constructed – whether we speak of the Off-world colonies, J.F. Sebastian's apartment with human acting toys, replicants with implanted memories, the person Roy Batty created out of himself, or the values Deckard and Rachael will discover.

Also postmodern is the visual fragmentation of the film. Director Ridley Scott never lets our eyes rest on anything familiar or comfortable, nor are we allowed enough light or perspective to fully orient ourselves. Characters, apartments, rooms, streets, offices, are always dominated by shadows. We first see Deckard in darkness with a store window behind him as he waits for a seat at the "noodle bar" in the street. The store window contains television monitors with images that never shed their static or grain. The neon sign contains foreign characters – probably Japanese, but do we know?

When Gaff takes off with Deckard in the "spinner," we might expect some visual perspective on the city as their vehicle lifts off, climbs above the buildings, and a hint of natural light breaks across Gaff's features. Shots of the city, however, are broken by bars separating the glass panels of the "spinner." Every "look" is fragmented by the camera angle. We notice a few familiar things on the flight – a building, a Cuisinart advertisement, the ever-present rain – but we never get to know where we are or have been.

We also experience auditory disorganization. On the streets people use "cityspeak," a language mixing German, French, Spanish, Japanese. We hear words from Gaff in at least French, Japanese, and German though he is played by Hispanic James Edward Olmos. Adding to our disorientation is a futuristic soundtrack that never leaves us a place to rest.

## Testing for empathy

Not surprisingly, the humans in *Blade Runner* find it difficult to distinguish human from not-human. Despite the film's high tech genetic engineering, the characters test emotional responses to sort humans from replicants, and the test closely resembles C.G. Jung's word association experiment developed first in 1904.

In *Blade Runner* the opening scene descends to a window high in the Tyrell Corporation pyramid, showing us Holden, a Blade Runner, standing and looking away from the camera. He's looking to nothing – the long horizontal window is too high above him to provide a view; and the light reveals only a blue-gray, soot-filled sky. He smokes a cigarette, drinks a cup of coffee, and a ceiling fan revolves above two chairs facing each other across an expanse of empty desk space. Visually the scene is a postmodern pastiche of a *film noir* past and a bleak technological future

A woman's voice announces the entrance of Holden's prey, "Next subject. Kowalski, Leon. Engineer, waste disposal . . . " This is "database talk": test subject period. last-name-first comma first-name period. job title period.

The woman's flat voice intensifies the stripped-of-human-warmth blue-gray. The thick concrete walls in the background, the smoke, and the blue-gray light weigh oppressively on us. This is hardly the place to test for empathy. Holden uses the Voight–Kampff test for empathy in an attempt to identify one or more of the replicants.[2] Replicants score much lower than humans on empathy, except perhaps the more intelligent Nexus 6 replicants who received implanted "buffer" memories to build on.

Holden's questions don't test for empathy as we are told or as we are likely to believe. Rather, his questions project into Leon the qualities of a sadist who would torture an animal, a not-human sadism. Holden's condescending tone and arrogant control of the interview reveal that he is the sadist, and Leon (Brion James) the helpless victim . . . until Leon revolts. The highly on-edge interview begins:

HOLDEN:   You're in a desert, walking along in the sand when all of a sudden you look down and see a . . .
LEON:     What one?
HOLDEN:   What?
LEON:     What desert?

Moments later,

HOLDEN:   So you look down and see a tortoise . . . You reach down and flip the tortoise over on its back, Leon. . . . The tortoise lays on its back, its belly baking in the hot sun, beating its legs trying to turn itself over. But it can't.

We hear Leon's heart beating faster, beating in our ears, his heartbeat blends into the soundtrack.

HOLDEN:   Not without your help. But you're not helping.
LEON:     What'ya mean, I'm not helping?
HOLDEN:   I mean you're not helping! Why is that, Leon?

Leon is about ready to crack when Holden grins.

HOLDEN:  They're just questions, Leon. In answer to your query, they're written down for me. It's a test, designed to provoke an emotional response.

Not only is Leon flipped on his back by Holden but he is also Tyrell's helpless creature – programmed to die on schedule. Leon is on the list of "endangered species."

The camera pulls back, we see both men in chairs marked with the name, "Tyrell Corporation" – they are both the corporation's slaves. Holden continues:

HOLDEN:  Describe in single words. Only the good things that come into your mind. [*Pause*] About your mother.
LEON:    My mother? Let me tell you about my mother!

Leon will not be trapped and exposed nor will he submit to Holden's arrogance by revealing poignant "good memories" associated with the photograph he carries of "his mother" – a photograph that accompanied his "inception." The photograph was given to Leon by a genetic engineer as a token in place of memories. In response to Holden, Leon leans forward, fires the gun he holds beneath the table, and then stands to blast Holden once more. The first blast sends Holden through the wall. Holden will live, Bryant tells Deckard, "as long as nobody unplugs him." Leon escapes for now.

There are no mothers in this film except in photographs. We never see children and only see couples in a nightclub scene, and these couples do not look like they left children at home with grandparents. Dialogue never hints at spouses, lovers, or parents. We see no families or friends, and the only bonds of affection and loyalty are between the four replicants and briefly between Pris, described as "a basic pleasure model," and J.F. Sebastian, one of Tyrell's engineers. Sebastian has a natural bond with the replicants because he worked on them and because, like them, he is aging prematurely and dying – Sebastian's name for his condition is "Methuselah's Syndrome," while Roy calls it "accelerated decrepitude." The human characters otherwise seem to have no life outside the immediate frame.

Sunlight is missing except once on the 800th floor of the Tyrell Corporation. Earth and plants are missing, and even potted soil has no place. Future civilization – 2019 – is characterized not by its achievements but by its losses. This motherless world is what we fear.[3]

## The class system

Ridley Scott's vision of 2019 embodies the same social structure we see in cultures organized by a hierarchy of power. Technologies, populations, and languages have changed but not the stratification of power. As in Indo-European cultures for thousands of years, the pyramid (from Tyrell back to the Pharaohs) reflects the social stratification. At the top are worldly kings or other-worldly priests; their power is maintained by a warrior class, and the entire structure is supported by the broad base of shepherds and farmers, often by slaves, and now by "workers" or simply "everybody else."[4]

Dr Eldon Tyrell is at the top of the pyramid – a structure that rises above and dominates the landscape, supposedly over 800 floors tall. The pyramid is a throwback to modernism and the triumphs of technological and financial power. Tyrell's office is 80 feet by 80 feet of mostly empty space and decorated with 20-foot-high columns and an immense window that gives us our only view of the sun (Sammon 1996: 124). The office reflects Tyrell's narcissism and power that together allow him to create replicants and to retire them without feeling. His replicant "experiments" make Dr Frankenstein look naive and primitive.

The warrior class – the Blade Runners and the police patrolling in aerial vehicles – also includes the genetic engineers and others who build and support the Tyrell Corporation's profits. Similarly, our warrior class today includes not only the military but also the professional class of scientists, engineers, lawyers, stockbrokers, "mid-level" managers, etc. All are soldiers in the war of economic competition for profit.

Finally, at the base of the pyramid are the streets littered with "techno-trash," drenched with acid rain, and crowded by featureless people hurrying god-knows where. No one seems to speak the same language, and despite the crowding there is no human contact (Sammon 1996: 114). The one condition shared by everyone, however, is slavery. Everyone serves the same god and shares the same prison – though some can afford to decorate their cells comfortably. Even Tyrell, despite his power, serves the "profit-god" – minutes before his death he is making a stock market trade.

## The maximization of profit

We cannot understand our relationship to technology today or in *Blade Runner* without first understanding profit. If we personify profit, this god is not evil; in fact, he gets people bristling with ideas and energy and creates as much excitement as he does misery. In a still "gendered" world, "he" seems to be the fitting pronoun. Profit is an unstable god who views personal interests – art, leisure, love, family, pleasure, religion, etc. – as *competing* interests. When the "profit-god" achieves success, its warriors and workers must nonetheless remain vigilant to the envy of less fortunate souls and the energy of younger, more energetic warriors.

Evolving technologies are limited and contorted by their service to the "bottom line." Narrowly focused vision becomes impaired vision. The blinders don't come off. The problem with profit-driven vision is not what we see but what we are prevented from seeing. Decision-makers and consumers do not notice the hazards – especially long-term hazards – of new technologies, nor do they notice creative potentials that cannot be measured by profit. New technologies, therefore, only do old tricks: make more money, provide distractions, stimulate other products, etc.

Genetic engineers work wonders in *Blade Runner* because it is profitable. Since our scientific and technological skills grow exponentially, these skills are exploited by corporations to maximize profits. The speed of technological evolution has profound consequences for cultural evolution: culturally we are always unsuccessfully trying to catch up with technology. Technological evolution has no time to serve hoped-for cultural visions because it is too focused on and driven by profit. Since new technologies are evaluated for their profit potential, we learn about them primarily from sources like the *Wall Street Journal*, the Financial News Network, or common advertisements, and seldom from sources of spiritual, psychological, social, or creative meaning.

Technology has been appropriated by financial interests, but it had other origins. Our early ancestor was *homo habilis*, the tool maker. In the beginning I think our hunting and gathering technologies were probably inspired by a mixture of need, curiosity, and play. Our tools, like cave paintings and rituals, were probably expressions of creative magic and play that made life human and meaningful. I think we all value those moments when we experience a playful, interested attachment to our techno-goods and tools. Dolores Brien suggests the word "technophilia" to better appreciate and express our innately human "emotional affiliation with technology."[5] The word "technophilia" encourages us to appreciate the intimate emotional and imaginative ground of all of our technological creations. With this appreciation we discover an immediate counterweight to "technomania," the euphoric, frenetic embrace of technology marked-up for profit and status.

*Blade Runner* would have us believe that overarching scientific and technological ambition is our tragic flaw. We have, in the eyes of the film, made a Faustian bargain with technology. Genetically engineered humans have returned to earth and are, we are told, a threat to human existence. Detective Bryant tells Deckard: "This is a bad one, the worst yet . . . If the [Voight–Kampff] machine fails, we're in deep trouble." The fact is, however, that the replicants are not so dangerous. Except for Roy Batty who dies of "unnatural" encoded causes, the replicants are quickly tracked and retired. Yes, they are powerful, but when they display their super-human physical prowess, they do so with a proud adolescent flair. They may be desperate and angry, but they are not malevolent. They hardly know what to do with their exceptional talents. Leon puts his hand into a freezing liquid and removes it unharmed; with her bare hand Pris retrieves an egg from boiling water in Sebastian's apartment. These feats signal an adolescent sense of omnipotence more than menace. Their emotions may be unrefined or immature but they *are* human; given time and life, these replicants would learn to feel intelligently.

Our flaw is not the unnatural use of technology, nor even our desires for profit and power, but rather our *obsession* with power and profit. Tyrell tells Deckard proudly, "Commerce is our goal here at Tyrell. 'More human than human' is our motto. Rachael is an experiment, nothing more." How cold! Fittingly, the night Tyrell is killed we see the high priest of profit in an opulent bed, surrounded by candles, and reading a market report. We hear him speak to an automated trader, "66,000 Prosser & Ankopitch. Trade." It is commerce that created this world's devastation, that created "Off-world" colonies, and that created replicant-slaves and Blade Runners.

As Jungian analyst Wolfgang Giegerich has argued, our obsession with "the maximization of profit," has eclipsed religion, the life of the individual, and psychological individuation. As Jungian analysts it is critically important that we understand the psychological dominance of this one organizing principle – profit. The pursuit of profit alters all human relationships and all attitudes toward love and work:

> What we are witnessing at present in our world is a gigantic revolution that makes the industrial revolution look harmless. In the entire economy a radical and extremely powerful process of restructuring, downsizing, of rationalization is going on. It is a process that renders hundreds of thousands or millions of employees redundant and assigns to those remaining ones the logical status of a collective manoeuvrable mass. Parallel to "just-in-time" produc-tion, there is a tendency to "just-in-time" employment ("MacJob"). In Germany, people with limited-term contracts are sometimes

referred to as "Durchlaufmaterial", which might be rendered as "transit material".

(Giegerich 1996:
http://www.cgjungpage.org/articles/giegerich1.html)

C.G. Jung came close to identifying profit as the core complex driving technological development: "This task [science and technology] is so exacting, and its fulfilment so *profitable* [italics mine], that he [man] forgets himself in the process" (Jung 1990: para. 557). When we forget ourselves, we are easily lured by the intense pleasures and social powers of money. We purr to sounds of "The Dow is up. The Nasdaq is up." One-sidedness, however, is our peril. At the end of his life Jung wrote these words:

> we stand in need of a reorientation, a *metanoia* . . . We must . . . no longer succumb to anything at all, not even to good. A so-called good to which we succumb loses its ethical character. Not that there is anything bad in it on that score, but to have succumbed to it may breed trouble. Every form of addiction is bad, no matter whether the narcotic be alcohol or morphine or idealism.

(Jung 1965: 329)

*Blade Runner* shows us a world where people – depersonalized replicants – have become profitable objects of manufacture, servants of worn-out obsessions with security and profit. Since the futures we imagine are often slightly exaggerated images of the present, *Blade Runner* is an instructive mirror. Haven't we already become interchangeable parts on corporate payrolls – today's version of "cannon fodder"? As consumers, our identities and purchasing statistics are for sale to retailers and advertisers. Now, with the Human Genome Project so far advanced and cell technology soon capable of regenerating human tissue and organs, we are not so far from *Blade Runner*'s replicants. Despite the risks of rewriting biological human instructions, I find the potential exciting because of the human hopes and visions it may inspire. As a realistically distrustful consumer, however, I am highly suspicious of the likely merger of genetics and capitalism. We need, therefore, time to think about our pending decisions. Time would allow us to respect our hopes and fears, to think about them, to reflect upon the fantasies and dreams embodied by genetic technologies and upon the fantasies and dreams we are likely to overlook.

Eric Lander, head of the Whitehead-MIT Center for Genome Research, remarked in the July 3, 2000 issue of *Time*, "Once you start to see human beings as a product of manufacture, you cross a line and you may never be able to return." With "products of manufacture" we approach the post-human boundary. We have not crossed the line, however, because we have not surpassed ourselves as Roy Batty and Rachael surpassed their maker. Nor have we realized what it may mean to be human or to create a humane world. Eric Lander's observation, no matter how insightful, urges us to maintain educated fears but fails to acknowledge the value of educated hopes.

## Hyperextension

In Carl Jung's early work, *Symbols of Transformation*, he described how one goal – the maximization of profit, for instance – can usurp all other claims of allegiance (Jung: 1967: 141). To explain the process of transformation Jung introduced the concept of the "canalization of libido," a process biologists and others today call "hyperextension." Hyperextension is as commonplace as a young person with long muscles and a physique made for swimming who trains competitively for a scholarship or an Olympic gold medal. We hyperextend our endurance to meet deadlines or our computational resources to map human DNA.

Jung wrote about how we all make analogies between emotionally charged themes (sex, for example) and alternative images (planting seeds in the earth, for instance). Our ancestors learned how to transform energy or libido from one aim (mating) to another (farming). The ongoing use of such symbols of transformation and "countless analogies" has permitted us to hyperextend virtually any human potential. In *Blade Runner* we witness effects of the hyperextension of technology and power but also, gradually, the effects of hyperextended consciousness and love.

In the analytic container we concentrate on spontaneous symbols as they occur in dreams and in other imaginative states; this concentration promotes the transformation Jung called "individuation." In the collective sphere powerful groups use emotionally laden symbols (sex, wealth, pleasure, aggression, etc.) to hyperextend our abilities to compete aggressively, to work excitedly, to feel intensely, to think deliberately, etc. We have learned, for instance, to feel that cars, cell phones, faster computers, and reshaped bodies are not only sexy but necessary for our survival. We think about the sex appeal of cell phones or new computers, but we fail to reflect on the fantasies, dreams, and tangible consequences of pursuing and fulfilling our wishes. Daily we hyperextend our athletic abilities, our intelligence, our consumer habits, our gender differences, our cultural differences, our youth, our interest in money, etc. In *Blade Runner* the Tyrell Corporation hyperextended genetic engineering to create more-than-human replicants – but only in the service of profit and nothing greater. In today's world, as in *Blade Runner*, profit equals Darwinian "fitness," and fitness, as evolutionary biologists know, is all.

Jung's theory of symbols of transformation provides a language to understand the permutations of desire in cultural psychology. Freud's contrasting theory of sublimation provides insight into those cultural changes based on fear, on the conflict between the amoral Id and the fear of castration, between, for instance, loving big cars and homes and fearing global warming and climate change. The two theories of transformation and sublimation, when brought together with the theories of psychological complexes, object relations, psychological defenses, and archetypal processes, can deepen our understanding of the world we inherited and the world we are creating. With a new understanding, we may avoid the disturbingly familiar future of *Blade Runner* where "the good life" is still corporate: "There's a place for you at Dominguez and Shimata Colonies" . . . a "chance to begin again" in the "golden lands of opportunity and adventure," a chance to help "America into the new world." With con-sciousness – which Jung called the second creation – we can also approach a future that is the best we can imagine and think (Jung 1965: 339, 256).

## Technology is not neutral

*Blade Runner* urges us to believe two things about technology that we are all too ready to believe: the first is that technology itself is neutral. Deckard says, for example, "Replicants are like any other machine. They can be a benefit or a hazard. If it's a benefit, it's not my problem." The same can and has been said about nuclear power, about money, about drugs, and in the US we hear this argument frequently used against gun control legislation. The argument is seductive but false. We can only believe that guns are neutral if we ignore the aggressive fantasies that inspire their creation. Each technology is initiated by human psyches, each technology arises from psychological fantasies, wishes, and fears. The human psychological ground is forever a part of technology, regardless of how technology is actually used. Like any psychological complex, emotionally charged associations (images, thoughts) cluster about every tool or technology. Our technologies and the human relationships that sustain them exist within a "body" of associations, potentials, promises, hazards, dreams.

Precisely because technology is not neutral, we are afforded chances to know ourselves through what we make. Our technological creations – vaccines, antibiotics, spreadsheets, "instant messengers," etc. – are our dreams. Our creations will inevitably affect us, frequently in unanticipated ways. The computer brought the world to a flat screen on our desktops. Through e-mail, ICQ, chat rooms, streaming video, and web pages; we have the magic "access" to the world – definitely desirable. Access, however, also brings atrophied muscles, a stream of advertising, invasions of privacy, cyber-sex, more work, repetitive motion disorders, and other questionable fruits. What else can we create at our desktop computers? Can we explore the imagination at any new depth? Can we carry on new conversations over time and across boundaries of nationality and age, conversations that would have been impossible just a year ago? And what kind of conversations and to what ends?

Through more conscious relationships with our technologies, we will learn more about who we are but also more about who we may become and how we may change. A technology may reveal something new about itself and ourselves just as a dream can express something we never imagined or thought.

The second conclusion urged upon us by *Blade Runner* is that we must limit our technological ambitions. Fear hovers over this conviction: technology may be unstoppable, evolution may abandon carbon based compounds and select silicon, or a superhuman intelligence, once created, may decide that humans should be "terminated," or as *Blade Runner* would have it, surpassed and "retired."

We understand what directs and drives growth – fear and desire, wishes for security or excitement, obsessions with profit and power – but we do not understand how or when to limit ourselves. The answer, I believe, already exists in the analytic practices of self-reflection, psychological conversation, and responsiveness to oneself and others. These analytic practices are perhaps easily overlooked because they have been culturally assimilated over the course of the last psychological century. Unfortunately, such deliberate psychological practices are seldom exercised in relation to the challenges of a post-human world; nor do they enjoy the personal conversations, air time, shelf space, or bandwidth they deserve.

Sublimation should help us with the limits and self-reflection necessary to slow the speed of technological momentum, but its reach is less influential than a genuine change of attitude. Jung's appreciation of the process of transformation, therefore, fosters a more hopeful perspective:

We do not know how far the process of coming to consciousness can extend, or where it will lead. It is a new element in the story of creation, and there are no parallels we can look to. We therefore cannot know what potentialities are inherent in it. Neither can we know the prospects for the species Homo sapiens.

(Jung 1965: 340)

All of the practices of analysis – containing, expressing, remembering, imagining, dreaming, listening psychologically, thinking symbolically, interpreting – encourage the development of a "responsive self," responsive to the inner world, responsive to present and remembered others, and responsive to the surrounding world. The "responsive self" is an analytic ideal. If the image of a "responsive self" inspired our best energies, it could become a cultural ideal. Whether or not we name this "self," every session of psychoanalysis engages in practices that ultimately foster and sustain such a "self."

## Responsive self, sacred union

The subplot of *Blade Runner* centers on the relationship between Deckard and Rachael, Tyrell's experiment. The meaning of a film is usually carried by its subplot – in our case, the theme of love over power and the question of what it means to be human. We watch Deckard and Rachael become increasingly responsive to the emotional complexities of their situation. No one comes close to the subtle depths of *Blade Runner*'s post-human future except Deckard, Rachael, and Roy. Deckard risks the difficult knowledge that Rachael is more human than any human he knows. Rachael learns to trust, later to love, the person assigned to "retire" her. Roy sees the immeasurable value of everything he has witnessed and lived, so much so that he saves Deckard's life, the life of the man hunting him. Finally, Deckard witnesses the mystery of Roy's soliloquy and death with silent respect. His response to Roy's transformation is to rescue Rachael and tie his fate to hers. Replicants and humans alike are far more than sets of coded DNA instructions.

Deckard's life is saved twice – first by Rachael (she shoots Leon with Deckard's gun) and then by Roy (he catches Deckard's hand at the moment he slips from the rooftop ledge). He is twice reborn to greater human depths. Deckard learns from these unexpected exchanges that "human" is a category that transcends the circumstances of one's creation – sexual reproduction or genetic engineering.

*Figure 6.2  Blade Runner.* Deckard (Harrison Ford) and Rachael (Sean Young). (Ladd Company/Warner Bros, Courtesy Kobal)

*Blade Runner* ends twice – first with Roy's internal solitary union and second with the union chosen by Deckard and Rachael. Deckard and Rachael leave his apartment, staking their lives on each other and on their escape from L.A. Their union symbolizes the best of what a post-human future may be. Watching these three people carefully we see the outlines of what it means to be human in *Blade Runner*'s post-human future:

- *The bestowal of value.* Chew, an ancient Asian, makes genetically engineered eyes in the deep cold of his lab. All he can see is his work as he insists that Roy and Leon leave because he is "Busy. Busy. You go away. Make appointment." He only sees the squishy cold eyes he labors over. Chew doesn't even experience a moment of curiosity or wonder when Roy says, "If only you could see the things I have seen with your eyes."
- *The refusal to disavow human evil.* Roy and Rachael can be ruthless *and* self-sacrificing. They remain present, they do not dissociate, and they know their own evil, although theirs stands pale before the evil humans enact. Humans in *Blade Runner* are blind to their dehumanization of replicants ("skin jobs") and of anyone with lower status (Bryant: "If you're not cop, you're little people").

- *Complex moral judgments.* Rachael shoots Leon, a replicant like herself, to save Deckard whom she instinctively ("humanly") trusts and respects. Earlier, when subjected to the Voight–Kampff test by Deckard, she differentiates and contains emotions about cruelty to animals, about a husband's betrayal, jealousy, abandonment, sexual politics, and the test situation itself. She has far more emotional intelligence than Tyrell, her maker.
- *Acting empathically.* Only replicants sacrifice themselves for others or for something higher than their job description. Humans, by contrast, like their human status but do not act humanly. They think empathically about animals that no longer exist but then act narcissistically toward others.
- *Valuing memories.* The humans in *Blade Runner* never speak of memories; replicants long for memories. While we may suffer from memories, as Freud and Jung realized, today we may also suffer from impoverished or absent memories. Unlike everyone else in the film, Roy does experience, reflect, and remember. After saving Deckard's life, Roy sits in the dark rain on the rooftop and, with Deckard as his witness, speaks. His soliloquy celebrates his memories. Knowing that he is dying, he says, "I've seen things that you people wouldn't believe . . . Attack ships on fire off the shoulder of Orion . . . I watched c-beams glitter in the dark near the Tanhauser Gate . . . All those . . . moments . . . will be lost . . . in time, like tears . . . in the rain. Time . . . to die." He attains, in his death, a mystical union within himself.
- *Seeing beauty in the face of meaninglessness.* Rachael lovingly looks at the family pictures on Deckard's piano while he rests – lovingly, though she has no reason to believe that Deckard's "family" is any more real than the family she "remembers" (implants). She begins to play the piano. When Deckard awakes having dreamt music, Rachael explains that she doesn't know if she took piano lessons or only has Tyrell's niece's implanted memories of piano lessons. Deckard responds with the fewest loving words we might imagine: "You play beautifully."
- *Creating new forms of love.* Deckard tells Rachael that she is a replicant; he also loves her. He says, "Now you kiss me," and Rachael responds, "I can't rely on my memory . . ." Her memories – Tyrell's sixteen-year-old niece's memories – have not reached this far. Deckard teaches Rachael words of love and sex – "Say, 'kiss me.'" She responds, "Kiss me." She then finds her own words, "Put your hands on me." When Deckard goes back to his apartment for Rachael,

they leave to forge a new race, however small and endangered, in a foreign place. They leave to build memories, to define themselves, and to explore what it will now mean to be human.

Jung considered the opposite of power to be relationship, not power-lessness.[6] Not only was he right but he captured in this one line the predicament of our time. We choose power. We ignore the consequences of our actions on others, on ourselves, on the world around us, and on the future, and in exchange we lose our bearings. The power we choose is the power to dominate, not the necessary power to have our own thoughts, to define ourselves, and to take care of ourselves and others. We cannot afford to disavow this deeper sense of power. To be responsive to this world, our love must respect power and our technological or financial passions but must also liberate us from obsessions of all kinds. Love that will transcend the limits of power can embrace the past generations who gave birth to us and the future generations whom we can now only imagine but who will inherit the world we create.

We can find hope in the psychoanalytic practices that value remembering and connecting memories with images, feelings, insights, and relationships. These practices are forms of psychological love. The greatest influence on our sense of relationship in this century is again the psychoanalytic practice of all persuasions. Nowhere do we find a container more suited to the creation of a responsive self than in the analytic relationship. It is natural and necessary, then, that psychoanalysis take up the challenge of responding consciously to the profit-making, power-gathering shadow of our century and to our technological selves that have been profit's slaves. It is our task to articulate a new psychology for new times. The emotionally rich metaphor of the union of Deckard and Rachael is more satisfying than strictly rational alternatives such as cost–benefit analyses, scientific risk assessments, superego restraints, changes motivated by fear, or fundamentalist religious responses.

By celebrating the union of humanity and technology in Deckard and Rachael, I think *Blade Runner* provides us with the metaphor for a self responsive to others, ourselves, the planet, and the future. Deckard and Rachael are not cast out of Eden to work and suffer; they escape a spoiled Eden to attempt their experiment in being human. Relationship means deliberate, conscious respect for the "other" and a willingness to take responsibility for oneself and for the other. Respect calls us to take responsibility for the consequences of what we create and to use our technological intelligence to serve the best of what it means to be human. If we accept our post-human condition, we accept the challenge to be human by thoughtful, responsive choices, not human by default. In cultivating a responsive personality, I imagine that we will reach a deeper understanding of Jung's statement – and the alchemists before him – that "man is indispensable for the completion of creation; . . . in fact, he himself is the second creator of the world" (Jung 1965: 256).

## Notes

1  *Blade Runner* (1982) Dir. Ridley Scott. Writing credits (in credits order): Philip K. Dick, Hampton Fancher, David Webb Peoples. Cast: Harrison Ford . . . Deckard, Rutger Hauer . . . Roy Batty, Sean Young . . . Rachael, Edward James Olmos . . . Gaff, M. Emmet Walsh . . . Detective Bryant, Daryl Hannah . . . Pris, William Sanderson . . . J.F. Sebastian, Brion James . . . Leon, Joe Turkel . . . Tyrell, Morgan Paull . . . Holden. Produced by Michael Deeley, Hampton Fancher, and Brian Kelly.

2  The Voight–Kampff, like the word association experiment developed by C.G. Jung from 1904–1907, identifies "feeling-toned complexes" (or their absence) by noting reaction times to stimulus words, physical reactions (pupil dilation in *Blade Runner*, Galvanic Skin Response, and other involuntary physical reactions with the word association experiment), idiosyncratic responses, etc. Jung's research provided the experimental validation of Freud's theory of repression, Jung's theory of psychological complexes, psychosomatic disturbances, and later object relations theory.

3  See *Mad Max*, *The Terminator*, etc.

4  Cf. Georges Dumezil's theories of Indo-European social structures.

5  Dolores E. Brien, as editor of the Psychology and Technology section of the C.G. Jung Page (www.cgjungpage.org), has published articles and interviews online that bring a rich Jungian perspective to techno-psychology.

6  "Where love [relationship] stops, power begins" (Jung 1990: para. 580).

## Bibliography

Barash, D. (1986) *The Hare and the Tortoise: Culture, Biology, and Human Nature*, New York: Viking.

Cameron, J. (1984) Dir. *The Terminator*, Exec. Prods J. Daly and D. Gibson.

Dick, P.K. (1975) *Do Androids Dream of Electric Sheep*, New York: Ballantine Books.

Giegerich, W. (1996) "The Opposition of 'Individual' and 'Collective' – Psychology's Basic Fault," *Harvest: Journal for Jungian Studies*, 42, 2: 7–27.

Hayles, N. Katherine (1999) *How We Became Posthuman: Virtual Bodies in Cybernetics, Literature, and Informatics*, Chicago: University of Chicago Press.

Jung, C.G. (1965) *Memories, Dreams, Reflections*, New York: Vintage.

Jung, C.G. (1967) *Symbols of Transformation*, London: Routledge & Kegan Paul.

Jung, C.G. (1990) *The Undiscovered Self with Symbols and the Interpretation of Dreams*, Princeton: Princeton University Press.

Lander, E. (2000) in "Mapping the Genome," *Time*, July 3, New York: Time Inc.

Miller, G. (1979) Dir. *Mad Max*, Exec. Prod. B. Kennedy.

Rothenberg, D. (1993) *Hand's End: Technology and the Limits of Nature*, Berkeley: University of California Press.

Sammon, P.M. (1996) *Future Noir: The Making of Blade Runner*, New York: HarperPaperbacks.

Schmookler, A.B. (1995) *The Parable of the Tribes: The Problem of Power in Social Evolution*, New York: SUNY.

Scott, R. (1982) Dir. *Blade Runner*, Exec. Prods. B. Kelly and H. Fancher.

Vinge, V. (1993) *The Coming Technological Singularity: How to Survive in the Post-Human Era*, http://www-rohan.sdsu.edu/faculty/vinge/misc/singularity.html

Winner, L. (1989) *The Whale and the Reactor: A Search for Limits in an Age of High Technology*, Chicago: University of Chicago Press.

# Chapter 7

# 2001: A Space Odyssey
## A classical reading

*John Izod*

## Background

In the iconography of myth, ghosts have interesting first and second cousins in UFOs (Unidentified Flying Objects) and fictional spaceships respectively. They are related, of course, through their signifieds rather than their signifiers (their connotations rather than their looks). It was the mythological connections of flying saucers that engaged Jung's interest in the 1950s. During that decade many sightings were claimed, and these phenomena attracted much public attention.

Jung argued that the UFOs of that era were a collective manifestation of the fears aroused in Western nations by the Cold War. Indeed, although he did not use the term, he was in effect showing how the cultural unconscious could energize and launch a symbolic cluster with archetypal roots that responded to the pressures of the time. Demonstrating that such images have a history, which at the very least reaches back to the sixteenth century, he wrote an *amplification* – not only of reports of sightings but also of their images and associated ideas. He showed how, whatever other passengers they might be suspected of conveying, flying saucers were most certainly carriers of archetypal energies.

Among other factors, Jung considered the pervasive nature of geometric and numeric symbolism associated with the UFOs, and demonstrated how the same symbolism traditionally represented images of divinity (Jung [1959] 1964: paras. 771–4). He also found that the masculine–feminine antithesis occurred in some graphic descriptions of UFOs, with, in one case, cigar-shaped objects opposed to others that took a saucer or lens form (ibid.: para. 662). That kind of opposition characterizes images of the unified, monotheistic self such as the syzygy. In addition he observed that manifestations of UFOs took the form of revelations from heaven; as such, they often developed traditional representations of the divine. Not surprisingly, then, they also built upon and in turn heightened the familiar contrast between a higher world which is perceived as being the locus of the enigmatic, the fabulous, the mythological and the divine on the one hand, and the ordinary lower world on the other. When he took all the evidence into account, Jung found abundant reasons to associate UFOs with the central archetype of the self that his earlier work had differentiated (ibid.: paras. 771–6). It follows that they are close to the idea of the divine.

It is a commonplace observation for Jungians that dreams occasionally take a predictive form, and certain visions may do the same when the contents irrupting from the unconscious indicate a coming change in disposition of which the dreamer is not yet consciously aware. In 1968, Arthur C. Clarke published *The Promise of Space* in which he advanced an idea that complements the Jungian perspective on visions collectively experienced. He observed a powerful interaction between science and literature – in both directions. From our perspective, it is particularly fruitful to recognize that the fiction of space travel did a great deal to draw humanity closer to the goal of interplanetary travel, which it only began to realize more than three hundred years after the first fictions were written. Clarke makes a persuasive case that from the second half of the nineteenth century onwards, the human hunger for space found expression in fictions and dreams. These in turn eventually excited interest in the great labor needed to convert dreams and aspirations into the intricate material technologies of actual space travel (Clarke [1968] 1970: 21–32).

The *Promise of Space* was published in the same year that the celebrated film *2001: A Space Odyssey* was released, the screenplay for which Clarke had written with its director Stanley Kubrick. The film's distribution was synchronized with a time when worldwide consciousness of space travel was acute. It was the period when the Cold War was at its most intense. The race for superiority in outer space between the then two super powers, the Soviet Union and the USA, had been hard fought, ever since the Soviets had launched the first artificial satellite Sputnik 1 in 1957. Hypnotized by the paranoid belief that control of space would lead to military superiority, the American government responded over the next decade with massive investment in a fast-track space program. This phase of the race reached a dramatic culmination on July 20, 1969 when the American space team achieved the first landing of a human being on the moon. In the aftermath of this triumph the main themes celebrated by the popular media in the capitalist world were twofold. The first theme concerned the clear evidence of American technological superiority over the Soviet Union – a superiority which was widely understood to entail the reasonable certainty of safety from surprise nuclear attack by Inter-Continental Ballistic Missiles. The second was less xenophobic and imperialist, and centered on the prospects for humanity in a new era, which this first step appeared to have opened.

Kubrick and Clarke alluded to the former and developed the latter theme in *2001: A Space Odyssey*, but they did so in a manner which changed both topics and linked the film ideologically with records of UFO sightings and the associated literature cited by Jung.

The first thing to recall, for all those who have not had the opportunity to see the film in its original format, is that no screens in today's cinemas other than those in specialized IMAX venues (such as theme parks) can compete with Cinerama for size. On that giant screen Kubrick created vast empty zones to provide a visual simile for the idea of galactic space. The screen's sheer dimensions, together with the splendor of the images and music that filled it, endowed both the fictional odyssey and the film itself with a sense of majesty. In addition, the movie progresses at a distinctively slow pace from start to finish. Its deliberate rhythm ensures that there is time for the extraordinary images, effects and sounds to register their points with audiences. The measured tempo of the action adds to the sense of awe engendered by its scale.

All the above factors emphasized the epic nature of the action. However, because throughout much of their history until the end of the 1960s Hollywood studios tagged every lavish feature production with the slogan "Epic" for publicity purposes, it is worth reminding ourselves what the term means when applied more stringently to narrative form. While a true epic is a narrative which may well have a large number of characters in it, the fundamental point is that its action should be on a grand scale, its themes involving the fate of an entire people, or indeed, as here, the entire human race. Nothing inhibits the presentation of large heroes and villains with strongly marked personalities, but such characters should in some way further the noble purposes of the epic as leaders of a people, or their all-too-threatening enemies. Characters are likely to be used as vehicles to convey substantial moral statements, whether by words or deeds. These observations, which fit the formal outlines of literary epics from Homer's *Odyssey* through Milton's *Paradise Lost* and on to Melville's *Moby Dick*, can be applied with equal accuracy to *2001*, vindicating its claim to present an epic odyssey for the twentieth century.

The narrative has an outer frame, opening and closing to the triumphant musical annunciation of Richard Strauss's "Thus Spake Zarathustra." When immediately after the title sequence, the film starts to this accompaniment, the Sun slowly rises over two aligned planets – Earth and Jupiter. The plot's ambitious claim to enter both universal space and time is immediately indicated.

## Act one

The first of four distinct acts, "The Dawn of Man," starts in the era of pre-consciousness. Family groups of large apes nose around looking for greenery to eat. They forage, having the capability neither to grow food nor decisively to defend their territory. What brings these creatures to the new consciousness that marks them out as prototypes of humanity is the advent of a sign, a black monolith that appears without forewarning in the territory of one of the groups. It stimulates in them an appetite for rudimentary knowledge and understanding. After touching and being touched by it, their leader works out how to use the bones of dead beasts as weapons. As he puzzles how to make inanimate objects work for him, Richard Strauss's "Zarathustra" sounds once more and emphasizes the high significance of the moment.

The leader soon arms his companions, and their new power enables them to kill for food and to drive aggressive rivals away from their water hole on penalty of death. However, this is only one side of their story. The discovery by the emergent race of human beings that a bone can be an implement brings the ability not only to take up arms but also to use tools. Kubrick articulates visually the entire history of humanity's skill with implements in one of the most celebrated cuts in cinema. The leading ape-man hurls his bone hammer into the air, exulting in new power. The image cuts from the bone hovering at the zenith of its flight to a space ship approaching its docking zone millions of years later. This extraordinary juxtaposition leaves the audience recognizing that, whilst the complexity of both weapons and tools has multiplied many times during the history of our species, the fundamental moral opposition remains unchanged. The nature of the power that distinguishes humanity – the capacity for constructive thought – brings with it the inescapable consequence that we can use it either for good or evil. Power itself is morally neutral; but the use of it always has moral repercussions.

The monolith can be interpreted as analogous to the presence and activation of an archetype in that it awakens latent capabilities. However, the range of archetypes that it might body into symbolic form is limited by its characteristics. This is obviously not one of the figures commonly found in both personal and collective psychologies that take a personalized form (such as the anima, animus, shadow, trickster, wise old woman, or man do); rather, its minimalist abstraction, the high seriousness and ascetic rigor of its signals link it firmly with the transpersonal. One of the few clues to its function on this first appearance is the alignment of its vertical plane with the Sun and the Moon. It points metaphorically to something unknown, at a high level, and yet to be discovered. That the monolith is vertical implies, given that the ape-men have limited knowledge of their environment, the need for the species to stir out of uroboric pre-consciousness to deepen their conscious understanding of their world. And indeed the advent of this signal starts for humanity the long journey into the ever more intense consciousness that the film charts.

In earlier factual records and fictional evocations of human experience, the coming down to Earth of UFOs is typically presented as the arrival of the gods pressing in upon consciousness from a higher order of the archetypal unconscious. In *2001*, however, there is a double trajectory, the new element being that humans go out to meet the unknown. We shall return to this topic later.

## Act two

Aeons after the awakening of humanity and at the end of the twentieth century, scientists discover a second monolith buried beneath the surface of the Moon where it has lain some four million years. The second act of *2001* is set in a time when global conflict (the Cold War between the superpowers still current at the time of the film's release) has been superseded by relatively cordial, if somewhat suspicious, political relations between the Earth's great powers, the USA and the Soviet Union. Lunar exploration has become routine and devoid of mystery, and international tensions are not the major issue for the space travellers. Rather, global terror, fear of the unknown, is. So the discovery of the monolith is not the source of awe that we might have expected from its previous manifestation. It causes instead acute anxiety in the top echelons of US scientists and bureaucrats who know of its existence. When a senior scientific administrator Dr Heyward Floyd (William Sylvester) goes on a fact-finding trip to the moon, his visit is conducted under conditions of the utmost secrecy to prevent word reaching the Earth's populations. (The fact that the US authorities have circulated a cover story alleging that a serious epidemic has broken out at the site of the secret excavation speaks volumes symbolically about their anxiety.) His purpose is to advise the authorities when and how to break the news; but the ideological straitjacket within which he and his superiors have bound themselves is revealed when he addresses a meeting at the American Lunar base of the board of scientists who discovered the monolith. All are soberly suited, their formal language and the over-cautious atmosphere just like that of countless board rooms on Earth in the second half of the twentieth century. One sentence from Floyd's speech gives the register:

> "I'm sure you're all aware of the extremely grave potential for cultural shock and social disorientation contained in this present situation if the facts were prematurely and suddenly made public without adequate preparation and conditioning."

Behind the bland abstractions it is evident that the authorities take it for granted that the Earth's population will need to be "conditioned." There is, to say the least, a loss – not only of civil liberty but also of freedom of thought and imagination entailed in the intense secrecy. Much later we discover that the authorities have decided not to let any information permeate outside the security cordon. The Earth's nations have been kept in ignorance of the monolith's existence.

In the second and third acts, technology is represented with deliberate ambivalence. The film played to many in the audience of the late 1960s (including the present writer) to whom its wide-screen vision of passenger-carrying space craft and the great wheels of orbiting space stations was a source of wonder. We have mentioned ways in which the aesthetics of the screen were deployed both to excite and gratify a sense of wonder and awe. However, on the screen itself, the twenty-first century characters make the electronics and advanced equipment the object of rational but unemotional attention. For them the wonderful has become the merely routine. What is more, the clichéd scientific jargon of the fictional astronauts' speech renders, with only slight exaggeration, the wooden communications lingo of NASA's men in the 1960s – so there was a direct connection with the present for the audience of the day. The banality of this impoverished human discourse contrasts with the majesty of the music. The latter carries both the power and the subtlety of the emotions generated by the awesome circumstances in which the characters find themselves, but which their limping words, sanctioned corporate-speak, are incapable of touching. (I owe this observation to Jane Ryan and Miriam Sheer.) The contrast between the two ways of perceiving – the one dominated by the uses and control of a complex technology, the other by the musicality and poetry of the experience – develops into an unstated, but real, conflict of values. The film's scientists and astronauts focus on *the means* of space travel. The film itself – and eventually one of the astronauts – encourages its audience to contemplate *the purposes* of such a voyage.

The focal point of Dr Floyd's visit to the Moon is an on-site examination of the excavated monolith. Here the high significance of what we are witnessing is signaled to the audience by the fact that no radio communications between the team can be heard. Instead we listen to a ceremonial incantation composed by Ligeti, which is like the chorale sounding when the first monolith was discovered by the scientists' distant forebears. For a moment or two the incredible presence of the sheer-sided block imposes itself on the men. Floyd moves forward and touches it, just as the lead ape-man had done. However, the awe communicated through the music and the slow movements of the group of scientists toward the monolith quickly dissipates. The team then trivializes the occasion by posing for a group photograph in front of it. At this moment it emits a radio signal that pierces their ears and (we later discover) succeeds in focusing their minds on the proper issues at hand. This is the only signal it transmits. Thereafter it remains as inert as it had done for the four million years it was buried under the surface of the Moon. But the exact timing of its emission also suggests not only that it has a message to deliver, but also that the visitors may be close to a hubristic undervaluation of its significance – a mistake which the monolith itself corrects.

The amount of data on the monolith available to the audience is not large, but it does license two parallel readings. It has been on the Moon four million years and produces a strong magnetic field which first led lunar explorers to it. The latter believe that it must have been deliberately buried. It emits just the one radio signal, and does so at the precise moment that its vertical plane is aligned with Jupiter and the Sun. This transmission is the trigger that causes the US government to dispatch a mission to Jupiter.

Among the many uncertainties which this scant information leaves open, one question in particular tantalizes. Is there a chain of monoliths (four in all by the end of the journey) which signal to each other? Or is there just the one, the manifestations and movements of which are beyond the capacity of reason to comprehend? The first proposition stimulates the thought that there must exist an older, more advanced species capable of rigging such a signaling system across our galaxy. The second idea fits sweetly with the recognition that the monolith stands for and leads humanity ever deeper into the unknown – and that it has therefore a connection with the transpersonal or collective unconscious.

I intend to produce a reading of *2001* which respects both these possibilities, arguing that the monolith is a visible metaphor for the evolving self of Western humanity. In this context we should note that on its second appearance, the monolith is once again vertical. Again during this phase in human development consciousness must dominate the endeavors of the species which require focusing on technology to enable travel to the more distant planet.

## Act three

The third act is set eighteen months later on board the *Discovery*. The mission to Jupiter on which it is bound has been prepared under conditions of secrecy so stringent that the crew have not been briefed on their ultimate goal before departure. None of them even know that there is a secret purpose to their mission. Dave Bowman (Keir Dullea) is in command, with Frank Poole (Gary Lockwood) his deputy. Three further crew members who comprise a survey team are in a state of hibernation and will be awakened when they reach their destination.

Once again we see the potential for boredom inherent in a routinely perfect environment. The crew members have little to do other than keep themselves fit by running the inner rim of the great wheel of their living quarters. Once again blandness governs verbal discourse and shuts off the emotions, whether in conversations between Dave and Frank, a birthday greetings message from Earth to Frank, or in a news item about the voyage. Nonetheless, there is conflict latent here – and it centers on the use of the rational and conscious intellect and the extension of its powers through the on-board computer.

The HAL 9000 series computer (voiced by Douglas Rain) has a perfect operational record, a fact of which it is well aware, being apt to remind humans of its superiority whenever it can. Since it has an intelligence comparable to that of its human makers (but functions with greater speed and reliability) and is programmed to converse with people on equal terms, it is assumed for all intents and purposes to be conscious too. Of course what it actually has to a high degree is the capacity to undertake logical processing – a capacity which it demonstrates by trouncing Frank at chess. This very same skill appears to provide it with the framework for another game in which the stakes are altogether higher. We may deduce from what later happens that HAL, knowing its superior powers of reasoning, has worked out a totalizing logical argument. It calculates that anything less than a total belief in its accuracy on the part of the crew would mean that they were less than wholly in thrall to its authority. In that case they would be less than perfectly committed to the mission. The machine decides to test the men for their loyalty. It does so by fabricating a bulletin anticipating the supposed breakdown of a piece of communications equipment.

When the crew test it they can find no fault. Nor can the identical HAL 9000 at mission base. Mission control reports that they suspect HAL is in error in predicting the fault. Frank and Dave lock themselves into one of the Pods – the small space vehicles that *Discovery* carries. They cut audio communications with HAL and confer in secret. Reaching the obvious (but wrong) conclusion that HAL has malfunctioned, they agree that if further problems occur they will have no alternative but to switch off its functions of higher consciousness and transfer control of the mission to the machine at base.

Although HAL cannot overhear Dave and Frank, it can see them and knows how to lip read. The syllogism that it has worked out is brutal in its totalitarian simplicity. It has concluded that what it says must by definition always be correct, because it has powers of perfect logical reasoning. And this will remain the case even when, as in the present instance, it has itself falsified the data on which its first premise is based. HAL requires unquestioning faith from the human crew members. When it encounters anything less, it deals with that as if it were mutiny.

Is HAL a tool or a weapon? Perfected for its capacity as the former, it evolves into a weapon which turns its life-controlling powers against the crew of the *Discovery*. This occurs as a logical consequence of it applying to the maximum its most advanced function – ruthless logic. Earth's smartest tool turns on its makers and becomes a deadly weapon directed against them because its "mind" has no capability for any other mode of functioning. Though a machine, HAL becomes in dramatic terms an epic villain, no less single-minded and dangerous than Milton's Satan, its formidable strengths combined with great weaknesses. Appropriately enough HAL's demise will have some of the absurdity that surfaced in Satan's defeat.

The action moves fast after HAL has made its decision. When Frank goes outside the *Discovery* to replace the unit that has been tested, HAL sends his Pod after him to cut his oxygen line and hurl him into space. Dave boards his own Pod to recover the body, and while he is out of the ship, HAL kills the three hibernating crew members. Dave returns to the parent ship, but the computer refuses to open the bay doors and admit him. HAL tells Dave that it knows of the plan to disconnect it. It concludes: "This mission is too important for me to allow you to jeopardize it." Dave's response to the crisis facing him, since he cannot match HAL in logic, has to be arrived at through the application of his other, human, strengths. His emotions (fear for his own life, grief for his dead friend, cold rage against the computer) combine with knowledge, courage and determination and make him an opponent formidable in ways with which HAL cannot compete.

Having left his helmet behind in his rush to get to Frank, Dave has no safe means of regaining entry to the *Discovery*. He has no choice but to put his life at risk by blasting his way in through the emergency hatch. While doing so he must survive in an environment without air until he can manually close the hatch behind him. This is an option which HAL could not anticipate, because the practice of self-sacrifice runs counter to the priorities with which it has been programmed. Then, donning his helmet as precaution against the risk that HAL will try to starve him of oxygen, as it has done the sleeping crew men, Dave enters the computer room and disconnects its higher functions. As he does so HAL is reduced to idiocy, eventually singing a little ditty before its voice grinds towards silence. As its conscious functions die, a security lock fails and the mission-briefing tape plays. Only now does Dave discover his true goal.

## Act four

The fourth act, "Jupiter and Beyond the Infinite," opens as *Discovery* approaches Jupiter, where the black monolith now orbits. An ancient mystical symbol is evoked by a shot of Jupiter's meniscus encompassing the crescents of two of its smaller moons. Reminiscent of the impossible image of Earth's old Moon cradling the new Moon in its arms, Kubrick's picture includes an important variant in that the spaceship can also be seen against the dark sphere of the planet. Since in profile the shape of the *Discovery* plainly recalls a spermatozoon, the visual conjunction of male and female principles could hardly be more explicitly stated. What is more, to continue the theme of fertility, the Pod in which Dave now embarks from the parent ship for the last time also carries with it the metaphor of the delivery of seed. The imagery of fertility anticipates what is still to come.

As Dave approaches the monolith (now oriented in the horizontal plane relative to both him and the audience), the Pod moves into alignment with it, Jupiter and the Sun. Now the journey beyond the great outer planet to the infinite commences. The astronaut first witnesses streams of light, radiant, saturated in colour, hurling him through dimensions of time and space beyond the known – but not beyond the imaginable. The lights from the Pod's instruments reflect onto his face like warpaint. Every hero fights, and Dave's battle is to hold onto consciousness. Even when his face is splayed in a silent scream against the glass of his porthole, and through every extremity of peril, he watches. While supernovae explode, galaxies wheel and plasma streams from stars in pinpoint formation, his eyes remain alert. As the journey continues he observes, foretelling what is to come, the development of a star that contains the smudged outline of a fetal shape. And then, while his eye still blinks as he watches intently, the speed of travel seems to slow while he is hurled across weird solarized unlandscapes. The celebratory choral voices that have accompanied him give way to steely scratching and deep electrical clangor, and suddenly everything "naturalizes" again. Except that the natural is also totally strange.

Dave's Pod has "landed" in an approximate simulacrum of a Regency style hotel suite. The resemblance is approximate because, unlike most hotel suites, this is a chamber of light. Even the floor, which is white, radiates luminance. This materially impossible room is best understood as a metaphor, an expression adapted to the requirements of our times for what John Milton referred to three and a half centuries ago as the "doctrine of accommodation." By this he meant that numinous mysteries can only be expressed to humanity in a language that is comprehensible within the limitations of the human mind. In the final minutes of *2001*, image, music and sound replace speech, but the intention to express deep mysteries is comparable to Milton's endeavor – as the bewilderment of many commentators has made plain.

From this point time jumps forward in a succession of carefully marked elisions. Still in his Pod, Dave looks into the room and sees himself there, still in his space suit. But now he is a considerably older man of perhaps sixty years of age. This figure space-walks nervously into the bathroom, and looks at himself in the mirror, observing with the frank gaze that has characterized his whole solitary journey. Hearing a slight noise from the principal room, he looks round. The Pod has vanished, but a man about eighty years old is dining there. This too is Dave, and he too has heard a sound and checks the bathroom; but his younger self has disappeared. Resuming his meal, the old man knocks his wine glass onto the floor where it breaks. As he ponders this mishap he detects the faintest breathing and looks at the bed where, as an ancient man, he lies quietly waiting for the end of his life. In his final gesture, Dave slowly raises his arm and points at the black monolith, which has now reappeared at the foot of his bed. The viewpoint reverses, and we look back down at the bed from where the monolith stands. The venerable man has vanished into an effulgence of light in the womb of which coalesces the image of the fetal star child. We now track into and through the monolith and find ourselves once again among the planetary and stellar bodies where, to the triumphal heraldry of Richard Strauss's "Thus Spake Zarathustra," the Star-Child Dave hangs softly luminous in the firmament.

## The personal and the collective journey

By the end of *2001: A Space Odyssey*, an extended chain of symbols has been presented to the spectator. Their meaning bewilders every audience, but amplification and the active imagination help bring sense out of the puzzle. Our cue that it is appropriate to work in this fashion comes from the "room" itself, which exists like a metaphoric frame upon the action that occurs within it. In effect it puts quote marks on the sentence of time within which the existence of the hero Dave is framed, as also (because he too is de-realized) is the existence of the species. It lets us perceive that human life has two dimensions: the personal, represented by the aging and death of Dave; and the collective, indicated in the absence of distinctive marks of character and the celebration of the new birth – a moment of growth for the species.

Dave Bowman's journey through rainbow light can be compared with the revelations of the wonders of the numinous higher world that Jung found typical of visitations by UFOs. Where the descent of the UFO/god can be taken as a metaphor for an involuntary coming to consciousness, Dave's odyssey, which he carries out for all humanity, is a voyage of discovery – an exploration of the unknown which deliberately extends the realm of consciousness by penetrating the mysteries. Dave's final voyage is a hero's journey – but this time into an over-world rather than the underworld that so many heroes have to endure. But like his chthonic counterpart, he encounters terror and emerges in a remade form. The further it progresses, the more Dave's journey becomes a dynamic image of the self as evolving, progressing, recurring through the generations. It is that great journey, characteristic of the human experience, to the very edge of the known, looking into the unknown, which is here couched in terms exactly right for our age. The symbolism of flight has long associations (through birds and insects before ever humanity grew wings) with the entry into the realm of the spiritual. Here it is updated to encompass space flight.

If we have any doubt about this, the journey beyond Jupiter to the infinite is punctuated by extreme close-ups of Dave's eye blinking as it takes in the many wonders that the journey presents him with. As Hellen and Tucker (1987) remark in relation to this episode, the eye used for intelligent observation makes an obvious symbol for increasing consciousness. Dave's eye, which changes color every time he blinks, can be interpreted as symbolizing the essential observing self that, enhanced by his experiences, will endure after the death of his body. The same authors are, however, surely mistaken in implying that the eyes of HAL have a similar meaning to Dave's (1987: 38–9). On the contrary, HAL's eyes, which keep under surveillance every inch of the *Discovery*, seem to be anything but windows to the soul. We never see more than one at a time, so they bring to mind the Cyclopes of Homer's *Odyssey*, who, as Grimal reminds us, were a race of gigantic savage beings with one eye, tremendous strength and murderous disposition (1986: 113). Each of HAL's eyes is cold because despite the best attempts of voice programmers to simulate a personality it has none. The longer we know HAL, the more his red eye seems to signal danger – in contrast to the life-sustaining warmth associated with the astronauts' cockpits. Always alert, never blinking, each of his eyes is an instrument of espionage and control.

## Alchemical amplifications

The basis for Hellen and Tucker's generally helpful observations lies in a number of connections between *2001* and typical images in the writings of alchemists. In order to take the point, we need to clarify the significance of the work of these precursors of modern science for our present undertaking. Their goal was to accomplish a process of chemical transformation by refining common matter into gold. However, their complex experiments implicated more than physical matter alone and in this respect their objectives differed from today's scientists. In attempting to refine dross into gold, they did so in the confident belief that they were also trying to bring about a spiritual purification of themselves.

Jung spent years investigating the writings and emblematic imagery in the alchemists' publications. He observed the intensity of their labors which could last for years as they pursued investigative procedures that (as is obvious in the light of today's science) must have faced them with more reversals and blind alleys than successes. He deduced that the very difficulty of those procedures enhanced the force of the alchemists' projections and imaginings, so that the attempt to bring about chemical transformation became also a process of striving for individuation. In seeking appropriate images to act as vehicles for their thoughts and projections, they brought into play imagery from diverse sources, resuscitating among them certain figures familiar in the classical literature of ancient Greece and Rome. Under the pressure of the alchemists' less than fully conscious needs, these icons became imbued with a strongly archetypal cast, as Jung's immensely detailed account of their work repeatedly demonstrates. And this is the relevance that alchemy has for us.

Of the iconic figures reclaimed by the alchemists none was more prominent than that of Hermes (also known by his Roman name Mercury or Mercurius). There are strong resonances between the personal traits of Hermes/Mercurius and the figure of Dave. To take the most obvious starting point, there is a suggestive link with his surname "Bowman," since Hermes was the archer of the gods (Hellen and Tucker 1987: 37). He was the god of flight, and, according to some authorities, the messenger and servant of Jupiter. Universally known as the messenger of the gods at large, one of his tasks was to bear the souls of the dead to Hades (we can recall Dave's ceremonious releasing of Frank to the void). Because of this he was given the name Psychopompus, "accompanier of souls" (Grimal 1986: 198–9). In *2001*, however, there is one development of the classical mythology which has high significance: Dave is a messenger *to* the gods rather than from them. This too fits his connection to Mercurius, since the latter was the travellers' guide; and Dave, if our reading of him proves correct, will be the pathfinder for the rest of humanity.

Dave Bowman shares with his divine winged forefather not only the characteristics of the psychopomp but also those of the god of revelation. Like the latter, Bowman unites the opposites (see Jung [1953] 1968: para. 404). One instance of this occurs with the conjunction masculine/feminine which Jung had identified in early pictures of UFOs: it is clearly present in the film, as we have noted on a number of occasions. The conjunction in opposition of the sexes characterizes many images of the monotheistic, unified self, of which the syzygy is a case in point. In *2001* the fertile union of masculine and feminine principles is symbolic. It does not involve Dave and a woman but the conjunction of conscious with the unconscious. And it produces the new third thing, the Star-Child born mysteriously through Dave's death.

A further reinforcement of the same symbolic theme is found in the configuration of the monolith. Its rectilinear form stands in opposition to the spherical shape of the planets. In its own right, too, the monolith conveys the idea of opposition. We have seen it sometimes appear upright, sometimes horizontal, seeming to pull in the first instance toward deepening consciousness, in the second toward venturing into the unconscious. Mapping the two orientations onto each other produces the imaginary outline of a cross. And as we know from Christian use of that image, the cross readily signifies both the marriage of conscious and unconscious and the necessity of sacrificing the old life in order to be reborn into a new one. Both meanings fit with our reading of Dave's ultimate journey.

The final manifestation of the monolith at the deathbed is vertical. Dave had previously opened himself to the unconscious as directed by the stone's horizontal stationing in Jupiter's orbit. Now his successors (in story terms the new generations, but in terms of the address from the screen, ourselves) are offered the chance to recognize the need to deepen consciousness once again, in order to bring into the frame of human knowledge an understanding of what has been witnessed but only partially comprehended. So once again the conjunction of opposites in the collective conscious and unconscious is implicated in this symbol as in the other figures.

Yet another way of expressing the same conjunction was first spotted by Hellen and Tucker (1987) in that the monolith has the qualities of the *lapis philosophorum*. The *lapis* is the Philosophers' Stone familiar in the alchemists' treatises where it frequently has a central place in the process when used to symbolize both the beginning and the goal of the alchemical labor (Hellen and Tucker 1987: 33–6). The ancient physics, as Evola said, was also a transcendental psychology in which each physical perception had simultaneously a psychic component which animated it (cited in Jung [1953] 1968: para. 342n). Thus the alchemists often thought of their endeavors as falling into a pattern that conformed with the path followed by the mystic. That is, the pattern was a circular progress in which the end is contained in the beginning and the beginning in the end. Read in a manner which respects the alchemical process, the monolith takes on a double presence – firstly as the *prima materia*, the unrefined source material, and secondly as the philosophical gold (the *aurum philosophicum*) which is produced from it at the end of a long and arduous process of refinement.

The narrative structure of *2001* incorporates both a linear voyage of exploration and a circle. It is a circle in respect of the cycle of one man's life, both in his own being and for the countless generations which he represents. This paradox is hard to think of in terms of simply a human figure, but it is a familiar mental step in the case of the human who (like Christ) is also a god. So whilst we have been developing (and will continue with) the argument that *2001* conveys religious experience through imagery that reflects human knowledge and understanding in the later twentieth century, it is also important to recognize that it embodies oblique, intuitively grasped references to older types of reborn hero-gods. It is thoroughly grounded in the old mythological forms, notwithstanding it varies and develops them in a fascinating manner.

At an earlier point in the chapter, the idea was canvassed that the four sightings of the monolith might amount to the discovery of a signaling network planted in the solar system by a more advanced species. For this plot line to be fulfilled, Dave must by the end of his journey either have encountered the invisible species itself, or (more plausibly, since there is little sign of that having occurred) have come to the last symbol that it is within his power to comprehend. Either way, what he is shown in the Star-Child is simultaneously himself and the choiring generations that will follow him. So, if an advanced form of life has through its network of signals enticed humanity into the four-million-year journey, what it finally discloses is identical to what a Jungian reading of mythological and archetypal imagery reveals – namely, that the potential for the human race lies within the self, both individual and collective. This advanced life form may not yet even exist, but be coming into being as humanity itself.

All these indications that the final scenes of *2001* can legitimately be read as symbolizing an encounter with the self complement the second thrust of the narrative: the powerful linear movement outwards that the entire journey depicts. If we accept that at the height of his nobility Dave Bowman undergoes an apotheosis and then can be understood as a godlike figure, it will be productive to view him in the context of Jung's concept of the god within us.

## Encountering the self

Images of the self convey a numinous energy of overwhelming religious intensity, subsuming (but not obliterating) the individual's ego and consciousness to the totality. Jung identified the self with the image of the divine, but in a very specific sense as the god within us, a figure that is unlike the Christian deity in that it combines both good and evil:

> [The self] might equally well be called the "God within us." The beginnings of our whole psychic life seem to be inextricably rooted in this point, and all our highest and ultimate purposes seem to be striving towards it . . . When, therefore, we make use of the concept of a God we are simply formulating a definite psychological fact, namely the independence and sovereignty of certain psychic contents which express themselves by their power to thwart our will, to obsess our consciousness and to influence our moods and actions.
>
> (Jung [1938] 1966: paras. 399–400)

The key that I wish to use to aid comprehension of the theological dimension of the film's final act can be found in its representation of energy. God-men such as Christ and the Buddha (whether within us or outside us) have always been linked with light and energy, and even seen as sources of such power themselves – the halo ringing them being an obvious expression of it. But in *2001* there is a shift. The human image is by no means abandoned, but there is a strong visual and narrative suggestion that the god image is transmuting into energy. The balance of power personally commanded by the image of the god or goddess in his or her human form shifts away from the older model with which the Western world is thoroughly familiar through Christianity. Now impersonal power surrounds Dave. His final home, the site of his rebirth, hums with energy that radiates from its walls and floor, and is expressed by the abundant light in the apartment. (Perhaps the room itself suggests the form that our species, in struggling to shape that energy through culture, has given to life. The uneasy mock-Regency design nicely embodies that mix of the banal with the elegantly attained which Kubrick shows as typical of the works of humanity in its current stage of development.)

In the past the gods within (and outside) us have been figured as all-powerful, often as variants of the wise (or foolish) old man or woman. By contrast, Dave is an ordinary person. He possesses no extraordinary powers other than unflinching determination; he shows no sign of devotion to an organized faith. He enters the cycle of rebirth simply because he gives himself fully to what Kubrick and Clarke show to be the most profoundly religious of human impulses – the passion to know both the universe and the self more deeply. This is Dave's choice, both voluntary and moral. But having committed to that ultimate journey, he then has no further alternative but to submit to the overwhelming power which molds his fate. This force does not dress itself in quasi-human form, but is the raw energy that forms the stars.

Energy can express itself both through physical matter and through psyche. As Jung put it, "There are indications that psychic processes stand in some sort of energy relation to the physiological substrate . . . In spite of the nonmeasurability of psychic processes, the perceptible changes effected by the psyche cannot possibly be understood except as a phenomenon of energy" ([1954] 1969: para. 441). He went on to speculate that there might be not only a connection between the psyche and physiological and biological phenomena but some form of continuum linking psyche with physical events (ibid.: para. 442). Such interconnection is a distinctive characteristic of the universe represented in *2001*, and when Dave enters outer space on his final journey, his experience bears out these speculations. Hard-edged divisions familiar to us from our usual habits of classification dissolve. Matter and mind appear no longer to occupy wholly separate categories, and Kubrick makes the self a fluidly integrated part of the vast scene where the boundaries between physis and psyche bend and dissolve. A star forms and takes the shape of a fetus; the Regency room is alive with sound; and, conversely, space in its entirety is lodged within the head of the pioneering visitor. Apotheosis, the elevation of a mortal to the rank of a god, is not a new phenomenon either in religion or mythology. But the normal pattern with such a mythologem is that the hero is lifted away from the world, leaving humanity behind. Another factor that makes Dave Bowman's journey different is that the audience witness his story unfolding.

The nature of Kubrick's universe actually inflects the archetypal image of the self. This odyssey differs from Homer's in that this Ulysses does not return home. On the contrary, the god within us is travelling out, and in imaginary form entering the wider universe in order to take up a new position in the fluid pantheon of energy. Dave Bowman, like both Ulysses and Mercurius in their times, guides us on a new journey, heralding new adventures of the psyche.

## Jung's "Answer to Job" and the numinous as vital energy

In his late years, Jung wrote a speculative treatise, his "Answer to Job," addressing a topic which had gripped his attention since boyhood. The question was how a good god can visit appalling evil on the world he himself created. A mark of its importance to Jung is that in this thesis he did something unique in the canon of his writings, discussing God as an *actuality*, a universal entity, rather than exclusively as the "god within us" that we have been dealing with hitherto. In this important respect I want to part company from him since I do not believe that the notion of a "god out there" is essential to recognizing energy as the source of both universal and human life. On the other hand, I do want to make use of Jung's treatise as a means of describing what seem to me to be changes with immense potential for the future found in the image of the "god within us" that are projected through *2001: A Space Odyssey*.

On Jung's reading, the Book of Job focuses sharply the abundant evidence revealing the God of the Hebrew Bible, Yahweh, as not only a loving god but also a tyrant capable of acts of great harm. His deliberate persecution of Job is the result of a wager with Satan to test whether the devotion of the most loyal of Yahweh's servants can be corrupted by tormenting him beyond measure. In Jung's opinion, the endless punishments visited on Job have no purpose other than for Yahweh to prove his own power to himself. God appears to have been bamboozled by Satan into forgetting his omniscience and proving his might at the expense of love for his creature ([1952] 1958: paras. 587–8). But in doing so he reveals his dual nature to Job, and the latter perceives the unconscious split in his God's nature. The very fact that Job can see this is immensely significant, because it entails that Yahweh has also to learn to know himself. It is inconceivable that one of his creatures could have knowledge of Yahweh that the latter does not have of himself. "Whoever knows God has an effect on him. The failure of the attempt to corrupt Job has changed Yahweh's nature" (ibid.: para. 617). Thus began the long process that was to culminate in God becoming man with the advent of Christ. These events brought about, Jung argues, nothing less than a world-shaking transformation of the divinity: "The encounter with the creature changes the creator" (ibid.: para. 686).

In this, Jung advanced a radical thesis about the interdependence of god and man, arguing that this interdependence was vital to both parties, not just to poor weak humankind. The utterly new element was the hypothesis that the godhead needed to become human in order to activate his omniscience, for although Yahweh had possessed this power, he did not seem to use it. His consciousness seems not to have been more than a primitive awareness, his actions and perceptions paralleling the blindness of one who acts from the instinctive unconscious (ibid.: paras. 638–40). But the entry into the Christian era was designed to express changes in the old regime:

> The father wants to become the son, God wants to become man, the amoral wants to become exclusively good, the unconscious wants to become consciously responsible.
>
> (Jung [1952] 1958: para. 675)

Considering this thought strictly in the context of the god within us, Yahweh's urgent need to become human corresponds to the need of the archetypal image of the self to bring itself ever more fully into consciousness in order the more fully to know itself.

However, this was by no means the end of the story. Jung had no difficulty in showing that, although the Christian God became more loving than Yahweh in letting himself become man, he did not lose the capacity for harm. The signs are numerous. For example, to pick first on a minor tribulation, there is the disquieting hint in the Lord's Prayer in Christ's petition to his father, "Lead us not into temptation," which leaves open the possibility that God might be a devilish tempter (ibid.: para. 651). This is to say nothing of the altogether more savage fact that the Christian God of love and goodness is so unforgiving of his own creatures that he can only be appeased by a human sacrifice – and the killing of his own son at that (ibid.: para. 689). All in all, Jung concludes:

> God is not only to be loved, but also to be feared. He fills us with evil as well as with good, otherwise he would not need to be feared; and because he wants to become man, the uniting of his antinomy must take place in man. This involves man in a new responsibility. He can no longer wriggle out of it on the plea of his littleness and nothingness, for the dark God has slipped the atom bomb and chemical weapons into his hands and given him the power to empty out the apocalyptic vials of wrath on his fellow creatures. Since he has been granted an almost godlike power, he can no longer remain blind and unconscious.
>
> (Jung 1952 [1958]: para. 747)

The fundamental problem encountered in attempting to discuss the godhead is, as Jung recognizes, that whenever we speak of religious matters we are operating in a world of images which point to something ineffable. It is particularly interesting from our point of view to note his concession that, "we can imagine God as an eternally flowing current of vital energy that endlessly changes shape just as easily as we can imagine him as an eternally unmoved, unchangeable essence" (ibid.: para. 555). However, despite this recognition, Jung does not test the merits of conceiving the godhead as a current of energy, but – understandably, given both his Christian background and the nature of his argument as to the burden on humanity – he preserves the image of God in the image of a powerful father figure, as we have seen. Nonetheless, there are distinct benefits to be gained from reducing the personal component of the imagery that touches on the numinous.

## *2001* depersonifies the numinous

Depersonalizing the numinous in the way that *2001* does shows humanity as the servant of overmastering energy. That energy is perceived as rushing through both physical matter and the psyche, and as bringing life to both the conscious and unconscious mind. We have already said that revising the image of deity does what all religions have striven to achieve in the time of their greatest conviction. It both revitalizes the image and brings it as close as possible to the knowledge and experience people have of the world – both physical and cultural – that they inhabit. But locating the source of the numinous in energy does more than that. It allows a rapprochement of religious experience with the forms of knowledge uncovered by the natural sciences. Also, it makes it easier, since energy is wholly amoral, to understand how we are profoundly capable of acts of both the finest good and the greatest evil.

A film with the impact that *2001* had can bring to consciousness, and then leave latent in the cultural unconscious for years afterwards, a trace which modifies the culture by seeding a new image of great potential. In *2001* it is not just what *arises from* the unconscious that is so exciting, but also what consciousness *gives back to* and animates in the unconscious. What is at stake, in the stage of development to which Clarke and Kubrick show humanity to have arrived, is nothing less than enhancing knowledge and consciousness of the unconscious and the unknown, both personal and universal. Theirs is a revised version, updated for the late twentieth century, of the religious responsibility with which Jung believes humanity is charged.

It would be false to claim that the image of the numinous recognized in the western world has changed radically in the thirty-three years since 1968. But change in the collective unconscious can be a slow process that may be measured in hundreds rather than tens of years as the psyche reaches out and finds symbols that better express its needs. We began by speaking of the phenomenon that dreams and visions of extraordinary power sometimes predict future constellations of meaningful symbols. The imagery of inner and outer space that Kubrick, Clarke and (after them) many other artists have offered the twentieth century is emotive and powerful, and could yet become a popular and enduring symbolic cluster to convey our sense of what is magical about human experience of the universe and the self.

## Bibliography

Clarke, A.C. ([1968] 1970) *The Promise of Space*, Harmondsworth: Penguin.

Grimal, P. (1986) *Dictionary of Classical Mythology*, London: Penguin.

Hellen, A.J. and P.M. Tucker (1987) "The Alchemical Art of Arthur C. Clarke," *Foundation: the Review of Science Fiction* 41, 30–41.

Jung, C.G. ([1952] 1958) "Answer to Job," *Psychology and Religion: West and East, CW* 11, London: Routledge & Kegan Paul.

—— ([1959] 1964) "Flying Saucers: A Modern Myth of Things Seen in the Skies," *Civilization in Transition, CW* 11, London: Routledge & Kegan Paul.

—— ([1938] 1966) "The Relations between the Ego and the Unconscious," *Two Essays on Analytical Psychology, CW* 7, London: Routledge & Kegan Paul.

—— ([1953] 1968) *Psychology and Alchemy, CW* 12, London: Routledge & Kegan Paul.

—— ([1954] 1969) "On the Nature of the Psyche," *The Structure and Dynamics of the Psyche, CW* 8, London: Routledge & Kegan Paul.

# Chapter 8

# "Let's go back to finding out who we are"

## Men, *Unheimlich* and returning home in the films of Steven Spielberg

*Christopher Hauke*

### Seriously popular movies?

> Popular movies are cultural standard-bearers; they carry with them the values, beliefs, dreams, desires, longings, and needs of a society and, thus, can function mythologically.
>
> (Martin and Ostwalt, 1995: 66)

While Adorno and Horkheimer ([1944] 1973) were fretting about how popular cinema films – usually meaning Hollywood – simulated reality so well that the viewing subject was robbed of all sovereignty and manipulated in thought and emotion by the skill of the movie-makers, Jung was taking a rather different point of view:

> The cinema, like the detective story, enables us to experience without danger to ourselves all the excitements, passions, and fantasies which have to be repressed in a humanistic age.
>
> (Jung, 1931, *CW* 10: para. 195)

So-called "escapist" movies do just that. They help us escape – but not simply escape from "reality" (whatever that is), but also escape *to* a different reality, one that tends to be ignored or devalued in our day-to-day lives. They offer us an experience that is non-ordinary, one that is uncommon in daily life; uncommon by virtue of the passions involved, the events witnessed, and, importantly, uncommon because of the individuality of the characters and the story. And yet, despite all this unusualness, the novelty of scenes, narrative and imagery that grips our attention, we still recognise enough to, unbelievably, *identify* with the characters and the story of the film. For all its escapist *difference*, the best of these movies also convey a familiar human quality that compels our interest right through to the credits. As Phillip Taylor notes, "When our emotions can be so readily manipulated, cinema can tell us something about ourselves" (Taylor, 1999: 33).

Adorno and Horkheimer feared that,

> The more intensely and flawlessly [the film-maker's] techniques duplicate empirical objects, the easier it is today for the illusion to prevail that the outside world is a straightforward continuation of that presented on the screen . . . Real life is becoming indistinguishable from the movies. The . . . film . . . leaves no room for imagination or reflection on the part of the audience.
>
> (Adorno and Horkheimer, [1944] 1973: 126–127)

Without any such qualms, Spielberg has said of his movies how he wants to "take that technique and hide it so well that never once are you taken out of your chair and reminded of where you are" (Kroll, 1977: 98). There is a sense here that makes the aim of movie-making analogous to the function of dreams under Freud's original rationale where dreaming had the biological function of keeping sleep undisturbed. Escapist movies keep our fantasy undisturbed by "outer reality" so that finishing watching a movie is a bit like waking up from a dream. This should not surprise us for, after all, where else do we find ourselves experiencing the "excitements, passions, and fantasies" – and the extraordinary and the dangerous – we guard or repress from our ordinary conscious lives other than in dreams?

In other words, the fact that popular films are commercial commodities – at one level, just more product from the industrialised, capitalist world – should not distract us from their significance. On the contrary, I argue that their very popularity – that is, their success as a desirable object/experience – says an awful lot about what people want and need in their lives that movies, amongst other fantasies, are used to provide. Just because the vehicle that delivers this need also makes big money for studios, actors, directors and investors, this is no reason to ignore what the popular "escapist" movie is supplying for the culture as a whole.

Perhaps this has become true more recently in what we now refer to as a postmodern era; up until the late 1950s we *were* supplied with cultural fodder that pre-empted our discrimination, as Adorno and Horkheimer warned, but the arrival of the postmodern consumer on the wave of a contradictory capitalism where competition between the producers and an emphasis on the consumers' power – and "right" – to choose, has led to a self-reflective perspective on the commodities we have been "told" we want. There can be few adult consumers in 2001 who remain unaware of the role of hype in their lives. And it is at the movies, above all, that *we* make the difference between a successful film and a turkey – despite the millions the studios may pour into a product and its promotion. As the film scholar Stuart Kaminsky so moderately puts it,

> the more popular a film (the more people who see it), the more attention it deserves as a genre manifestation. If a film is popular, it is a result of the fact that the film, or series of films corresponds to an interest – perhaps even a need – of the viewing public.
>
> (Kaminsky, 1985: 3)

In addition to this, when it comes to Spielberg's films, the audience – the paying consumer – is particularly respected. Although his dramatic skills excel in their ability to grip our emotions, Spielberg is never tempted to over-explain a character or plot. He assumes he is speaking to an audience as visually and aurally literate as him through the films and media we have all grown up with, so "he never 'talks down' to his audience with tedious explanations but merely 'knows' what they know" (Mott and Saunders, 1986: 40).

Steven Spielberg is, perhaps, *the* most successful and prolific director/ producer/writer of popular films ever.[1] While his long-standing colleague George Lucas's *Star Wars* films have attracted Jungian film criticism,[2] Spielberg's work has not received the same attention. Perhaps this is because his themes seem better dealt with through other forms of film analysis and appreciation – the postmodern, self-referring, nostalgic angle that von Gunden (1991) takes, or Taylor's (1999) and Mott and Saunders' (1986) reductionist references to his childhood, or Kolker's (1988) Marxist–Freudian–Lacanian approach, for example. Other texts, such as *Projecting the Shadow* (Hocker Rushing and Frentz, 1995), clearly indicate a Jungian influence mixed with feminist and other social-cultural critique. In this book, the authors discuss *Jaws* and other movies within a Jungian myth-making paradigm – especially as it relates to other American myths, the frontier, the cyborg and the hero – but they remain cautious in admitting Jungian thought to be the powerful influence their text otherwise shows. My own post-Jungian approach in this present chapter seeks to show how certain themes in Spielberg's work which are often mentioned by other critics – men, the community, authority, "home" and the Other – may be tracked for their changing significance and development through a selection of films from *Duel* to *Saving Private Ryan*. I intend to show how certain Spielberg films are not only tracking the maturing imagination of an individual film-maker, but how changing approaches to reoccurring themes echo changes in the collective culture – thus making these movies compelling viewing for that culture. This resonance between Spielberg and his audience not only helps us understand how he can wrench our emotions with films as vastly different as *E.T.* and *Schindler's List*, but how, in following his own individual intuition and artistic decisions, he is also expressing a collective trajectory.

I have commented at length in the book *Jung and the Postmodern: The Interpretation of Realities* (Hauke, 2000) on how much of Jungian and post-Jungian psychology is in line with postmodern critique. Unlike Freud, Jung regarded the unconscious as far less the repository of repressed infantile and sexual material, and far more as a creative source of our collective human potential which has gradually been marginalised in modern times (especially since the Enlightenment). The emphasis on a mechanistic, scientific rationality, logocentrism, and a reliance on hierarchical thinking has delivered a great deal in terms of technological progress and the domination of Nature. However, the resulting dominant consciousness excludes and devalues much: the spirit, the feminine, emotional knowledge, intuition, the non-material and the religious. The last thirty years have witnessed a growing hunger for that which seems absent from Western culture at large and excluded from the dominant consciousness in particular. Jungian psychology serves as a response to modernity in the way that consciousness is regarded as seeking compensation for that which is left out and which remains unconscious. On both the individual and the collective level, the unconscious seeks to make itself known so that these contents may be once more integrated in our psyches and our lives. This chapter suggests that this process may be detected in the directorial work of Steven Spielberg which I describe. To a certain extent, aspects of this might be found in all of his films, but, for now, I have selected six movies: *Duel, Jaws, Close Encounters of the Third Kind E.T. – The Extra Terrestrial, Schindler's List* and *Saving Private Ryan*. By tightening my focus I wish to initiate a new perspective and revaluation of the popular "escapist" cinema of Steven Spielberg through a post-Jungian, and, indeed, postmodern, lens.

### *Duel:* "We are back in the jungle"

There are two main characters in Spielberg's first major directorial success *Duel* (1971): a suburban businessman, David Mann (Denis Weaver) and a filthy black, eighteen-wheel truck whose driver is never identified. David

Mann's name emphasises not only his "everyman" nature but also his struggle against the Goliath-scale foe who pursues him on the highway in a paranoic cat-and-mouse chase. In this early film, the role of women and the family is left very much in the background. Although we begin by witnessing Mann's car pull out of a nondescript suburban drive-way we see little of his background from then on. There is an important exception to this when Mann phones his wife back home – a scene shot "through a dryer glass window darkly" (Mott and Saunders, 1986: 20) in a launderette where he has stopped. This is cut with domestic scenes of his wife receiving the call, with children at her feet and looking every inch the pastiche of the suburban wife of 1950s ads and sitcoms. She accuses David of not sticking up for her "like a man" on a recent social occasion and we begin to see how his potency has come into question, just as later when he repeatedly fails to avoid the truck getting the better of him in scenes which escalate rapidly and dangerously. Parallel to the theme of lost, but finally refound, potency is the way that Mann loses faith in "civilised" behaviour he had previously assumed without question. The aggressive behaviour of the truck (which initially means its driver but later we are not so sure) and the lack of sympathy Mann receives when he discusses his plight with others on his journey, signals the collapse of social roles – "we are back in the jungle", he says to himself.

The turning point comes when Mann stops to phone the police at a garage that also has a collection of live snakes to attract customers. The truck turns back and roars around and around the garage, ripping up the phone box, smashing the aquaria and releasing the reptiles. We are alerted to the release of primitivity in the duel on the road for which the only solution has to be Mann's abandoning of his suburban values to discover his own primitive aggression which he is going to need in his bid to overcome and outwit his diesel-powered foe.

Mann is unarmed, struggling to keep ahead in a modest car that is badly overheating. What resources does he have to finally overcome the truck? In the Old Testament, David looked seriously out-gunned with his pathetic sling and stones, not so much a weapon as the common tool of his shepherd-boy livelihood; in *Duel*, Spielberg comes up with David Mann's only resource. This is the suburban businessman's companion and sign: the briefcase.[3] Mann lures the truck to a blind bend which hides a steep drop off the edge of the road, he jams his briefcase against the throttle pedal, leaps clear of the vehicle and watches as his car plunges down, followed by the truck which smashes on the rocks below.

The story of David Mann and his duel with the truck is no hero myth;

*Figure 8.1   Duel.* David Mann (Dennis Weaver).
(Universal Company, Courtesy Kobal)

there is no quest at the outset, no problem to solve or helpful folk along the way like in other myths, folk tales or *Star Wars*. This is a narrative of individuation, where accidental events throw predictability and assumptions about what the bourgeois, suburban life is meant to be completely to the wind, leaving the "ordinary man" to find a way to survive or perish in the attempt. In several films of this type, the central character becomes marginalised as "mad" as if this is the sole path to the discovery of non-ordinary qualities which the extraordinary circumstances require of him. Mann behaves irrationally and eccentrically in the café roadhouse where he thinks the truck driver is lurking; as his assumptions around civilised life are dismantled, he becomes "dismantled" into madness in the eyes of the other customers who, in a manner of speaking, do not have nearly so much on their plate. In just the same way, Roy Neary (Richard Dreyfuss) in *Close Encounters*, obsessed with the image of the UFO landing site, is compelled to carve the shape of Devil's Tower in his plate of mashed potato and in his mound of shaving cream to the frightened incomprehension of his wife and children. Both cases emphasise the loneliness of those who find themselves in unique, individual circumstances which are both unexpected and outside personal control. These conditions then compel them and inspire them to act outside conscious, conventional, "civilised" standards – not out of "choice" (the suburban consumer's "right") but out of primal *necessity*.

This is a major psychological theme in these Spielberg films and one which serves to grip the modern audience in an unconscious fashion that goes deeper than the surface narrative. The association of individual development with the necessity to temporarily abandon conventional, "sane", rational consciousness and to encounter the unconscious is a powerful Jungian theme. Jung himself claims he discovered much of what he knows of the unconscious through letting himself "drop", as he puts it, into the underworld where he encountered personifications of the collective unconscious (Jung, 1963: 203). Since the 1960s, postmodern culture – led by writers like R.D. Laing (1959, 1967), Deleuze and Guattari (1972), and Foucault (1967) – has found value in "insanity", not only as a critique of an over-rational consciousness and society, but also as a positive form of regression which can eventually lead to the rebirth of a healthier consciousness. This attitude to "insanity" is very much in line with Jung's recommendation that individual psychic development cannot proceed without an often painful encounter with the unconscious which may, at times, overwhelm the ego, and will certainly place the individual outside conventional society when the conditions of development become extreme. While Jung couched this path in terms of Greek mythological narratives and the esotericism of the alchemical path, contemporary film narratives achieve their powerful effect by displaying the character affected against a backdrop of familiar, suburban, hyper-ordinariness. The threatening mystery of the unconscious is a hair's breadth away from our comfortable, safe, ordinary lives.

## *Jaws*: fingernails on the blackboard

Ordinary life comes in the form of a sunny seaside resort town (with the friendly name of Amity) getting ready for the summer tourist season in Spielberg's first huge success *Jaws* (1975). Indeed, by using "a bevy of reflectors, augmented by three brute arc lights . . . set up to fill in the intensely strong sunlight" (Cribben, 1975: 276), film technique and art direction is used to enhance reality to the level of pastiche or a simulacrum (Baudrillard, 1994) – a postmodern hyper-reality which contrasts with the darkness to come. In a sense, it is the very brightness of suburban reality – as if there are no shadows – that produces the huge shadow of the shark that looms over Amity as the film progresses.

This time the story involves the paths of three male characters, and, while women and children are featured a little more, they remain a two-dimensional part of the ordinariness against which the men's extraordinary adventure unfolds. Spielberg cut the sub-plot which featured in Peter Benchley's original novel where Brody's (Roy Scheider) wife, Ellen (Lorraine Gary), has an affair with the marine scientist Hooper (Richard Dreyfuss). The wife is very much "left behind", just as Captain Ahab leaves his young wife at home in the comparable story of *Moby-Dick* by Herman Melville. The sea – and the task of individuation that is the hunt for the monster – is very much "man's work".

This brings in a need for us to analyse the splitting off of the feminine begun in *Duel* that comes into these narratives. What has this to do with what we have already said about the path of individuation and the ordinary versus extraordinary and marginalised status of the adventure? In *Jaws* there is a sense in which the shark itself, just as the whale in *Moby-Dick*, acts as the Other to the men's heroism – and split-off masculinity – by incorporating elements of the feminine in a negative form. It could be said that at this stage in Spielberg's narratives the feminine is still darkly unconscious, still the rejected shadow of the masculine, set in the dark and the deep and feared for its awesome power. The *vagina dentata* of the shark's jaws and the way that Quint (Robert Shaw) – the least "feminised" male on board – gets swallowed up seems to be a blatant sign of this; but – noting Fredericksen's chapter in this volume – the shark as *symbol* rather than mere *sign* points to more mysterious elements that find connection with the "feminine". While Hooper is the intellectual, and rich, scientist, Brody (Roy Scheider) is the "social" (and "soft") man who wants to act for the community and keep the beaches safe for all – especially the women and children. In doing so he is involved in a struggle with a narrower masculine character, the Mayor (Murray Hamilton), who, driven more by politics and economics, wishes to deny the danger of the shark to keep the beaches open, the cash flowing in and his political popularity untarnished. These three men, the ones not to die in the struggle, may be viewed as cultural males each struggling with the feminine – neglected and relegated to the unconscious and culturally projected in its negative form as the shark. In "*Jaws*: Faces of the Shadow", Hocker Rushing and Frentz (1995) use Jane Caputi's (1978) analysis of the shark as "an archetypal symbol of the fearsome feminine" and note how each of the three main male characters in *Jaws*, "the savage, the technological and the soft man . . . relate[s] differently to his community and to the prey" (Hocker Rushing and Frentz 1995: 89).

Quint (the "savage" man) is the most "traditional", unreconstructed male of the lot whom the feminist movement seems to have passed by. While it is he who mentions women and the feminised other frequently, he does so in the context of lewd and salty-dog imagery. As Hocker Rushing and Frentz point out, Quint's masculinity also "seems to derive from his rejection of the system and of its technological 'progress'" (ibid.). We see him gaining attention in an anti-social fashion by scraping his fingernails across a chalkboard; he smashes the radio when Brody wishes to call for help from "other men". But his extreme form of masculinity features particularly in his relation to woman and the feminine. He tells how he got one scar when he was "celebrating the 'demeese of my third wife'" (ibid.: 90). His toast to Brody and Hooper when they team up to hunt the shark is: "Here's to swimmin' with bow-legged women", and twice he limericks us – once to Ellen Brody with:

> Here lies the body of Mary Lee,
> Died at the age of one hundred and three.
> For fifteen years she kept her virginity,
> Not a bad record for this vicinity.

and later, near his end, he sings:

> Farewell an' adieu t'ye fair Spanish ladies,
> Farewell an' adieu you ladies of Spain . . .

The effect of having the three males in this film is to deliver a narrative where males combine qualities – Brody the soft man has to "introject" the technology of Hooper plus the savagery of Quint – to overcome the threat of the shadow feminine that lurks offshore. Hocker Rushing and Frentz see this as a new take on both the cinematic and American myth of the frontiersman, and the parallel struggle with "nature", while Jane Caputi (1978) emphasises the patriarchal conquest angle.

Jung's term for the archetypal feminine in men was the *anima*[4] which he theorised as a vital link through which the consciousness of males accesses the unconscious and the resources of the Self. Jung noted that Western culture and consciousness in general was typically masculinist and governed by hierarchical, linear, goal-oriented thinking. This is the psychological expression of patriarchy, and post-Jungians such as Loren Pederson (1991) note how the *anima* is aligned with the *shadow* in the psyche of contemporary males, and this then becomes projected onto women themselves. Women are made negative through men's projection of that which they are unable to tolerate in themselves – not so much individually but due largely to the limits of what our present culture and the dominant consciousness will support or allow. As we shall see shortly, this splitting off of aspects of the psyche also has implications for the denial of other aspects of our nature (as men *and* women), which includes the spiritual and religious. In this way, *Jaws* is a drama of masculinity against "Nature" but one in which the "natural" – the shark – receives the shadow projections of the Other, which includes the feminine, Nature, and the Spirit.

## Close Encounters of the Third Kind

### "They're here . . . "

In any psychological analysis of film it is all too tempting to become reductive and to look for the "meaning" of movies and their narratives in a psycho-biography of the directors and writers concerned. Too many film critics follow this type of analysis when a psychological perspective is not otherwise to the fore (see Mott and Saunders, 1986; Taylor, 1999; and von Gunden (1991) especially). I think this only goes to demonstrate how the culture of psychoanalysis and the cultural fantasy of the aetiology of childhood have taken such a grip throughout the twentieth century – one which shows no sign of abating. So it is with a degree of irony that I am going to mention, in the context of our discussion of male roles in Spielberg's films, how he was the eldest of a suburban, middle-class family with three younger sisters whose father left the family when he was 15, with the young Steven as its nominal (male) head.[5] Despite my resistance to such reductionism, as far as the developing imagery of men, women, children and suburbia appears in Spielberg's early films, certain biographical connections appear relevant. Spielberg has admitted how, "In many of my films I find I have created the family warmth which I wish I had experienced" (Taylor, 1999: 54) – note the use of "I find . . . " which suggests a non-conscious influence. And Spielberg's mother has said that when the single-parent family sit down for pizzas in *E.T.*, "'You are viewing our family at the dinner table'" (Hartman, 1983), suggesting the source of Spielberg's, "almost archeological, attention to suburban detail" (Pye and Myles, 1979: 24).

But whether this background *predicts* the role of the male in Spielberg's films in a causal fashion – and, more importantly, how this theme changes as Spielberg gets older – it is not possible to judge. Ironically, what *is* at stake is not the determining power of his childhood environment but the

way in which the creative expression of this in his art has led Spielberg
on to projects that deal with his themes in an increasingly differentiated
way. I discuss this when we come to his "mature" films – as they have
been dubbed – *Schindler's List* and *Saving Private Ryan*.[6] It might be said
that what we are witnessing is the individuation of a particularly creative
individual – but through the same period (1972 to 1999, the last quarter
of our twentieth century, the postmodern – and post-feminist – period)
this conveys the individuation of a generation of creative males as
their masculine perspective differentiates to include more than ever
before, much as patriarchal society as a whole seems to have developed.
What this involves is not only the integration of the unconscious feminine, but how the masuline has been joined and changed by a range of
Others previously excluded by Western culture. That is, much that
was abandoned to the unconscious and in need of reintegration, as Jung
frequently noted – not only the "feminine" but the instinctual, the chaotic,
the childish, the spirit and, above all, a sense of wonder: the difference
between looking down from the heights in smug confidence and looking
up in amazement and awe.

In virtually no other movie has the scale of wonderment and awe been
better portrayed than the experience Spielberg grants us of the gigantic
Mothership (*sic*) as it slowly fills the top of the cinema screen in *Close
Encounters of the Third Kind* (1977). Furthermore, if the Other of the
previous two films was agressive and predatory, *Close Encounters*
involves a complete contrast. In a reversal of so many cinema narratives
of encounters with aliens, the Others here turn out to be benign and
beneficent – although we have to travel a long way with the hero Roy
Neary (Richard Dreyfuss), in his struggle with the mainstream paranoic
assumptions of the political, scientific and military state, before we are
assured of this twist. This is no Terrible Mother pole of the archetype
at our core, but her opposite aspect offering an unspecified addition to
human life on the planet. At the end of the film, all that was lost is returned
– the missing airmen, the little boy Barry (Cary Guffey) and Neary's
sanity when his, and, importantly, his female co-adventurer Jillian
Guiler's (Melinda Dillon) harrowing experiences all make "sense" at last.
And it is not the "sense" of the suburbia from where they began – or the
way in which, earlier in the film, mysterious "UFO" lights "make sense"
by turning out to be police helicopters after all – it is the (non-)sense of
the Other at its non-terrestrial extreme.

Spielberg said of *Jaws* that, "the film illustrates that Common Man
can become a hero by dealing with . . . what has to be dealt with" (Taylor,
1999: 88). What Neary has to deal with in *Close Encounters* is more

*Figure 8.2  Close Encounters of the Third Kind.* Roy Neary (Richard Dreyfuss).
(Columbia, Courtesy Kobal)

terrifyingly Other than Nature, the shark, or even a wild lorry. For this
adventure, Common Man needs to be joined by Common Woman, an
extension of the humanity they jointly express and jointly restore, just as
Guiler's lost child is returned from the (Great) Mothership. Both Neary
and Guiler suffer stigmata from their encounters with UFOs – red, burnt
skin on the face – a phenomenon Jung comments upon when he finds it
in a patient's dream. Jung notes how the UFO seeks his dreamer out and
irradiates her with magical heat, "a synonym for her own inner affectivity
. . . a projection of her unrealized emotion . . . it points to an 'indelible'
experience whose traces remain visible to others" (Jung, 1958, *CW* 10:
para. 643). Jung also points out a religious significance when he says,
"One immediately thinks of the intolerable radiance that shone from the
face of Moses after he had seen God, of 'Who among us shall dwell with
everlasting burnings?' (Isaiah 33:14) and of the saying of Jesus: 'He who
is near unto me is near unto the fire'" (ibid.: para. 641).

Note that it is not Neary's own wife and children who get involved
in the quest; on the contrary they are abandoned – or, rather, they reject
him in fright – as he makes his descent into the unknown by way of his
obsessive, non-rational, mashed-potato carving, earth-and-bushes assem-
bling play. Neary has an inner vision of something beyond the daylight

of consciousness as compulsive as are all encounters with the unconscious. The image of the Devil's Tower has a numinosity Neary and Jillian cannot resist, and, like the image of the Grail, they have to follow where it leads them even if it means losing everything along the way.[7] This is why I disagree with Kolker when he asserts that: "All of Spielberg's films operate to prove the validity of, and to recuperate any possible losses to, the domestic space" (Kolker, 1988: 286). Although this may be a valid reading of Brody and Mann in their triumphs and return to normality, Neary's departure from the planet at the end of *Close Encounters* and Captain Miller's (Tom Hanks) death in *Private Ryan* offer no such recuperation or validation. In many instances, the suburban domestic space is precisely that which must be let go of for the sake of a spiritual triumph.

Not only does the (non-wife, non-domestic) woman join the man in *Close Encounters* but here we also see the start of Spielberg's involvement with the Child and the Child's Things in the course of the narrative. The child Barry's enchantment at the alien animation of his toys – and his beatific smile at the aliens when we in the audience do not even know what they look like – contributes to the Otherness of what everyone is experiencing. But while the majority of adults (Neary's wife, the military, the police) act out of fear and suspicion, the purity of wonder is placed not only with the child (and the old couple on the hill, similarly marginalised through their "seniority") – it also lies with the wonder of the scientists, especially Lacombe (Francois Truffaut). Sometimes the scientists act with a child's playfulness, such as when they discover the location of the landing site by grabbing the globe from their superior's office and rolling it down the hall like a beach ball.

This theme of *retaining* the Child's view – as opposed to the Christianised relinquishing of St Paul's, "When I was a child . . . I reasoned like a child. When I became a man, I put childish ways behind me" (1 Corinthians 13: 11) – and an ambivalence towards science, scientists and technology, become major leitmotifs in the next discussion around *E.T. – The Extra-Terrestrial* (1982).

## *E.T. – The Extra-Terrestrial*: "Home"

Spielberg made two other "boys'" films between *Close Encounters of the Third Kind* and *E.T.* (1982) – *1941* (1979) and *Raiders of the Lost Ark* (1981), both, in different ways, recalling the movies and TV series he and George Lucas had enjoyed as boys in the 1950s.[8] But in 1980, with *E.T.* in the planning stage, Spielberg went back to *Close Encounters of the Third Kind* and re-edited new versions for cinema release and a slightly longer version for the first TV showing. On a security-tight, closed set he continued filming *E.T.* under the revealing working title of *A Boy's Life*. If the other two were the boys' films he had always wanted to make (and wanted so much he made two more Indiana Jones sagas), *E.T.* was the film *of* the boy's life which Spielberg *had* to make.[9] Spielberg claims the idea for *E.T.* came to him when he was feeling down and alone on location for *Raiders* and started concocting the image of the secret or invisible friend every lonely kid has yearned for at some time. More than that, the theme of an alien actually landing among us and making friends and teaching us was the direct sequel to *Close Encounters of the Third Kind* that never got made. The theme of the friendly alien was right for that generation that wanted to leave Vietnam and Watergate – and the Cold War paranoia that had fuelled alien movies like *Invasion of the Body Snatchers* – behind them. With *E.T.*, Spielberg entered childhood as fully as any film-maker has done, relying on the child actors' performances rather than special effects, a sentimental story and relationships and more references to his own childhood experience – actual and Disneyfied – than ever before. It is as if the "man" in him could let go after having already proved so much as a director. And the audience let go with him too as Martin Amis describes:

> "Towards the end of *E.T.*, barely able to support my own grief and bewilderment, I turned and looked down the aisle at my fellow sufferers: executive, black dude, Japanese businessman, punk, hippie, mother, teenage, child. Each face was a mask of tears. Staggering out . . . I felt I had lived out a one-year love affair . . . in the space of 120 minutes."
>
> (Amis, quoted in Taylor, 1999: 130–131)

But lest we are distracted by a *Bambi*-type sentimentality, or that of Disney's *Old Yeller* (1957), also note how *E.T.* has as much in common with Bryan Forbes's *Whistle Down the Wind* (1961) "and all those movies about children who keep an alien creature hidden from adults who 'wouldn't understand'" (Michener, 1982: 63). For those familiar with *Memories, Dreams, Reflections* (Jung, 1963), the manikin Jung carved as a child and kept hidden in the attic of his house comes to mind. In *E.T.*, the little alien is kept hidden – not only from the world of adults but specifically from the all-male scientist hunters, who are consistently photographed from a child's-height point of view with their phallic key-chains rattling from their waists. There is no Brody or Neary in this narrative, just Elliott (Henry Thomas), his big brother and his spunky little sister (Drew Barrymore). Their single-Mum features but Dad is absent and movingly recollected by the smell of Old Spice on an old shirt of his the children find in the garage. In other words, the men have gone – replaced by a finer spirit in Elliott and the little alien.

In fact, the "hero" of this narrative is the Other; and now there are two Others: E.T. and Elliott himself, both "aliens" marginalised at the edge of the larger suburban and "troublesome adult world" (Kolker, 1988: 290). And Spielberg's skilful manipulation of our emotions in the audience aligns us more fully with the Other than ever before. Just as Elliott mysteriously participates in E.T.'s experiences – when E.T. gets drunk at home or watches the clinch from a love scene in an old movie on TV, Elliott goes through the same thing away at school – so does every member of the audience participate in the plight of this pair and their *folie a deux*. We are required to identify not with the heroism of a conscious struggle against the Other, but with the Other itself. In this way, in as much as suburbia and rational science are signs of the dominant consciousness, with Elliott and E.T. we are riding the emotional roller-coaster of the unconscious – that which is kept hidden and repressed.

All E.T. wants is to "go home". Elliott hides him inside his own home – in the closet as a home within a home while he himself manages to stay home from school by faking a high temperature. But E.T. is not at home in our world – like a child away at camp for the first time he wants to "phone home". The alien Other is *uncanny* – not only *unknowing* but also *unheimlich*: un-home-like. This is the unconscious for Freud; while we are at home with our conscious mind, the unconscious is where we are least at home. But like with spiritual experiences – and descents into madness that have been mentioned earlier – the encounter with the uncanny takes us away from home in the profoundest way. For Jung this is a necessary journey, but one from which we must return if we are not to remain "mad", cut off from ordinary shared humanity. The sea in *Jaws*, the terror of the road in *Duel*, the imagined and then the actual Devil's Tower in *Close Encounters of the Third Kind*, the place of the Lost Boys in *Hook*, the island in *Jurassic Park* (the "Lost World") are all versions of the un-home-like *uncanny*. In *E.T.*, however, the theme becomes more complex with its two aliens: it is as if the truly uncanny E.T. seeking to return to another home expresses that aspect of Elliott – and by association, ourselves – which will forever feel not quite at home in the type of conscious world created, maintained and valued by the dominant consciousness.

## Schindler's List and Saving Private Ryan

Modernity's blind trust in the achievements of our highly differentiated consciousness found its most articulate critic of recent times first in Friedrich Nietzsche. Nietzsche's philosophical approach was rapidly followed by Freud's rediscovery of the unconscious and ultimately by Jung's development of these ideas into a psychology of the unconscious – or, in other words, a psychology of everything we forget at our peril. During the same period, 1900 to 1950, Western culture experienced cataclysmic upheavals – the two world wars, the Holocaust, and the atomic bomb – which demolished late nineteenth-century confidence in the achievments of Western civilisation, and which required that civilisation confront itself with humility from thereon. Early in this period, Jung had written of how:

> The frightful catastrophe of the first World War drew a very thick line through the calculations of even the most optimistic rationalizers of culture . . . as is the psychology of humanity so also is the psychology of the individual. The World War brought a terrible reckoning with the rational intentions of civilisation.
>
> (Jung, 1917/1942, *CW* 7: paras. 72, 74)

Spielberg's last two films depict the European psyche at two such turning points: they do this so darkly and with such *réalité* that we forget this is the guy who made the "kids' films", let alone the "shark'n'truck" horror stories. What remains familiar, though, is the way our hearts are wrenched – this time not by fantasy, no matter how significant for us that fantasy is, but by a version of events that we know to be horrifyingly true.

*Schindler's List* (1993) and *Saving Private Ryan* (1998) seem to be so different from the five earlier Spielberg films I have disussed so far that, at first glance, they hardly seem approachable within the same chapter and thrust of analysis. These are not entertainments. Of *Schindler's List*, Spielberg has said, "You go to all of my movies to be entertained – except for this movie: you go to be informed" (BBC TV, 1994). He wishes us to view them as imperfect and partial records of two historical occasions, linked via the politics of their era – World War Two and the Nazi attempt to rule Europe. Therefore they are not "escapist" movies in the sense of the films I have been discussing; in the case of *Saving Private Ryan*, Spielberg was very wary of the history of Hollywood in glamorising World War Two on the one hand, and providing jingoistic encouragement for the allied nations on the other. Others of his generation had already made war films – *Apocalypse Now* (Coppola) and *The Deer Hunter* (Cimino) for example – which had dealt with Vietnam in all its atrocious reality and its effects on those who returned to the States. Through the period of youth protest against the war, and in the years afterwards, Spielberg seems to have had no similar political urge to comment either personally or through his art, but responded more in terms of, as Kolker says, the great fantasist of recuperation (Kolker, 1988: 286). For Kolker, and for Taylor (1999), the themes of "returning home" refer more to the way US culture was anxious for a sense of restoration of what they felt they had lost through the assassination of the Kennedy brothers and Martin Luther King, Watergate, Vietnam, and the Iranian hostage crisis; hence the "celebration" of suburbia in all its "normality". In a comment that seems to be left over from an earlier edition of his book, Taylor actually says Spielberg's "films do not after all confront us with difficult or unpalatable issues that require painful or agonizing moral decisions" (Taylor, 1999: 33). At that time, Spielberg had not made *Schindler's List* and *Saving Private Ryan*, and few would have predicted that he would – or could.

But even though these films deal with the horror of the Nazi persecution, the dehumanisation and murder of the Polish Jews, and the visceral horror of the Omaha beach landing and the subsequent Allied advance against Nazi Germany in 1944, respectively, they retain several elements that we have found and referred to in the previous "escapist" movies. Technically the recent films are as expert as ever, but they employ very different methods. *Schindler's List* is filmed in black-and-white,[10] frequently with a hand-held camera lending the film a *cinéma vérité* or news reportage style which underscores the historical reality of what is being reproduced for us.[11] Spielberg films scenes where dialogue is not always cut from close-up to close-up as is the Hollywood style, but shown from a distance so the audience can watch the participants, choosing where to place their gaze rather than being led by the camera angle and the editing as is usually the case. The same technique is used to film dialogue in *Saving Private Ryan* where, later in the film, we see conversations between the US soldiers in long-shot in the context of the destruction of a city that surrounds them. At the beginning of this film, Spielberg captures the horrific reality of war by placing the camera/viewer within the troops as they disembark or take shelter to avoid bullets and shrapnel; he does this by using certain lenses and camera-shaking mechanisms which refuse to allow the audience any distance from the relentless progress of the violence of mechanised warfare. He has tried to recreate the immediacy of Capra's black-and-white photographs of the landing and other documentary film where blurs and shakes enhance the fact that the photographer was also a participant in the combat. The film is on coloured stock but with about 60 per cent of the colour desaturated out so we are left once more with the sense of witnessing something from the past with an – albeit simulated – level of technical quality that is there to confirm our sense of watching "history".

Once again we find, within these very "differences", Spielberg still using his technical ability with cameras, shots, lighting and editing to enhance the drama the film has to portray – fully aware of cinematic history and its relevance for his aims. He is still the dramatist selecting the most appropriate tools to support the drama. As in *Jaws*, *E.T.* and all his films, the dramatic narrative is still key. And in both *Schindler's List* and *Saving Private Ryan*, we are once again back with the narrative of the *men*. In the former, Schindler (Liam Neeson), Stern, the Jewish accountant (Ben Kingsley) and Goeth, the Nazi commandant (Ralph Fiennes) carry the tensions of the story in a structural style harking back to Brody, Hooper and Quint in *Jaws*. These men are here in the thrall of the Nazi genocide machine itself; this is the Other that grips all three according to their structural position in relation to it and the complexities of their characters. Schindler, the German capitalist war profiteer who also risks his life to save Jews; Stern, who articulates for us the quality of surviving each hour as if it could be one's last as was the experience of the ghetto and the camps; and Goeth, the embodiment of evil and cruelty, shooting Jews for sport, but also an apparently "civilised" European.[12] Once again it is the rescue of a community of women, children and other men which lies at the core of the drama played out through these three men. This time, though, the story really happened; this time millions really died; the Other of the Nazi regime came not from the Deep or from Deep Space but from the deepness of a human potential for evil that, Jung warns, we all need to recognise. As in most Spielberg films the drama is about, "a protagonist who is no longer in control of his life, who loses control and then has to regain it" (Taylor, 1999: 39). The Other of National Socialism robs all three men of control of their lives. This is even true of Goeth for whom historical circumstances grant him opportunities to indulge his inhumanity with an impunity no recent era ever would have allowed.[13] Through Schindler and Stern, and those on their List, we witness how, under the same circumstances, life can be regained, against all odds, as well.

In 1982, an article in *Time* said: "Film-making has been a profitable form of psychotherapy for Spielberg" (Taylor, 1999: 58). Along with many of his generation – and in line with the hyper-reflectivity of postmodern times – Spielberg's work has frequently been informed by his own subjectivity and personal history. But as with a proportion of all cultural figures, the subjective concerns within his work coincide with collective concerns of the culture as a whole. Spielberg comes from a non-practising Jewish family and was subjected to anti-Semitic taunts in the WASPish and redneck suburbs he grew up in: "I was the only Jew . . . the object of a lot of discrimination" (BBC TV, 1994), he tells us. His father served in Burma in World War Two and would have his war buddies around for drinks at the house – an evening that started off merry enough but, as Spielberg again recalls, one which disintegrated into tears as the night went on (BBC TV, 1998). The last two films still have a subjective core, but, because they deal with historical events, that core now also expresses a *collective* concern – the "never again" lesson of the Nazi era – in a recognisable way that overrides the individual. Speaking for my own response, like Amis's audience (see above), I too cried in *E.T.* and was in awe of *Close Encounters of the Third Kind*; but after watching *Schindler's List* I was struck dumb in anguish – nothing I had seen or read had conveyed the horror of the Holocaust like this before. I kept thinking, "But this all happened. This was a movie but it had not been a movie." After *Saving Private Ryan* I was again shocked into an awareness of the sacrifice of the allied troops brought home particularly by Miller's dying words to Ryan, "Make sure you earn this." Spielberg has acknowledged in a recent interview (BBC TV, 1998) how he had to give up a certain type of sentimentality – as expressed in *E.T.* – in favour of a rawer emotional tone which he has only found possible since he has been older.

*Saving Private Ryan*, with fewer female characters than ever before, again uses the story device of an adventure initiated for the sake of the female – this time Private Ryan's mother who has already lost three sons and for whom the "authorities" decide that her surviving boy, Ryan, should be found, relieved of duty and returned safely home. Tragically, other sons and husbands have to die along the way. The ordinariness of Captain Miller (Tom Hanks) is once more underlined by the insertion of fantasised memories of being with his wife back home. As Spielberg has said of Miller, he is "that quintessential guy who finds himself in charge, but just wants to win the war and go home" (in Taylor, 1999: 155). The "home" in *Schindler's List* moves out of fiction as Spielberg includes footage of Jewish survivors "at home" in Israel, placing stones on graves in a sign of respect. In his maturing style, Spielberg retains themes like the return home, but now home is not the local subjective suburbia of his own childhood coinciding with a collective longing for the romanticised

American childhood; it is a sense of "home" that symbolises a restoration of the fullness of human potential on a much larger cultural scale that Jung so often draws our attention to.[14] In addition to, but also quite beyond the "growing-up" of Spielberg the man, these "popular" Hollywood films demonstrate an individuation of Western culture as it too enters maturity.

In summary, what this chapter has drawn together is the way that the most financially successful movie director of all time, a director of "escapist" popular entertainment, has produced a body of work that bears serious examination along Jungian cultural and psychological lines. I have limited the analysis to six films which demonstrate a chronological development of themes that appear central to Spielberg as an individual, on the one hand, and to collective Western culture on the other. These have been the themes of men and the Other, the feminine, community, authority, descent into "madness" and loss, and the meaning of "home", the *unheimlich* and the return.

It is fascinating to note how, in his Introduction to *Flying Saucers – A Modern Myth of Things Seen in the Skies* (1958, *CW* 10: pp. 309–433), C.G. Jung links his need to comment on such phenomena with his 1936 text *Wotan* which was concerned with the rise of National Socialism: "I feel myself compelled, as once before when events of fateful consequence were brewing for Europe, to sound a note of warning" (Jung, *CW* 10: para. 589). In his cultural-psychology the link between the two phenomena is *projection*:

> the unconscious . . . in order to make its contents perceived . . . does this most vividly by projection, by extrapolating its contents into an object, which then reflects back what had previously lain hidden in the unconscious.
>
> (Jung, *CW* 10: para. 609)

Psychological projection has extreme forms like hallucinations, normal forms where we see the mote in our brother's eye without seeing the beam in our own, strange cases such as UFO sightings and also political propaganda (ibid.).

> Projections have what we might call different ranges, according to whether they stem from merely personal conditions or from deeper collective ones. Personal repressions . . . manifest themselves in our immediate environment, in our circle of relatives and aquaintances. Collective contents, such as religious, philosophical, political and

social conflicts, select projection-carriers of a corresponding kind –
Freemasons, Jesuits, Jews, Capitalists, Bolsheviks, Imperialists, etc.

(Jung, *CW* 10: para. 610)

Before movies were ever invented, human beings collectively projected
the unconscious psyche onto the stories, myths and folk tales handed
down from generation to generation in oral tradition. As consciousness evolved, differentiating exponentially over the last 600 years, the
unconscious has held more and more of our collective human potential
that the present era excludes. The dominant consciousness of modernity
eclipses an Other comprising the feminine, the mytho-poeic, the religious,
mystical, spiritual, subjective and uncanny while promoting the fantasy
of a detached, objective rationality as the dominant *Weltanschauung*.
In our postmodern times, the technological achievments of this type of
consciousness have, ironically, delivered us a technique of projection that
is now returning what we have lost on a massive collective and cultural
scale: the projection of the celluloid "moving" image on the cinema
screen. The cinema has become the place where we gather in the dark
together to witness the story and participate emotionally in the sharing of
the projection. Spielberg seems to understand this as well as did Jung and,
coming back to how this chapter began, although he operates within the
commercial pressures of an industry driven by the need to ensure mass
popular support of its projects, Spielberg says:

> "that's a blessing in disguise because it will bring us back to the story
> and the characters. It will compel us to return to the source of all great
> story-telling – the human soul and how it suffers and celebrates. *Let's
> go back to finding out who we are – not necessarily what we are
> capable of constructing*."

(Taylor, 1999: 72; italics added)

## Notes

1 *Duel*, his first movie, originally made for TV in 1968, achieved widespread
critical acclaim in 1973, and within seven years – after his cinema debut
of *Sugarland Express* (1974) – Spielberg released *Jaws* which, in 1975,
broke all box-office records at that time. He was still under thirty. Since
then, as a director, he has gone on to make the *Indiana Jones* trilogy (1981,
1984, 1989), his alien stories *E.T. – The Extra-Terrestrial* (1982), *Close
Encounters of the Third Kind* (1977), *1941* (1979), plus a version of Peter
Pan called *Hook* (1991), films of the novels *The Color Purple* (1985) and
*Empire of the Sun* (1987), and recently *Jurassic Park* (1993), with an

acknowleged maturity emerging into his movies with the Oscar winning *Schindler's List* (1993), and *Saving Private Ryan* (1998).

2   Mainly for their Joseph Campbell *monomyth* narrative (Campbell, 1949) which has influenced many screenwriters and directors, including George Miller's *Mad Max* films.

3   As a sign of suburban male belonging, the briefcase, and its applications, is often evident in movie semiotics – I am reminded, for example, of the way in which Michael Douglas's character in *Falling Down* uses his briefcase, his only property, in several unconventional ways as he too descends from normality into violent eccentricity. In this movie his displacement of "useful" suburban citizenship is underscored by how the briefcase is revealed as empty of any real "work" and only contains his lunch. Curiously, it is part of the Spielberg myth that he first got onto the Universal Studio lot at the age of 17 by putting on a suit and carrying an empty briefcase past the guards at the gate who assumed he was some well-known director's son.

4   See John Beebe's chapter in this volume.

5   "In *E.T.*, that's my bedroom! . . . Gertie (Elliott's sister played by Drew Barrymore) is an amalgamation of my three terrifying sisters", Spielberg once stated (Taylor, 1999: 56); and Spielberg's father once woke the whole family and drove them out to see a meteor storm in the middle of the night, similar to Roy Neary in *Close Encounters of the Third Kind*.

Further differentiation along gender lines in Spielberg's early family influences is emphasised by texts which indicate the possible significance of the fact that his father was into science and engineering (and was a pioneer of the early modern computers) while his mother was an accomplished pianist. "Being the only son in 'a house with three screaming sisters and a mother who played concert piano with seven other women,' Spielberg feels he 'was raised in a world of women'" (Mott and Saunders, 1986: 8, quoting Michael Sragow, "A Conversation with Steven Spielberg", *Rolling Stone*, 22 July 1982, p. 28). Apparently, even the family dog was female.

6   *The Color Purple* and *Amistad*, I believe, express an important but different branch of this "maturity" which I do not have space to discuss here

7   See John Hollwitz's analysis of *Field of Dreams*, and Jane Ryan's and Lydia Lennihan's chapters in this volume, for discussion of the Grail theme in Jungian thought.

8   The three *Indiana Jones* movies are the successful indulgence of a nostalgia for the cliff-hanging adventure films Spielberg and Lucas loved as boys in the 1950s, despite Spielberg's TV consumption being censored by his parents. The apocryphal tale about this details how Mr Spielberg senior would disguise the TV by covering it with a cloth and putting flowers on top to stop Steven watching the forbidden late night adventure shows. And even though a head-hair was placed on the on-switch so any disturbance could be detected a-la-James Bond by father Spielberg, Steven remembered its position precisely, he claims, and replaced it so that his secret viewing could go undetected (Mott and Saunders, 1986: 9).

9   Made for only $10m, a child-size price and the lowest cost of any Spielberg film, it managed to do more business than any other film in history and held that record for ten years – until it was broken by Spielberg's own *Jurassic Park*.

10  The exception of course is the pale red coat of the little girl who appears through the movie. This strikes me as a good example of an ineffable symbol in a film, along the lines of Don Fredericksen's understanding in his chapter "Jung/sign/symbol/film" in the present volume.

11  Spielberg says there was no formal story-board planning for this film (as, indeed, none was done for *E.T.*) but, "I created the scene and wandered into the scene like an eavesdropper . . . making the camera very second nature to what was happening in front of the camera" (BBC TV, 1994).

12  With a revolting example of distorted rationalisation, Himmler apparently wrote in his diary that the Nazis' ability to overcome disgust at witnessing their own murderous barbarity was a confirmation of their superior "civilised" status.

13  Spielberg has commented of Goeth, "On the surface he's an evil man . . . he's the devil personified." He is an example of "good casting by the Third Reich . . . these people might have been in jail in a normal time in Germany . . . they would be regarded as psychopathic" (BBC TV, 1994).

14  Such as in 1935 when he wrote, "Our present-day consciousness is a mere child that is just beginning to say 'I'" (Jung, 1935, *CW* 10: para. 284).

## References

Adorno, T.W. and Horkheimer, M. ([1944] 1973) *Dialectic of Enlightenment*, trans. J. Cumming, London: Allen Lane.

Baudrillard, Jean (1994) *Simulacra and Simulation*, trans. S.F. Glaser, Ann Arbor: University of Michigan Press.

BBC TV (1994) Steven Spielberg on *Schindler's List*, BBC 1, 8 March, London.
—— (1998) *War Stories: Steven Spielberg*, BBC 2, 13 September, London.

Campbell, Joseph (1949) *The Hero With a Thousand Faces*, Bollingen Series xvii, Princeton: Princeton University Press.

Caputi, Jane (1978) "*Jaws* as Patriarchal Myth", *Journal of Popular Film* 6: 307–308, 311.

Cribben, Mik (1975) "On Location with *Jaws*", *American Cinematographer* 56, 3 (March): 276.

Deleuze, G. and Guattari, F. (1972) *Anti-Oedipus: Capitalism and Schizophrenia*, New York: Viking.

Foucault, Michel (1967) *Madness and Civilisation*, trans., R. Howard, London: Tavistock.

Hartman, David (1983) Interview with Leah Adler, "Good Morning America", ABC-TV, 5 May.

Hauke, Christopher (2000) *Jung and the Postmodern: The Interpretation of Realities*, London and Philadelphia: Routledge.

Hocker Rushing, Janice and Frentz, Thomas S. (1995) "*Jaws*: Faces of the Shadow" in *Projecting the Shadow: The Cyborg Hero in American Film*, Chicago: University of Chicago Press.

Holy Bible, New International Version (1973–1988) London: Hodder and Stoughton.

Jung, C.G. Except where a different publication or translation is noted below, all references are, by volume and paragraph number, to the hardback edition of *C.G. Jung, The Collected Works* (*CW*) edited by Sir Herbert Read, Dr Michael Fordham and Dr Gerhard Adler, and translated in the main by R.F.C. Hull, London: Routledge.

—— (1963) *Memories, Dreams, Reflections*, London: Fontana.

Kaminsky, Stuart M. (1985) *American Film Genres* (2nd edn), Chicago: Nelson-Hall.

Kolker, Robert Phillip (1988) *A Cinema of Loneliness, Penn, Kubrick, Scorsese, Spielberg and Altman* (2nd edn), Oxford: Oxford University Press.

Kroll, Jack (1977) "Close Encounter with Spielberg", *Newsweek*, 21 November, p. 98.

Laing, R.D. (1959) *The Divided Self*, Harmondsworth: Penguin.

—— (1967) *The Politics of Experience and The Bird of Paradise*, Harmondsworth: Penguin.

Martin, Joel W. and Ostwalt, Conrad E., Jr. (1995) *Screening the Sacred: Religion, Myth and Ideology in Popular American Film*, Boulder, San Francisco and Oxford: Westview Press.

Michener, Charles (1982) "A Summer Double Punch", *Newsweek*, 31 May.

Mott, Donald R. and Saunders, Cheryl McAllister (1986) *Steven Spielberg*, Columbus Filmmakers series, Bromley, Kent: Columbus Books.

Pederson, Loren E. (1991) *Dark Hearts. The Unconscious Forces That Shape Men's Lives*, London: Shambhala.

Pye, Michael and Myles, Linda (1979) *The Movie Brats*, New York.

Taylor, Phillip M. (1999) *Steven Spielberg. The Man, His Movies and their Meaning* (expanded 3rd edn, with a new chapter by Daniel O'Brien which includes *The Lost World, Amistad* and *Saving Private Ryan*), London: B.T. Batsford.

Von Gunden, Kenneth (1991) *Postmodern Auteurs: Coppola, Lucas, De Palma, Spielberg, and Scorsese*, Jefferson, N.C. and London: McFarland & Company Publishers.

## Further reading

Loshitsky, Yosefa (ed.) (1997) *Spielberg's Holocaust. Critical Perspectives on Schindler's List*, Bloomington and Indianapolis: Indiana University Press.

Yule, Andrew (1996) *Steven Spielberg, Father of the Man. His Incredible Life, Tumultuous Times and Record-Breaking Movies*, London: Little, Brown & Company.

# Part III

# Studies in genres and gender

Chapter 9

# *Film noir*
## Archetypes or stereotypes?

*Luke Hockley*

> The pebbled glass door panel is lettered in flaked black paint: "Philip
> Marlowe . . . Investigations". It is a reasonably shabby door at the end
> of a reasonably shabby corridor in the sort of building that was new
> about the year the all-tile bathroom became the basis of civilisation
> . . . come on in – there's nobody here but me and a big bluebottle fly.
> (Chandler, 1949, *The Little Sister*)

## Introduction

The opening lines of Raymond Chandler's *The Little Sister* conjure
up vivid images that could easily have come from one of Hollywood's
numerous *noir* films. The setting and atmosphere are immediately
recognisable, the prose-style and Marlowe's character with its self-
mocking tone are no less familiar. Yet, unlike many of Chandler's other
novels such as *The Big Sleep*, *The Lady in the Lake*, or *Farewell My
Lovely*, *The Little Sister* was never made into a film. It is indicative of the
vitality of *film noir* that images from these films imbue the prose with
their underworld qualities. *Film noir* has become part of our contemporary
visual vocabulary; this makes us question why it has happened.

As viewers of films we are well versed in the intricacies of film
genres. We know what to expect from our films – (don't we?). While we
understand the surface meaning and generic conventions of a film well
enough, perhaps we are less aware of the psychological drama that is
being played out and why we find appealing such figures as the detective
and *femme fatale*. Perhaps in our haste to put our knowledge of genre to
work, we confuse stereotype with archetype. The aim of this chapter is
to suggest that drawing on post-Jungian ideas about the archetypal can
provide a useful analytical framework within which to understand the
enduring appeal of *film noir* and, by extension, other films. We will start

by examining the history of genre theory and the claim that *film noir* has for genre status. From there, we will use an approach derived from genre studies to understand the emergence of recognisable characters. Using the framework of analytical psychology, we will reflect on the psychological reasons for this development and on the significance that the themes and characters of *film noir* hold for us.

By way of balance and compensation, genre theory also throws up some interesting challenges for the interpretative conventions adopted by analytical psychology. The similarities and differences will reinforce and challenge each other. The aim is not to create a synthesis or hierarchy of theory: rather, it is to suggest that both genre and archetype theories offer different, but mutually supportive, approaches to reflecting on the interpretation and appeal of films.

## Genre theory and films

Genre theory is only one of many possible ways through which to classify and analyse films. However, for our purposes it is particularly interesting as, along with the visual surface of each genre (lighting, editing, camera framing, camera movement, etc.), it pays particular attention to the development of narrative themes, or, if you prefer, "patterns" or "structures" in films over time. Genre theory is also directly interested in the *mise-en-scène* of a film. This is a shorthand term that refers to some of the key elements in a film that inflect its meaning: character, lighting, location and movement.

Genre theory in film studies traces its intellectual roots back to the *Poetics* of Aristotle and its significance for eighteenth-century European classicism. This largely literary tradition provided a framework for twentieth-century film theorists to evaluate the relative artistic worth of film directors, the films themselves and the studios that undertook their production. Strangely perhaps, one of the most important groups in getting genre theory to be taken seriously was not, primarily, interested in genre films at all. The French group Cahiers, named after their journal *Cahiers du cinéma* first published in 1951, were fierce advocates of the auteur theory. They emphasised the importance of directors in the Hollywood Studio System, and the ability of the exceptional director to shape, control and indeed imprint films with his (the directors that were initially singled out by Cahiers were all male) unique vision and view of the world.[1] However, by the 1960s Cahiers were also encouraging film theorists to take the notion of genre seriously. (Albeit seeing individual genre films as examples of the work of an auteur.)

Since that point, genre theory has undergone numerous revisions and refinements. However, in all its variations there is a concern with three core elements: audience, institution and text.[2] Genre theory suggests that these elements cannot be treated as separate entities but rather should be seen as interconnected components. In turn, this leads to a model based on an equilateral triangle with one of each of these elements located at each corner. Thus, a study of the film as text needs to be informed by a consideration of audience and institution, and so forth. This finds some parallels in Jung's instance that interpreting dreams (texts) is a joint enterprise undertaken between the analyst, who brings a set of institutionalised interpretative conventions and theoretical frameworks, and analysand[3] (audience) who, jointly with the analyst, undertakes the work of understanding the dream and verifying its meaning:

> it makes very little difference whether the doctor understands or not, but it makes a difference whether the patient understands. Understanding should therefore be understanding in the sense of an agreement that is the fruit of joint reflection.
>
> (Jung, 1934, *CW* 16: para. 314)

Genre theory also stresses that films need to be seen as developmental and should not just be analysed solely as individual texts. In 1969, British writer Lawrence Alloway wrote in his catalogue for a screening of American crime films at the New York Museum of Modern Art:

> The emphasis in this book is on a description of popular movies, viewed in sets and cycles rather than as single entities. It is an approach that accepts obsolescence and in which judgements derive from the sympathetic consumption of a great many films. In terms of continuing themes and motifs, the obsolescence of single films is compensated for in the prolongation of ideas in film after film.
>
> (Alloway, 1969: 19)

These remarks suggest a useful parallel with analytical psychology. Examining films as cycles, genre theory suggests that meanings and cultural values are best understood as elements that develop over time. In much the same way, analytical psychology explores the development of the meaning of an image or set of images during a period of individual analysis. Analytical psychology also uses a process termed "amplification" in which the images under consideration are "amplified" by exploring similar images found in different contexts and by reacting to these parallels in an imaginative way. The process uses images from mythology, world religions, art and anthropology. It finds an echo in one of the approaches that is adopted in genre theory:

> In early genre criticism, this genre morphology was frequently combined with a genre/myth analogy, relating generic rise and fall in a mimetic relationship to changes in social consciousness. This audience-driven morphology assumes that film viewers either validate existing mythological forms or require that they undergo revision.
>
> (Berry, 1999: 29)

It is well known that the dream images that an analysand brings at the early stages of analysis can predict the direction that the analysis is going to take. Further, these initial images are best understood by the analyst in the light of subsequent dreams and other creative arts undertaken by the analysand, such as painting, sculpture and creative writing.[4] In other words, if we want to understand images from a psychological point of view, it is important to see them not just as individual events but as part of a related sequence.[5] This is one of the ideas that underpins genre theory, which sees films as constantly referring to each other and building up a series of characters, themes, and visual motifs that gradually become imbued with meaning.

> genres are not simply bodies of work or groups of films, however classified, labelled, and defined. Genres do not consist only of films: they consist also, and equally, of specific systems of expectation and hypothesis that spectators bring with them to the cinema and that interact with films themselves during the course of the viewing process. These systems provide spectators with a means of recognition and understanding. They help render films, and the elements within them, intelligible and therefore explicable.
>
> (Neale, 1990: 46)

## Film noir

As might be expected, the early films in a genre sometimes suggest the way that that genre is going to develop. In this respect, the case of *film noir* is an interesting one. Genre theorists argue that *film noir* emerged in American studio-based film-making of the 1940s. Films such as *Laura* (1944), *The Maltese Falcon* (1941), *Double Indemnity* (1944), *Farewell My Lovely* (1944) and *The Woman in the Window* (1944), share a menacing tone and are populated with erotically charged characters. Of course these films are predominantly the work of German and Austrian film-makers who had arrived in Hollywood during the late 1930s and early 1940s. They bought with them a dramatic style of film-making derived from their experience of producing German Expressionistic films. Fritz Lang's *The Woman in the Window* (1944), Otto Preminger's *Laura* (1944), Billy Wilder's *Double Indemnity* (1944) and Edward Dmytryck's *Crossfire* (1947), all show clear evidence of this tradition. The film scores of émigré composers such as Franz Waxman (*The Paradine Case*, 1948), Miklos Rozsa (*Double Indemnity*, 1944) and Max Steiner (*The Big Sleep*, 1946), along with those of other composers, also played an important role in setting the tone and mood for *noir*. This style was grafted onto the American literary hardboiled detective tradition typified by the work of Dashiell Hammett (*Red Harvest*, 1929; *The Dain Curse*, 1929; *The Maltese Falcon*, 1930; *The Glass Key*, 1931) and Raymond Chandler (*The Big Sleep*, 1939; *Farewell My Lovely*, 1940; *The High Window*, 1943; *The Lady in the Lake*, 1944). Many of these novels were subsequently turned into film-scripts and, when combined with the visual style of German Expressionism and the appropriate music and soundtrack, the result was *film noir*.

Historically, genre theorists, such as Raymond Borde and Étienne Chaumeton, argued that *film noir* was not really a genre at all but was, instead, a film style. The style, or appearance, of *noir* was characterised by high contrast lighting with deep black shadows and brilliant burnt-out white highlights. Its other stylistic features included canted camera framing, night-for-night shooting, a deeper than normal depth-of-field, cluttered *mise-en-scène*, the use of flashbacks, voice-over narration and chiaroscuro lighting. These expressive and stylistic devices provided a set of cinematic techniques with which to create psychologically rich pictures. The visual treatment was applied to a variety of films, and not just those with detectives. The gangster film *Angels with Dirty Faces* (1938), the melodrama *Mildred Pierce* (1945), and the horror movie *Cat People* (1942), all have a strongly *noir* appearance. This lack of thematic consistency led Paul Schrader, in his 1972 "Notes on Film Noir", to comment,

> Film noir is not a genre . . . It is not defined, as are the western and gangster genres, by conventions of setting and conflict, but rather by the more subtle qualities of tone and mood. It is film "*noir*," as opposed to the possible variants of film grey or film off-white.
>
> (Schrader, 1972: 53)

Coming from the 1970s, this commentary essentially looks backwards to the classic 1940s Hollywood *noirs*. Even so, his generalisation holds good for some of the more contemporary films that were released in the 1980s and 1990s. The gloomy streets of the crime thriller/alien invasion movie *Dark City* (1998) are heavily *noir*-inspired, as are *Reservoir Dogs* (1992) and *Dick Tracy* (1990). However, it is the new crop of films that maintain either a thematic, or character-based link with the classic *noirs* that are of particular interest. Here, I have in mind films such as *Blade Runner* (1982), and more recently *Basic Instinct* (1992) and *LA Confidential* (1997). E. Anne Kaplan, in writing the introduction to the new 1998 edition of *Women in Film Noir*, suggests that this style of film-making fits the postmodern inclinations of our contemporary society:

> It is not, I think, accidental that as I write, noirness seems to be back in style in both the movies and American culture more generally. Indeed, the very phenomenon of "noirness" or "retro-noir", in its repeating nostalgically of a cultural mode from another era, signals the 90s as a post modern moment.
>
> (Kaplan, 1998: 1)

To an extent this seems true, but these films are more sophisticated than this neat categorisation, with its allusions to notions of pastiche and imitation, might suggest. It is certainly the case that these retro-*noir* films feature what, at first sight, appear to be familiar and stereotypical characters; lonely isolated detectives and sexually powerful and manipulative *femmes fatales*. However, the characters in these contemporary *noirs* are not exactly the same as their counterparts in the classic *noirs*, of which more later. It is also the case that the themes of these new *noirs* are different to their 1940s predecessors: *Blade Runner* (1982), tackles issues of human subjectivity, the role of emotions and feelings in human identity, and the illusory nature of existence; *Basic Instinct* (1992), addresses male sexual fantasies and fears; while *Disclosure* (1994), although not *noir* in the visual sense but in terms of tone, theme and character, addresses issues of sexual control, power and manipulation in the workplace.

One way to understand this change is in terms of an unconscious dynamic. Jung hypothesised that in the unconscious part of our psyche were a series of common, unconscious structures, which he termed "archetypes". In much the same way that we all have a common genetic structure that regulates our ageing process, Jung suggested that archetypes provide the basis for psychological growth and maturation. The unconscious archetypal patterns make themselves known in the form of images in dreams and other creative acts, including making films. While the patterns remain constant, the images they adopt change according to external, personal and cultural factors. Jung also sounds a cautionary note:

> Not for a moment dare we succumb to the illusion that an archetype can be finally explained and disposed of. Even the best attempts at explanation are only more or less successful translations into another metaphorical language. (Indeed, language itself is only an image.)
> (Jung, 1951, *CW* 9I: para. 271)

In more contemporary language, Hauke makes a similar observation in noting, "Ultimately, all these so-called unconscious contents and unconscious processes are all and always, unknown . . . This in a nutshell, is the attitude to Jungian depth psychology that locates it as postmodern" (Hauke, 2000: 200–201). The application of this model to modern *noirs* suggests that while the archetypal pattern may have remained constant the images of the archetypes have indeed changed. While 1940s *films noirs* may have been thematically diverse, modern *noir* is remarkably consistent in its narrative concerns and characters.

Focusing on films as texts emphasises their visual and thematic elements. Buscombe, in "The Idea of Genre in American Cinema" (1970), calls for us to pay more attention to the iconographic elements of films; this fits well with analytical psychology's interest in imagery. The visual conventions, for Buscombe, provide a framework, or setting within which the story can be told. While he was writing mainly about the Hollywood Western, his observation holds good for other types of film genre – including *film noir*. Implicit in his approach was the assumption that film analysis had not paid sufficient attention to the details of costumes, props, locations and film sets. It is, perhaps, typical of the trajectory of mainstream film studies that this type of approach can be overly rationalised. A clear example of this is Eco's development of a system of icongraphic codes, which he outlined in his influential presentation to the Pesaro Film Festival in 1967. This is summarised by the authors of *New Vocabularies in Film Semiotics*:

> Eco, for his part, suggests a cinematic code of triple articulations of the image, consisting of a first articulation, called semes, i.e. initially recognisable meaningful units – for example "gangster wearing trench coat" – which can in turn be broken down into a second

articulation of smaller iconic signs such as "cigarette dangling from lip," all finally analysable into a third articulation having to do with conditions of perception.

(Stam *et al.*, 1992: 33)

What this approach, and many others in film analysis, leaves to one side is the way in which the story-space of a film functions as psychological space. This is where theory derived from analytical psychology can enrich film theory with the realisation that the *mise-en-scène* of a genre can have a psychologically symbolic significance. In much the same way that detail in dreams, which may appear trivial, can be important, so too, detail in the background of films can exhort a significance on the meaning of a film that is not readily apparent. Jung observes:

> The dream is often occupied with apparently very silly details, thus producing an impression of absurdity, or else it is on the surface so unintelligible as to leave us thoroughly bewildered . . . when at last we penetrate to its real meaning, we find ourselves deep in the dreamer's secrets and discover with astonishment that an apparently quite senseless dream is in the highest degree significant, and that in reality it speaks only of important and serious matters.
>
> (Jung, 1917, *CW* 7: para. 24)

For example, the city setting of most *films noirs* may not be as neutral as it appears. If we reflect on its possible symbolic significance, in the terms of analytical psychology, the city stands as a symbol of the psyche or at least the unconscious. That high contrast cinematography, with sharp whites and deep blacks, provides a symbolic reference to consciousness and the unconscious, respectively; that many of the activities of the detective happen at night further reinforces the underworld and unconscious dimension of these films. The detective's investigations into the underworld of crime are, in one sense, also an exploration of his own unconscious processes. The chiaroscuro lighting, the canted camera framing and shafts of light filtering through venetian blinds, all suggest the broken, disorientated and fragmented state of his psyche. Attempting to hold onto his sense of self-identity, the detective retains a strong persona built up of what Eco described as elements of his iconic code but which here form part of a psychological identity. The detective's cluttered office, heavy drinking, working alone and working through the night, form part of the self-identity of the 1940s *noir* detective, as do the trademark trench coat and cigarette.

## The *femme fatale*

Much of the work on the counterpart to the figure of the detective, the *femme fatale*, has been derived from a Freudian psychoanalytic perspective. Kaplan has neatly summarised this position:

> In the '70s and '80s, theories of the *femme fatale* figures of the male imaginary (or so we argued), imaged forth males' terror of, but fascinated interest in, that bleeding wound: the play of desire fear hovered around the castration that might happen if males followed their desire for the beautiful sexual and powerful woman. What many named the phallicization of these women aimed to reduce male fear of their castration – their own bleeding wound – so as to permit fulfilment of the sexual desire these women evoked.
>
> (Kaplan, 1998: 9–10)

Analytical psychology offers an alternative to this rather bleak view of male, and indeed human, sexuality. To recognise that the detective is more than just an iconic figure and that he cannot be fully understood in just psychoanalytic terms, we need to look past the surface image that he presents. To go past the archetype of the persona and deeper into the psyche will give a better understanding of the world of the detective. Jung was keen to stress that the persona, while it is important, represents what is only an outer layer of the psyche. Underlying this are other archetypes and a sophisticated system through which the psyche attempts to balance itself. If the psyche has become overly reliant on one element, then a compensatory opposite is thrown up. In the case of the detective, the over-identification with his persona leads to an encounter with the archetype of the shadow (as the criminal) and the contrasexual archetype (as *femme fatale*). As James Hillman observes, "The more a man identifies with his biological and social role as man (persona), the more will the anima dominate inwardly" (Hillman, 1985: 11).

Jung suggested that the contrasexual archetype, which he referred to as the *anima* or *animus*, is an archetype that deals explicitly with gender roles and identities. This is an area where Jung can easily be misunderstood, as his definition of the *anima* as the inner figure of woman in man, and the *animus* as the inner figure of man in woman, seems somewhat outmoded and old-fashioned. However, in essence, the suggestion is that both sexes have the capacity for the full range of human experience, but that culturally, certain types of behaviour have been ascribed to men and women. The inevitable result of this is that the *anima* exists in a state of tension with conscious masculine sexuality, as does the animus for women. Both sexes are drawn towards their contrasexual archetype, yet at the same time they are worried by an attraction that appears to transgress culturally acceptable gender divisions.[6] As Jung observed, in a very rare reference to films:

> Thus, I have noticed that people usually have not much difficulty in picturing to themselves what is meant by the shadow . . . But it costs them enormous difficulties to understand what the anima is. They accept her easily enough when she appears in novels or as a film star, but she is not understood at all when it comes to seeing the role she plays in their own lives . . .
>
> (Jung, 1954, *CW* 9I: para. 485)

While Jungian psychology may offer the opportunity for a theory of sexuality in which female and male qualities are valued equally, it is important to stress that the *anima* and the *animus* tell us nothing about the psychology of the other sex. What they do, is to shed some light on how, at any given time, men view women and how they understand their own sense of the feminine. The opposite also holds good: and the *animus* can tell us something about how women view men. As Christopher observes, "the anima and animus are symbolic modes of perception and behaviour within the psyche, which are represented internally by figures of the opposite sex" (Christopher, 2000: 37). These "modes of perception and behaviour" are shaped through the interaction between unconscious pattern (archetype) and personal/cultural pressures and change, as they react to different historical conditions. This reinforces the assertion that in encountering the contrasexual archetype, we find ourselves in the world of the imaginal – we are not working with a documentary understanding of the opposite sex.

So, what does this tell us about the figure of the *femme fatale*? In her chapter in Kaplan's *Women in Film Noir* (1998), Kate Stables makes a clear distinction between the *femme fatale* in classic *noirs* and the new 1990s *femme fatale*. She notes that the *femme fatale* now makes an appearance in non-*noir* films. Typically she is sexually more powerful than her 1940s predecessor, and has a more explicitly sexual persona with dialogue to match. Further, the *femme fatale* offers a site within which to contest and explore a range of sexual differences:

> The postmodern film, rather than containing and masking the social contradictions structured into its narrative, is structured to utilise

them for widely divergent interpretations of the same text. Thus
*Basic Instinct* could be variously reviled as a misogynistic fantasy
and celebrated as a feminist *tour de force*, condemned for blatant
homophobia and celebrated as the ultimate cult lesbian movie.

(Stables, 1998: 166)

*Basic Instinct* (1992) is certainly a film with multiple layers and numerous
knowing references to the *noir* tradition. However, it may be that one
reason why the film appears shifting and unstable is that it is dealing with
material that is essentially unconscious and archetypal. Interestingly,
Stables hints at this possibility:

> The *fatale* figure has been re-employed consciously because the
> *fatale* woman is a universal symbol for a global cinema that is forced
> to embrace archetypes. The *fatale* myth is common to all cultures
> and her iconography is widely recognised as a result of a blanket of
> nineteenth-century European representations as well as earlier cinema
> incarnations.[7]

(Stables, 1998: 167)

The idea that the *fatale* figure has been used "consciously" highlights the
institutional dimension to film production and the role that the cinema
industry plays in producing films that have a broad appeal. Traditionally,
this type of analysis has had a political agenda to explore the way in which
film genres are part of an institutional mode of representation that
influences our psychological sense of self-identity. Berry summarises the
position neatly:

> For the most part, however, ideological readings of film genre
> have been based on textual rather than industrial analysis. The 1970s
> and '80s genre debates in *Screen*, for example, tended to see genre
> as a sub-set of the journal's broader ideological critique of classical
> Hollywood narrative, since genres provided and regulated variety
> while still binding the viewer to the cinematic institution as a whole
> in a position of textually inscribed subjectivity.

(Berry, 1999: 36)

However institutionally focused, analysis can still be cast within the
framework provided by analytical psychology. On two accounts this
suggests a useful intersection between post-Jungian ideas and film theory,
both of which might be interesting areas for further investigation. First
is an examination from the perspective of analytical psychology of the

relationship between film studios (as creators) and the films they produce. Second, there is the more general observation that genres in many ways resemble archetypes. Both offer patterns that reoccur and define themselves over time through sets, cycles and images. Further, the relationship between narrative pattern and iconography is not unlike the distinction that archetype theory makes between structure and image. Berry's comments also prompt a consideration of the influence of marketing, global markets, and the role of universal appeal in determining the final shape of films.

This reminds us that all images, even archetypal images, have an ideological dimension. This is something that analytical psychology has a tendency to forget. The history of analytical psychology and the development of interpretative conventions are in danger of exerting a determining influence on the meaning of images. Post-Jungian theory is rightly wary of this and attempts to break new ground in this respect. For example, Hillman attempts a radical shift in classical Jungian thought when he insists on the centrality of images as a presentation, and not solely representation, of the world. From a different perspective, Andrew Samuels argues for a broadly deconstructionist approach, which highlights the dangers of treating images of archetypes in a literal manner:

> When we bring in either masculinity and femininity or maleness and femaleness, we are projecting a dichotomy that certainly exists in human ideational and functioning onto convenient receptors for the projections. Arguing that masculinity and femininity should be understood nonliterally, as having nothing to do with bodily men and bodily women in a social context, may be taken as an effort to come to terms with what is lost by the projection: but this has not led to a recollection of it.
>
> (Samuels, 1990: 301–302)

This is one way in which analytical psychology can be distinguished from the Freudian perspective. Psychoanalysis emphasises the "decoding" of Oedipal desires from images, and in so doing it adopts a more literal perspective. I want to suggest that the "*fatale* figure" has an unconscious dimension which has little to do with bodily men and women. It is this archetypal dimension that, unknowingly, we project onto the world and the people we meet. As Jung puts it:

> As we know, it is not the conscious subject but the unconscious which does the projecting. Hence one meets with projections, one does not

make them . . . Projections change the world into the replica of one's own unknown face.

(Jung, 1951, *CW* 9II: para. 17)

Extrapolating from the personal to the collective suggests that the unknown face of our culture's unconscious can at least be glimpsed in films. In this sense, the *femme fatale* has little to do with actual bodily women and is more helpfully seen as a male archetypal fantasy. As Jung implied above, the cinema screen becomes the recipient of physical projection (in the cinematic mechanical sense) and the psychical projections (in the unconscious sense) of a collective culture and fantasy.

There is the possibility that what we see in the figure of the *femme fatale* is a cultural imagining of the negative aspects of the anima. This is played out in *LA Confidential*. The film, based on the novel by James Ellroy (1989), is set in the early 1950s and depicts a lurid underworld of prostitution and drug dealing where a corrupt Los Angeles police force is attempting to run organised crime in the city. The film is not a *noir* in the classical sense (the lighting is mostly too naturalistic, although faces are sometimes lit chiaroscuro), but the characters are heavily *noir* influenced. For example, all the detectives are flawed, each has a strong persona that is strongly affected by shadow qualities. Captain Dudley Smith (James Cromwell) engages in brutal beatings, extortion and murder. Jack Vincennes (Kevin Spacey) is seduced by his second job as technical adviser to the television show *Badge of Honor*, to the extent that he will knowingly trap movie stars and politicians in compromising situations to provide photographs for *Hush-Hush* magazine. Ed Exley (Guy Pierce) is quick to take the moral high-ground when it suits his career and, while attempting to maintain the image of a clean-cut young cop, is prepared to shoot his corrupt boss in the back.

Central to the film is Fleur-de-lis, an "entertainment service" with prostitutes who look like movies stars – their slogan is "whoever you desire". This points up one of the main themes of the film, which director Curtis Hanson describes as, "the difference between image and reality" (*LA Confidential* DVD, 1997), which is a suitably psychological and *noir*-like motif. Lynn Bracken (Kim Basinger), a Veronica Lake look-a-like, is the film's *femme fatale*. In common with Catherine Trammell (Sharon Stone) in *Basic Instinct*, she is a sexually powerful woman who speaks crudely about "fucking" and relationships. She also has a sophisticated sense of her own identity. Hanson comments that, "She's sad. She's wise. She's the one character that knows the truth about herself and can see the truth in the other characters" (*LA Confidential* DVD, 1997). However, this does not make her immune to errors in judgement. For example, in an attempt to help Bud White, whom she has fallen in love with, and to humiliate his boss Ed Exley, she agrees to have photographs taken by *Hush-Hush* magazine of her and Ed having sex. Understandably, when Bud finds out he is furious. The lapse in Lynn's judgement is in part explained when we realise the way in which the persona, shadow and anima are interconnected. Far from being seen as separate and isolated entities, archetypes are better thought of as clusters of images or as groups of associated feelings and attitudes. This provides a partial explanation for Lynn Bracken's misjudgement in having sex with Ed Exley. As Hauke notes in *Jung and the Postmodern*:

> men need women to carry the deprecated image of femininity as a project of what is split off and denied in men, *with the result that women may be said to be carriers of an anima image that is contaminated by the masculine shadow.*
>
> (Hauke, 2000: 136)

Not only was Bracken carrying projections of numerous men's anima images, these became tainted with the shadow projections of Bud White. Bud recognises this because, along with Lynn, he is one of the few characters in the film who manages a degree of psychological insight. In symbolic terms, his surname hints at this capacity for consciousness, and his comments to Lynn, that other men only got Veronica Lake but he got Lynn Bracken, suggest an awareness of persona and ego. In terms of his *animus*, as well as his *anima*, it is significant that at the end of the film Bud decides to leave the police force to live with Lynn in the township where she grew up. Jung comments that, "It is normal for a man to resist his *anima*, because she represents, as I said before, the unconscious and all those tendencies and contents hitherto excluded from conscious life" (*CW* 11: 129). But Bud knows what he is doing. The move from the urban to the country, the shifting of persona roles, the commitment to his relationship with Lynn, and the acknowledgement of shadow life are all psychological changes that Bud has accepted.

## Conclusion

My conclusion is that a Jungian approach to film analysis emphasises an approach to films where character, theme and image are located in their archetypal contexts. The representational aspect of films is downplayed in favour of exploring their psychologically expressive qualities. This attitude steers us away from seeing films as populated with stereotypes, and points us clearly towards the imaginal and archetypal. The approach is not one of decoding, as in Freudian psychoanalysis, but of amplifying and analogising. As Eva-Maria Simms puts it:

> Jung clearly sees the social significance of art: it is not merely there to provide a protected domain for the pleasure principle, as Freud (1930) has it, but compensates for a cultural lack. Artistic images balance the tendencies of the collective consciousness by evoking primordial forms and injecting them into the discourse of a culture.
>
> (Simms, 2000: 53)

While going a long way with these remarks, I would like to suggest that the process is not wholly one of injection, but, in actuality, is more playful and creative. In the cases of film-making, and genre theory, what we find is an examination of themes and ideas, and of how they develop film after film. The exploration of how meanings are circulated between audiences, institutions and texts, offers a rich model that finds many parallels with post-Jungian psychology. The film theorist Berry comments that, "Genres are socially organised sets of relations between texts that function to enable certain relations between texts and viewers" (Berry, 1999: 41). This could almost be reformulated to read, "archetypes are psychologically organised sets of relations that function to enable certain relationships between images and consciousness". From this perspective, watching films and reflecting on them is a psychologically meaningful activity. Raymond Chandler once remarked that Hammett took murder out of the vicarage garden and put it back in the city where it belonged. Perhaps this approach to films goes some way to taking analysis out of the consulting room and putting it back where it belongs – in the cinema.

## Notes

1 This provides another avenue for exploration which is the extent to which the personal psychology of the director is present in the films that he or she makes. For an attempt at this type of analysis, cf. Clark Branson, *Howard Hawks: A Jungian Study* (Los Angeles 1987).
2 For a good overview of the historical development of genre theories, cf. Berry (1999).
3 The term "analysand" is used to refer to an individual who is in analysis.
4 Cf. Jung (1953) *Individual Dream Symbolism in Relation to Alchemy*, *CW* 12, paras. 52–121, (London: Routledge).
5 Someone new to the process of Jungian analysis can find an interesting introduction in two volumes by Daryl Sharp, *The Survival Papers* (1988)

and *Dear Gladys* (1989) (Toronto: Inner City Books). They are published in one volume as *The Survival Papers: Applied Jungian Psychology* (1990) (Slough: Quantum).

6   One post-Jungian position is to see archetypes as a site of tension between biology and culture; cf. Samuels (1985: 207–244).

7   It's not entirely clear here how Stables is using the term "archetype". Perhaps she unwittingly evokes some Jungian ideas.

## Bibliography

Alloway, Lawrence (1969) *Violent America: The Movies, 1946–1964*, New York: New York Graphic Society and the Museum of Modern Art.

Barnaby, K. and D'Acierno, P. (eds) (1990) *C.G. Jung and the Humanities: Toward a Hermeneutics of Culture*, London: Routledge.

Berry, Sarah (1999) "Genre" in Toby Miller and Robert Stam (eds) *A Companion to Film Theory*, Oxford: Blackwell, pp. 25–44.

Brooke, Roger (ed.) (2000) *Pathways into the Jungian World Phenomenology and Analytical Psychology*, London: Routledge.

Buscombe, Edward (1970) "The Idea of Genre in American Cinema", *Screen* 11, 2: 22–45.

Chandler, Raymond (1949) *The Little Sister*, Harmondsworth: Penguin.

Christopher, Elphis (2000) "Gender Issues – Anima and Animus", in Elphis Christopher and Hester McFarland Soloman (eds) *Jungian Thought in the Modern World*, London: Free Association Books, pp. 35–53.

Christopher, Elphis and Soloman, Hester McFarland (eds) (2000) *Jungian Thought in the Modern World*, London: Free Association Books.

Hauke, Christopher (2000) *Jung and the Postmodern: The Interpretation of Realities*, London: Routledge.

Hillman, James (1985) *Anima: An Anatomy of a Personified Notion*, Woodstock: Spring Publications.

Jung, Carl Gustav. All references are by volume and paragraph number to the hardback edition of *C.G. Jung, The Collected Works (CW)*, edited by Sir Herbert Read, Dr Michael Fordham and Dr Gerhard Adler, and translated in the main by R.F.C. Hull, London: Routledge.

Kaplan, E. Ann (ed.) (1998) *Women in Film Noir*, London: BFI.

*LA Confidential* DVD (1997) *Off the Record* Documentary, Warner Brothers.

Miller, Toby and Stam, Robert (eds) (1999) *A Companion to Film Theory*, Oxford: Blackwell.

Neale, Stephen (1990) "Questions of Genre", *Screen* 31, 1: 45–66.

Nichols, Bill (ed.) (1976) *Movies and Methods*, Berkeley: University of California Press.

Samuels, Andrew (1985) *Jung and the Post-Jungians*, London: Routledge.

Samuels, Andrew (1990) "Beyond the Feminine Principle" in K. Barnaby and P. D'Acierno (eds) *C.G. Jung and the Humanities: Toward a Hermeneutics of Culture*, London: Routledge, pp. 294–306.

Schrader, Paul (1972) "Notes on Film Noir", *Film Comment*, Spring.

Simms, Eva-Maria (2000) "In Destitute Times: Archetype and Existence in Rilke's Duuino Elegies", in Roger Brooke (ed.) *Pathways into the Jungian World Phenomenology and Analytical Psychology*, London: Routledge, pp. 49–64.

Stam, Robert, Burgoyne, Robert and Flitterman-Lewis, Sandy (1992) *New Vocabularies in Film Semiotics*, London: Routledge.

# Chapter 10

# Love-life

## Using films in the interpretation of gender within analysis

*Mary Dougherty*

In this essay I consider five popular films from the 1950s to the present as emblematic expressions of gendering practices as well as formative participants in those practices. I identify specific parts of the film narratives that represent how these practices both constrict and promote ways of being for women. I explain my use of film as metaphoric points of reference within analysis and how films can function as objective images to reveal compensatory psychic elements beyond ways we have been constricted by gender. Finally, I suggest that the symbolic power of film, especially when witnessed within analysis, has the potential to expand and deepen one's subjective sense of self through fostering an ongoing relationship to the unconscious.

There they were: Lauren Bacall, Betty Grable and Marilyn Monroe on the veranda of a New York penthouse – Lauren (the smart brunette) convincing the other two (not-so-smart blondes) that the three will need to share resources and sublet this classy apartment in a classy neighborhood in order to meet Rich Guys. She makes it clear that she is *through* falling in love with "gas pump jockeys" – that it's just as easy to love a rich guy as a poor one. "[Getting married], it's the biggest thing you can do in life. The way most people go about it, they use more brains picking a horse in the third at Belmont than they do picking a husband . . . It's your head you've got to use, not your heart." She continues: "If you want to catch a mouse, you set a mousetrap. So, all right, we'll set a bear trap. Now all we've got to do is one of us has got to knock off a bear."

The trap works. They get invited to a party as "companions" for businessmen visiting New York and each woman is then paired with a guy who looks like a promising rich prospect. These gals are acting as agents of their own potency – that is, the potency of their beauty to manipulate men for money and power.

Figure 10.1 *How to Marry a Millionaire.* Courtesy of 20th Century Fox

Or are they? Betty runs off with a married businessman to his hunting lodge only to fall for a forest ranger who she thinks is a timber tycoon. Marilyn misses her rendezvous with her oilman because she ends up on the "wrong" plane next to the "right" guy. Lauren determines to go through with her marriage to an old but rich man. But in the end, she can't – because she has fallen hard, and again, for another gas pump jockey.

In the last scene, the three gals munch burgers with their not-so-rich guys at the counter of an all-night diner. Lauren's gas pump jockey then pulls out this wad of dough, pays with a $1,000 bill and says, "Keep the change." He *is* rich, after all. The three women faint backwards off their stools. The all-knowing guys then drink a toast to their wives (now safely on their backs and unconscious).

Comedy in this film works by portraying the heroines operating both within and outside the prescribed gender roles of the 1950s. They are not Good Girls holding glass slippers waiting to be found; they are out there taking action to get what they want: a rich guy to buy their groceries, pay off their debts and marry them. At one point, they actually step outside the law by selling off the furniture in their sublet for extra cash. By the end of the movie, however, the normative gendered dynamics between the men and women are re-established: the men are portrayed as being the subjects of their own desires and the women as objects of that desire. The *mise-en-scène* of the movie maximizes the screen presence of these three fabulous women so that they became objects of either desire or identification for the men and women viewing it.

Certainly, the constriction of these gendered roles as well as the thinly veiled allusion to prostitution went over my 14-year-old Catholic school-girl head when I first saw *How to Marry a Millionaire* (1953). In fact, I can't remember what I thought – all I *remember* is the image of Marilyn in that red sequined gown multiplied in a parade of mirrors across the CinemaScope screen. Her luminous presence went into me like a physical event that quickened my life as a newly forming female person.

In retrospect, I understand my adolescent experience of Marilyn as my narcissistic identification with her cinematic presence that I internalized as part of my ego development and gender identity – an identification that privileged the power of being a desirable woman over the power of acting on my own desires. However, my experience was also an embodied emotional response to an image of female power, sexuality and beauty that was unavailable – even unacceptable – within the cultural and familial constraints of my everyday life. Marilyn's image carried for me the emotional charge of the shadow archetype – an image that my psyche metabolized at the level of body consciousness that awakened me to unlived aspects of my personality even as it disrupted the emotional equilibrium of my conscious sense of self. Suffice it to say that versions of this kind of emotional, visceral incorporation of film images account for the power of popular film to not only express our gendered roles but to actually participate in conditioning them.

My fascination with movies – especially with the portrayal of women in movies – became a more conscious endeavor over the years and functioned as a way to reflect upon and to understand my life, even when my feminist intuitions railed against the constriction of women's roles. The portrayal of women in films focused my attention on the gendered dynamics that conditioned women's lives. Paradoxically, it also allowed me to begin the process of deconstructing these dynamics in my own life. That is to say, beyond the ways in which movies reinforce traditional gender roles, they also unintentionally undermined conventional gender roles in their portrayal of women:

> If it is true, as many suggest, that Hollywood films repressed women and sought to teach them what they ought to do, then it is equally clear that, in order to achieve this, the movies first had to bring to life the opposite of their own morality. To convince women that marriage and motherhood were the right path, movies had to show women making the mistake of doing something else. By making the Other live on the screen, movies made it real. By making it real, they made it desirable. By making it desirable, they made it possible. They gave the Other substance, and they gave it credibility. In asking the question, What should a woman do with her life? they created the possibility of an answer different from the one they intended to provide at the end of the movie.
>
> (Basinger 1993: 6)

Jeanine Basinger's view provides an alternative feminist perspective to the one within the dominant academic feminist discourse. The latter condemns mainstream narrative film as inherently phallocentric: women are viewed on screen as the castrated passive objects of the male gaze – the active gaze of the fully endowed spectator. According to this theory, all that remains for the female viewer is the conflict between her identification with the power of the female image and its constraints within the film narrative (Mulvey 1990).

While I understand this theory and can align with aspects of it, I find myself in agreement with Polly Young-Eisendrath that "both women and men are poorly served by theoretical constructs in which gendered differences are defined in terms of lacks and deficits with pathological responses to those lacks as normative" (1998: 201). Similarly, I find that we are poorly served by film theories in which gendered differences as portrayed in mainstream narrative film are perceived to be rigidly and inherently structured by the cinematic codes of film-making itself: the techniques of its making and the contexts for its viewing. Such a theory proposes that the only way to circumvent the confinement of these cinematic codes is to create a passionate detachment between the spectator and the film images on the screen – for the spectator to become a critical observer rather than an illicit participant. This is an intellectual distancing from being manipulated as the spectator of the film. It is also a defense against being moved by the emotional experience of the film as well as a defense against the unconscious response to that emotional experience.

In contrast, a Jungian approach appreciates the capacity of film to bring ego consciousness into relationship with the unconscious through the emotional power of film itself (Izod 2000: 267–285). Jung understood the power of images as the natural language of the unconscious – that it is through images and dreams that the psyche reveals itself. Jung also emphasized emotion as "the chief source of consciousness. There is no change from darkness to light or from inertia to movement without emotion" (Jung 1954, *CW* 9I: para. 179, as quoted in Izod 2000: 271). Viewing film invites us into a transitional space of communal dreaming, in which the ego is immersed in the emotional experience of the film that can move us below consciously held attitudes. This is valuing film's capacity to open us to "a form of thinking through the body, often affecting us most forcefully at those junctures of experience that lie between our accustomed categories of thought" (MacDougall 1998: 49). Rather than intellectually distancing from the pleasure of viewing film to avoid being manipulated by what the movie lacks, the spectator is *revisioned* as a participant-observer who holds the tension between being moved by what the film expresses and being aware of what it fails to represent.

When I use Hollywood films as metaphorical points of reference with my patients in analysis, I work from within this awareness. As with fairy tales, films can speak to us of universal human issues at the level of the imagination, providing objective images to reveal compensatory psychic elements outside of our own subjective experience. When the tale or film is introduced into a therapeutic environment, there is a chance that the power of fantasy can be revived in order to soften the hardened fixations of the patient's internal world, a softening of the fixed order that allows the possibility of a different order (Kast 1998: 119). I believe this chance is increased with the utilization of film because of its capacity to evoke shared experience. When the patient or I reference a particular film in an analytic session, there is the chance that both of us have seen it; that we will have both been inside the same story; that we will have both experienced the same dream. Entering that shared imaginal space is not a detour from the transference/countertransference dynamics; rather, it can be an addition to the already established body of shared images and understandings woven into the fabric of the analytic relationship itself. Of course, the attunement of the analyst to the patient's ability to make use of such a therapeutic intervention is always a consideration.

Working with films as metaphorical points of reference in analysis is particularly relevant in exploring gendered dynamics with women analysands. Reflecting on specific gendering practices within film narratives provides a cultural lens through which they can begin to observe and to speculate on how gendered dynamics function in their own lives; on what human qualities are core to their subjective sense of self; on what qualities are left out, repressed and projected onto the opposite sex.

Both *How to Marry A Millionaire* and a 1990 variation on the same theme, *Pretty Woman*, depict the disparity in traditional gendered roles. While the *style* of the interactions between women and men has shifted in the thirty-seven years between the making of these two movies, the gender dynamics within them remain remarkably similar. That is to say, in these films women's subjective sense of self is confirmed within the boundaries of being the relationally vulnerable object of desire, of wanting to be wanted. Self-determination and essential human aggression are split off, repressed and covered over by a self-involvement in the emotional outcomes of others. Men's subjective sense of self is confirmed within the boundaries of being the assertive self-reliant subject of action. Relational vulnerability and feelings in general are split off, repressed, and walled off by a manic self-involvement in work.

*Pretty Woman* is a filmic fairy tale. It's about a handsome, sophisticated, wealthy Edward (Richard Gere) who, disenchanted with his privileged life, finds himself re-enchanted by his "hired" companion, Vivian (Julia Roberts). In *Pygmalion* style, she learns to remake herself within the accepted norms of the upper class. Unlike the 1953 version, however, she does some interior decorating of her own: she points out to Edward that they are in the same business: "We both screw people for money." Their week of love allows Edward to feel more vulnerable – capable of having feelings – and allows Vivian to feel more autonomous

– capable of going back to school. Both are changed by their relationship, albeit in mutually unrealistic ways.

This is a story about a prostitute and a businessman – and of her becoming the object of his sovereign subjectivity. The autonomous actions she takes are limited to spending his money – which does not add up to being a self-determining subject of her own desire. Despite the fact that she demands to be loved and not just wanted, the mutuality of their love is undermined by the inequality of power in the relationship. The outcome is traditional: she gives up her "work" in order to gain his "love."

Why would I use these two Hollywood movies as a therapeutic point of reference? Because analysands go to the movies and movies take up residence in the mythic layers of their psyches and are therefore psychologically relevant to their lives. I have used these and other films, depending upon the age of the woman, to interpret developmental lacks and neurotic splits that occur along gender lines. This might include, for example, confronting the false bravado in women whose autonomous action is limited to spending other people's money.

Despite Freud's famous prescription for human happiness, "Love and Work," our gender roles tend to promote the development of one or the other. Men get to be grown-ups in the world of work and babies at home, while women get to be babies in the world of work and grown-ups at home. This sexual arrangement determines that a major domain of human experience in both women and men remains undeveloped (Dinnerstein 1976).

*Broadcast News* (1987) is a story of three professional people caught in the intersecting demands of love and work, between relational vulnerability and autonomous self-reliance. Tom (William Hurt) is a charming TV anchorman with good looks, who is reasonably ambitious, but with limited intelligence and integrity. Aaron (Albert Brooks) is an intelligent news reporter with integrity, who is reasonably good looking and ambitious, but with limited charm. Jane (Holly Hunter) is an intelligent TV news producer with ambition and integrity, who is reasonably good looking, but with a limited capacity for relationship.

This movie reverses traditional gendered roles by its portrayal of Jane as an autonomous woman who gains career success at the expense of relational intimacy. This woman, neurotic in her self-reliance, lives out the ideals of self-sufficiency while splitting off her sexual desires. Throughout the movie she never makes it with either guy, although both give her plenty of opportunity. The only relief she allows herself from the pressures of work is to sob on cue when she is alone. Both men achieve varying degrees of success, but they also express their vulnerability and need for relationship – elements missing in the woman's character.

Clinically, it is not uncommon for women to feel cut off from and even ignorant of their capacity to experience sexual pleasure fully. If men are perceived as the active subjects of sexual desire and women as the passive objects of that desire, a self-determining woman might unconsciously avoid relational intimacy (Young-Eisendrath 1999: 63). At the same time, a relationally identified woman might also avoid sexual intimacy because it feels like one more way to meet someone else's needs. Whether a woman's subjective sense of self is formed in alignment with or against gendered expectations for women, if human sexual arousal and passion are defined only in terms of the male orgasm, her saying "No" to sex becomes a form of self-assertion.

I work with women in analysis on both sides of the struggle to become fully empowered subjects of their lives in both love and work. For the purposes of this essay, I will present two case examples. Sally is a married woman in her early forties who appeared to have it all, including a successful career and children. She began to see me for psychotherapy because she had fallen in love with a younger male colleague with whom she was having an affair. She was confused, anxious and deeply ashamed – but could not give him up. Their shared sexual experience awakened in her an intensity and a passion that she had glimpsed only as a much younger woman.

We tracked how and when she had put away any expectation for sexual satisfaction in her marriage. As a part of that tracking, the female character in *Broadcast News* became an emblem for both the focus she had brought to her professional pursuits as well as the distance she had imposed on sexual intimacy. She has come to see that her withdrawal from sexual intimacy was her attempt to avoid the constriction of married life – a constriction she saw her sister and mother endure. Gradually she has realized that while she had developed a mature sense of herself professionally, she had remained undeveloped emotionally. In her marriage, she had dissociated her relational and sexual needs as well as her husband's in order to avoid facing the real problems in their relationship.

In contrast, Ann, also in her mid-forties, had not yet reached her career potential. While she worked hard, promotions were always given to others. Ann sought psychotherapy because she felt herself losing out on career opportunities. She was vivacious, attractive and relationally adept.

As a younger woman, she could always count on finding a man willing to make things happen for her career, to a point. Through her analysis she began to realize that her expectations for success had never been met and that when they weren't, she would fall into learned helplessness. In time, she has come to understand that she has spent her energy trying to attract the help she needed rather than using her own self-agency to take actions on her own behalf. In reflecting on *Broadcast News* she came to realize that what was missing in her personality was a modified version of the focus and self-agency portrayed by Holly Hunter – a self-agency that in the past she projected onto men but that she now recognizes as her own responsibility.

Current gender studies suggest that our identification and dis-identifications with personality traits according to gender are culturally designated roles that permit societies to assign women and men different potentials and tasks (Young-Eisendrath 1998: 203). The projection of unlived or unacceptable parts of the self onto the opposite sex is a central component of gender conditioning. As our conscious personality develops, we identify with particular images, fantasies and experiences of gender, body and self. Alongside this conscious personality, an equally powerful counter-personality (or complex) develops in the unconscious. I and others assume that we must deconstruct and reformulate the images we have metabolized as part of our gender identity in order to integrate projected aspects of ourselves (Flax 1993).

Jung understood projection as a means by which unconscious contents can be made available to ego consciousness. The encounter of the "other" in the external world, including the "other" portrayed in film images, provides the raw material to be activated by projection. Such an encounter can initiate the process of accessing rejected parts of the self in the inner world thus allowing ego consciousness to differentiate between what has been lived and what remains repressed and undeveloped (Samuels *et al.* 1986: 113–114). In the case examples cited above, Holly Hunter's character serves as the raw material for the projections of both analysands: Sally has come to be aware of her repressed sexuality in alignment with the protagonist, while Ann has come to be aware of her undeveloped self-agency in contrast to the protagonist.

Gaining awareness of the projected unconscious aspects of self is an initial step in the ego's differentiation from and relationship to the unconscious. Further analytic work requires the conscious confrontation and understanding of the unconscious patterns of being that have constricted one's life. But this is not the final goal of Jungian psychology. Beyond this process, Jung envisioned the "optimum relationship between the ego and the rest of the psyche as a continuous dialogue. By definition, this is a never-ending process. What changes is the nature of the conversation" (Salman 1997: 55). Over time, both within the analytic process and beyond it, this dialogic relationship facilitates the confrontation and integration of contents from both the personal and the collective unconscious that expand and deepen one's subjective sense of self to include a sense of wholeness.

But what happens when life circumstances and psychological predisposition preclude any possibility of developing a conscious relationship with the unconscious – when repressed unconscious contents inhibit conscious functioning and subsequently break through ego control? Jung referred to this phenomenon as an *enantiodromia*: the eruption of compensatory contents from the unconscious in opposition to consciously held attitudes (Samuels *et al.* 1986: 53).

In the film *Thelma and Louise* (1991), we see two women caught in the extremes of an *enantiodromia* – a flip from a consciously held attitude into an unconscious opposite. Louise (Susan Sarandon) encourages Thelma (Geena Davis) to go away for a weekend. Thelma tries to ask her controlling husband for permission to go but can't – so she leaves him a note in the microwave and takes off. They stop at a dance bar, belt down a few drinks and dance with a couple of guys. One puts the make on Thelma and then tries to rape her in the parking lot – but Louise stops him. He continues his verbal abuse. Louise shoots and kills him. The rest of the film tracks their frantic effort to escape the law of the land and the law of psychic compensation as they swing frantically between manic aggression and hopeless desperation.

The tragedy of the film is that neither woman had life experiences that allowed them to see or trust other options. And why should they? Not only were they unpracticed at being the subjects of their own desires, but they had only experienced dominating aggression or passive resistance from the men in their lives. If a woman has not experienced her own capacity to make choices that impact on her life and the lives of others, she can't imagine that the possibility even exists.

As the two women try to make their escape, they experience the expansion of personality that comes from making choices as well as a manic compulsivity that results from a closing down of options. They end up robbing a store, blowing up an 18-wheeler and accosting a cop. In the middle of taking these desperate actions, they nevertheless experience new parts of themselves. Thelma says, "Something's crossed over in me. I can't go back. I mean, I just couldn't live." And later: "I feel awake. Wide awake. I never remember feeling this awake. Know what

I mean? Everything looks different. You feel like that, too? Like you got something to look forward to?"

When I saw this film, the women in the audience cheered for Thelma and Louise. My sense was that they identified with the two protagonists as the latter experienced new parts of themselves by acting on their own behalf. What was not portrayed, however, was how a woman can take her life into her own hands, leave home, drive down a road into a new life and *not* be driven over an edge. I have often had occasion to use this film clinically to differentiate between acting in *reaction* versus acting in *response* to life's circumstances, and to articulate how self-transformation accumulates through small actions over time accompanied by an awareness of one's limitations and strengths. I point out that the ironic tragedy for Thelma and Louise was that although their actions did accumulate into making choices, their final choice was to be the subjects of their own deaths rather than the subjects of a different kind of life.

*The Piano* (1993) is a film offering an alternative outcome in the struggle to choose between death and life – between the constriction and the expansion of one's subjective sense of self. It also offers rich opportunities for gendered and relational reflections: the penetration of sexual intimacy that awakens the soul; the fury of revenge against the unfaithful other; the rigidity of withdrawal as a protection for the self. However, the images from the closing sequence are the ones that most often find their way into clinical significance with my patients. These images evoke a palpable experience of the ongoing dialogic relationship between the conscious and the unconscious that Jung considered the *sine qua non* of individuation.

This closing sequence begins with Ada (Holly Hunter) and her lover, Baines (Harvey Keitel), returning to the isolated beach where she was first put ashore in New Zealand with her piano and her daughter. It was also the beach where we saw Ada's desperation when Stewart (Sam Neill), the man she was to marry, demanded that the piano be left behind because it was too heavy. Now, having survived the trials and passions that reconfigured their lives, Ada and Baines prepare to leave for a new life together. But this time, it is Ada who wants to leave the piano behind.

As they are paddled across the waters in a sea canoe, the precariously balanced piano is referred to as a "coffin." It increasingly threatens the stability of the boat and Ada demands that it be thrown overboard. As it plunges into the sea, her old attachment takes hold: she slips her foot into the coiled rope tied to the piano and in the next instant she is pulled under the sea. As the piano sinks, so does she. Floating above her piano, she holds her breath, and waits. Then a different decision compels her to free her foot and she flees to the surface to breathe new life.

Reflecting on these images with analysands permits us to witness those complexes that function as their "piano." We can re-experience the power of complexes to drag us down against our conscious intentions – and imagine how we unconsciously re-entangle ourselves in constricting habits-of-being precisely at the point when we have the capacity to move beyond them. We feel with Ada the regressive pull of old attachments – the lure of falling back into her silent, schizoid isolation in which the piano was her only object relation. We recognize her ambivalence in risking a love relationship that will require her to change and to develop. But we can also feel her refusal to stay unconscious – a refusal that compels her to the surface against ties to the piano. This scene embodies a truth about psychological change: that no one can claim new capacities without sacrificing their attachment to former ways of being (Williams 1998: 229).

And yet, as the next scene reveals, Ada's attachment to the piano was not severed, but transformed. We hear Ada's child-self speak with surprise that her will has chosen life and that she is learning to speak. We see her in the light of day slowly developing ego capacities, including being in relationship with Baines. Then the image and the voice-over shifts again to the silent realm below, with Ada floating in a non-verbal world still tied to her piano. Her child-voice continues:

> At night I think of my piano in its ocean grave and sometimes of myself floating above it. Down there everything is so still and silent that it lulls me to sleep. It is a weird lullaby and so it is; it is mine.
> There is a silence where hath been no sound.
> There is a silence where no sound may be,
> In the cold grave – under the deep, deep sea . . .
> (Campion and Pullinger 1994: 215)

This final scene of the *The Piano* invites an attitude toward images from the unconscious described by James Hillman: "We should not lose the dream in the light of day; rather, we should visit the land of dream and be affected by the peculiarities of that world" (1990: 6, quoted in Izod 2000: 276). As viewers, we are dropped into the "land of dream" to experience the peculiarities of Ada's lullaby – that is to say, to experience the image as a generative activity of mind in which the image functions as a link between a conscious subject and an unknown (Kotsch 2000: 226). Ada's lullaby revisits the image of herself tied to the piano, a symbol of the complex that once constrained her life but now lives within her psyche as a point of entry into the depths.

Making use of film with a woman in analysis can allow for the articulation of her gender identity and the confrontation of shadow components in her personality. As these shadow components are engaged within the dynamics of the analytic process – including transference dynamics – we lay the ground for understanding, accepting and having compassion for those habits of being that once constricted her life. However, it is in the active engagement of the symbolic power of images (including filmic images) emerging from within this process that the analysand is initiated into an ongoing dialogue with the unconscious, a dialogue with the potential to connect her to more than either she or I can know.

## References

Basinger, J. (1993) *A Woman's View: How Hollywood Spoke to Women*, New England, Hanover and London: Wesleyan University Press.

Campion, J. and Pullinger, K. (1994) *The Piano*, New York: Miramax & Hyperion.

Dinnerstein, D. (1976) *The Mermaid and the Minotaur: Sexual Arrangements and Human Malaise*, New York: Harper & Row.

Flax, J. (1993) *Disputed Subjects: Essays on Psychoanalysis, Politics and Philosophy*, New York and London: Routledge.

Izod, J. (2000) "Active Imagination and the Analysis of Film," *Journal of Analytical Psychology* 45, 2: 267–285.

Jung, C.G. (1954) "Psychological Aspects of the Mother Archetype", in *The Archetypes and the Collective Unconscious* (*CW* 9I).

Kast, V. (1998) "Can You Change Your Fate? The Clinical Use of a Fairytale as the Turning Point in Analysis", in A. Casement (ed.) *Post-Jungians Today: Key Papers in Contemporary Analytical Psychology*, London and New York: Routledge.

Kotsch, W. (2000) "Jung's Mediatory Science as a Psychology Beyond Objectivism," *Journal of Analytical Psychology* 45, 2: 217–244.

MacDougall, D. (1998) *Transcultural Cinema*, Princeton: Princeton University Press.

Mulvey, L. (1990) "Visual Pleasure and Narrative Cinema," in P. Evans (ed.) *Issues in Feminist Film Criticism*, Bloomington: Indiana University Press.

Salman, S. (1997) "The Creative Psyche: Jung's Major Contribution," in P. Young-Eisendrath and T. Dawson (eds) *The Cambridge Companion to Jung*, Cambridge: Cambridge University Press.

Samuels, A., Shorter, B., and Plaut, F. (1986) *A Critical Dictionary of Jungian Analysis*, London: Routledge & Kegan Paul Ltd.

Williams, D. (1998) "The Piano: From Constriction to Connection," in M.L. Kittelson (ed.) *The Soul of Popular Culture: Looking at Contemporary Heroes, Myths and Monsters*, LaSalle and Chicago: Open Court.

Young-Eisendrath, P. (1998) "Contrasexuality and the Dialectic of Desire," in A. Casement (ed.) *Post-Jungians Today: Key Papers in Contemporary Analytical Psychology*, London and New York: Routledge.

—— (1999) *Women and Desire: Beyond Wanting To Be Wanted*, New York: Harmony Books.

# Chapter 11

# The *anima* in film*

## John Beebe

The *anima* in film is much like the *anima* anywhere else:[1] a confusing, deceptive presence with the capacity to engender inner transformation. Perhaps the only advantage a filmgoer has (in common with the individual who can remember dreams) is that the archetype is visible as well as effective. For that reason, I have frequently turned to movies to understand better the typical role of the *anima*, and my hunger, as a clinician, to get a clearer sense of the functioning of this unconscious feminine presence has not gone unsatisfied. What I will offer here is a guide for exploring the *anima* through film, as well as an indication of some things film has helped me to discover about the *anima*'s function in relation to other archetypes of the psyche, most particularly the persona.

I do not think it is appropriate to call every woman in film an *anima* figure, although the luminous representation has the important characteristic of turning a human being into an image that can be manipulated to aesthetic effect by a supraordinate creative personality, the film director. The director's role in making a film is already, therefore, not unlike that of the Self in creating dreams. The Self seeks to achieve the goals of the total psyche by affective stimulation of the ego; it does this through images that are not so much representations of reality as feeling-toned complexes of unconscious life. These complexes are, however, often made to simulate conscious reality and especially significant persons so that consciousness will take heed of the "home truths" they are there to convey. Of these feeling-toned complexes that mediate, in the regulation of psychic balance, between Self and ego, none has such a memorable effect as the *anima*. (This is why so many women are not content with Jung's insistence that their mediating figure appears as a male, the *animus*.) In a movie, the importance of the female image in stimulating emotionally relevant fantasy is obvious. One has only to point

*Figure 11.1* Greta Garbo in *The Story of Gosta Berling* (1924) Image Courtesy of Jerry Ohlinger's Movie Material Store, Inc., New York

out the heavy emphasis the motion-picture medium has always placed upon its leading actresses.

Not every leading female character in a film is an *anima* figure, but often there are unmistakable signs that an unconscious, rather than conscious, figure is intended. It may be useful at the outset to specify some of these signs:

1   Unusual radiance (e.g., Garbo, Monroe). Often the most amusing and gripping aspect of a movie is to watch ordinary actors or actresses (e.g., Melvyn Douglas and Ina Claire in *Ninotchka*) contend with a more mind-blowing presence – a star personality who seems to draw life from a source beyond the mundane (e.g., Garbo in the same film). This inner radiance is one sign of the *anima* – and it is why actresses asked to portray the *anima* so often are spoken of as stars and are chosen more for their uncanny presence, whether or not they are particularly good at naturalistic characterization.

2   A desire to make emotional connection as the main concern of the character. One of the ways to distinguish an actual woman is her need to be able to say "no," as part of the assertion of her own identity and being.[2] (Part of the comedy of Katharine Hepburn is that she can usually only say no, so that when she finally says "yes," we know it stands as an affirmation of an independent woman's actual being.) By contrast, the *anima* figure wants to be loved, or occasionally to be hated, in either case living for connection, as is consistent with her general role as representative of the status of the man's unconscious eros and particularly his relationship to himself. (Ingrid Bergman, in *Notorious*, keeps asking Cary Grant, verbally and nonverbally, whether he loves her. We feel her hunger for connection and anticipate that he will come alive only if he says "yes." His affect is frozen by cynicism and can only be redeemed by his acceptance of her need for connection.)

3   Having come from some quite other place into the midst of a reality more familiar to us than the character's own place of origin. (Audrey Hepburn, in *Roman Holiday*, is a princess visiting Rome who decides to escape briefly into the life a commoner might be able to enjoy on a first trip to that city.)

4   The character is the feminine mirror of traits we have already witnessed in the attitude or behavior of another, usually male, character. (Marlene Dietrich as a seductive cabaret singer performing before her audience in *The Blue Angel* displays the cold authoritarianism of the gymnasium professor of English, Emil Jannings, who manipulates the students' fear of him in the opening scene of the movie. Jannings pacing back and forth in front of his class and resting against his desk as he holds forth are mirrored in Dietrich's controlling stride and aggressive seated posture in front of her audience.)

5   The character has some unusual capacity for life, in vivid contrast to other characters in the film. (The one young woman in the office of

stony bureaucrats in *Ikiru* is able to laugh at almost anything. When she meets her boss, Watanabe, just at the point that he has learned that he has advanced stomach cancer and is uninterested in eating anything, she has an unusual appetite for food and greedily devours all that he buys her.)

6    The character offers a piece of advice, frequently couched in the form of an almost unacceptable rebuke, which has the effect of changing another character's relation to a personal reality. (The young woman in *Ikiru* scorns Watanabe's depressed confession that he has wasted his life living for his son. Shortly after, still in her presence, Watanabe is suddenly enlightened to his life task, which will be to use the rest of his life living for children, this time by expediting the building of a playground that his own office, along with the other agencies of the city bureaucracy, has been stalling indefinitely with red tape. He finds his destiny and fulfillment in his own nature as a man who is meant to dedicate his life to the happiness of others, exactly within the pattern he established after his wife's death years before, of living for his son's development rather than to further himself. The *anima* figure rescues his authentic relationship to himself, which requires a tragic acceptance of this self-sacrificing pattern as his individuation and his path to self-transcendence.)

7    The character exerts a protective and often therapeutic effect on someone else. (The young widow in *Tender Mercies* helps Robert Duvall overcome the alcoholism that has threatened his career.)

8    Less positively, the character leads another character to recognize a problem in personality that is insoluble. (In Nicholas Ray's *In a Lonely Place*, the antisocial screenwriter played by Humphrey Bogart meets an *anima* figure played – with a face to match the cool mask of his own – by Gloria Grahame, who cannot overcome her mounting doubts about him enough to accept him as a husband. Her failure to overcome her ambivalence is a precise indicator of the extent of the damage that exists in his relationship to himself.)

9    The loss of this character is associated with the loss of purposeful aliveness itself. (The premise of *L'Avventura* is the disappearance of Anna, who has been accompanied to an island by her lover, a middle-aged architect with whom she has been having an unhappy affair. We never get to know Anna well enough to understand the basis of her unhappiness, because she disappears so early in the film, but we soon discover that the man who is left behind is in a state of archetypal ennui, a moral collapse characterized by an aimlessly cruel sexual

pursuit of one of Anna's friends and a spoiling envy of the creativity of a younger man who can still take pleasure in making a drawing of an Italian building.)

Simply recognizing a character in a film as an *anima* figure does not exhaust the meaningfulness of what an analytic approach to cinema can unlock. The true interest of this approach comes when, through it, the dynamics of a cinematic experience of the *anima* are revealed and one can see how the figure herself changes in relation to the character whose life she affects. In film, as in no other medium, we can actually see the behavior of the archetype; in life, we know her far more indirectly, as moods, impulses, symptoms, and as a shape-shifting fleeting personage in our dreams – if, indeed, we can remember them. In film, we can see the *anima* figure over time, in a more or less stable guise, at her strange task of mediating the fate of a protagonist. We are permitted to watch as the *anima* relates to the other complexes of a psyche.

A way to understand a film psychologically is to take its various characters as signifying complexes, parts of a single personality whose internal object relations are undergoing change.[3] These object relations are represented by the interactions of the characters, who usually include a figure representing the *anima*. Because the relation of the *anima* to other complexes is of particular interest to a therapist, I have often recommended to therapists that they use the movies they view in their leisure time to train themselves in visualizing the internal relationships involved. In addition to increasing their own enjoyment of films, those who have followed my advice have often found that their sensitivity, within analytic work, to dream and associative material is greatly improved. This exercise, following in the Jungian tradition of having analysts-in-training engage in the interpretation of fairy tales, has the advantage that the material studied for archetypal comparison to clinical material is drawn from the same culture as our patients. It also draws a therapist deeper into what is essentially a new ritual context for the immersion into visionary archetypal experience.

Film-making, at least in the hands of its acknowledged masters, is a form of active imagination drawing its imagery from the anxieties generated by current concerns, and film watching has become a contemporary ritual that is only apparently a leisure.[4] Going to movies has achieved, in this country, almost the status of a religious activity. As a teacher, I have found that seminars built around the showing of a movie rich in imaginal material have been more successful in getting students to enter into a dialogue with images than my similar efforts to work with materials drawn from a more remote culture form, and I think this is because the viewing of films is numinous for us. Few myths impact contemporary Americans the way the films of Spielberg, Coppola, and Lynch do.

I would like to examine here the work of a somewhat less immediately familiar triad of American directors, out of a potential pool of dozens of similar rank who have worked within our mainstream Hollywood tradition of using commercially established stars, cinematographers, and scripts to create works of art that are as meaningful as they are entertaining. The directors that I have chosen are undisputed *auteurs* who have particularly concerned themselves with the *anima*.[5] Both in their obsessive devotion to certain female stars and in the seductiveness of their ability to make good scripts built around movie formulas come alive enough to seem real, George Cukor, Alfred Hitchcock, and Peter Bogdanovich belong to the culture of *anima*, so much, in fact, that it sometimes feels as if the *anima* chose these directors to make her presence visible to us in our time.

In what follows, I will address films by these directors – *A Star is Born*, *Vertigo*, and *Mask* – that express the extreme of their inspiration by the *anima* archetype, films that I would call masterpieces of the *anima*. They are also exercises in personal film-making. In each of these films, the neurosis of the *auteur*, or at least that of his creative personality, is painfully evident.[6]

Each takes as its starting point a major malfunction of a hero's persona that threatens permanently to impair this male character's ability to work or find love. Each of these films, as is characteristic of movies about the *anima*, engages this wounded character with an *anima* figure who is symbolic of a deeper aspect of his suffering and who attempts to move his psyche beyond it. However, in these films, she fails. None of the films lead to an enduring, happy connection with the *anima* or to genuine transformation. The function of the *anima* here is significantly more tragic than therapeutic: her presence serves to deepen our sense of the hero's suffering, and to make us, and him, accept it as his fate.

These films were released in America between 1953 and 1985, but they share the distinction of finding special favor with critics and audiences grown sophisticated enough to appreciate their imaginal power at a particularly self-reflective moment in the history of film watching, 1983 to 1985, when the sense of a lull in the general level of current American films combined with the widespread availability of American movie classics on videocassette led a mass audience to undertake what until then only cinema buffs had been able to pursue – a basic reexamination of the entire corpus of the American cinema. This kind of reflection on an aesthetic tradition is itself an *anima* activity, one that the archetype will insist upon at times when its further evolution in life or in art seems blocked by an excessive insistence upon persona values. The period just before and just after Reagan was elected to his second term was such a time, when a one-sided interest in what the hero "can do" was in evidence. It is not unfitting that, at this point in our history, the great American war-horses of *anima* disappointment, *A Star is Born* and *Vertigo*, films about what the hero could not do, would be re-released in their restored or rediscovered wide screen formats and that they would generate in theaters the kind of interest that is usually reserved for new films. It is more surprising that Peter Bogdanovich, whose early career had involved him in the role of American film appreciator celebrating our *auteurs* of the hero archetype, Ford and Hawks and Welles, would be able to break through with *Mask*, a great new American film putting forward so solidly the *anima* theme of the hero's failure. Bogdanovich's film is in the tradition of the hard-boiled sentimentality and macabre kitsch of his earlier masters, who could satirize heroic aspirations, but it is less macho in its assertion that an ideal relationship to the *anima* on the hero's terms in not an American possibility and more gracious in its acceptance of the necessity for the defeat of the hero.

## A Star is Born

George Cukor's *A Star is Born* draws explicit life from the assumption that its audience will be steeped in Hollywood culture. It begins with the crackling of carbon arc lights coming alive to illuminate the skies of Hollywood for a premiere; much later in the film we will hear Judy Garland's electric voice cry out "lights!" as she begins to pantomime a production number she has been rehearsing for the cameras.

The story is about the birth of the star portrayed by Garland, but in Cukor's handling the real theme is the culture of film turning a searchlight upon itself. Judy Garland, as a band singer pulled into a new career in the movie business, becomes the image of a bewildered creative conscious-ness assimilating the many ironies of film-making itself. These ironies are presented as pitfalls of the studio system, but it is clear that the resonance is to the introverted problems of the creative process as well. Film-making is, above all, what Andrew Sarris has called "a very strenuous form of contemplation" (1968: 37), and in many films a leading actress becomes the personification of the director's meditative stance toward the materials of story, acting, photography, and music.

In *A Star is Born*, Garland becomes the image of Cukor's approach to creativity. The person she is here could not have been the prototype for any actual woman initiating a career: she is far too reactive to the man in her life and to Hollywood itself. Moreover, she is not particularly good at shaping herself even to these expectations. As a comeback vehicle for Judy Garland, the movie was a disaster, despite its excellent critical reputation and its part in securing her niche as cinema legend, but its depiction of the middle-aged commercial Hollywood artist's *anima*, the demonic energy, the androgyny, the slightly worn and worried look, and the now puffy, now beautiful head of Garland, and even the grandiosity and tiresome intensity of this fascinating but self-destructive star, work to the director's advantage. Making everything too much is a hallmark of the *anima*, and Garland indelibly conveys the intensity of the Hollywood *auteur* in imposing meaning on a commercial film. The frightening aspect of this dark film musical – and not just its plot, but the murky tones of its Technicolor qualify it as a true color *noir* film – is the way the *anima* of the film-making totally overtakes the persona, so that reasonable proportions give way to overproduction and melodrama. This is the subtext of Vicki Lester (Garland) supplanting Norman Maine, the Barrymore-ish star who discovered her. By the time of Maine's suicide, Vicki Lester is able to present herself accurately to her public as "Mrs Norman Maine."

Throughout Moss Hart's script, a grandiose Hollywood possibility is followed by a grim Hollywood reality (for instance: "the wedding to end all weddings" ends up getting held in a county jail, to avoid the press), but Hart's jokes at the expense of the Hollywood persona have for Cukor the larger meaning that the persona is losing control to another archetype. The songs of the score – most particularly "The Man That Got Away" – reemphasize the loss of masculine identity (protested for most of the movie by James Mason as the doomed Norman Maine) in favor of the archetypal emotionality represented by Garland. In the end, the movie's command of voice and dialogue and gesture (as ably defended by Mason's performance) give way to an overwhelming presence, mood, and intensity, as personified by Garland, whose unconscious energy is more interesting than her conscious skill at character portrayal. Yet Mason and Garland are in vivid relationship to each other. To watch Garland lust after James Mason's mastery, and Mason appreciate and envy Garland's magnetism, is to participate in a mystery at the core of cinema experience, the interplay between movie star and actor expressing a reciprocal tension between *anima* and persona. Cukor's appreciation of the neurotic dynamics of this relationship in the work of cinema artists is what makes this movie great, especially in its mad moments, like the one where Norman Maine walks into the midst of his wife's Academy Award acceptance speech to make a drunken pitch for a job and ends up smacking her in the face with the back of the hand he stretches out to make a point.

*A Star is Born* is not the only movie where a director works out of the tension between a command of style that is losing ground and a capacity for creative expression that is still vibrant (Federico Fellini's *Ginger and Fred* has exactly this theme), but I think it is by far the greatest one, raising this peculiar problem to the status of creative tragedy. In *A Star is Born*, Cukor delivers one of Hollywood's seminal lessons: even though movies are nothing without stars that can act, stars are finally more important than actors to the emotional effect of a screen experience. This is a truth that the actual Academy Awards loves to obscure, with its frequent honoring of thespians like F. Murray Abraham, Geraldine Page, and Jessica Tandy, and its slighting of authentic movie stars, like Chaplin and Garbo and Garland, and of *auteur* directors, like Hitchcock and Spielberg, who understand how to turn actors into images. (Look at *The Prince and the Showgirl* and watch what happens when Laurence Olivier is pitted against Marilyn Monroe.) What Monroe and Garbo and Garland understand with their star acting (which, despite their occasional ambitions, was never of the Broadway or London variety) is that film, unlike the stage, is not a medium of actors, but of actors' images. The actors are not up there on the screen, their images are; and this translation of person into image is crucially important psychologically, because it moves film past the personal and into the archetypal realm of psychological experience.

When, in the first decade of this century, Griffith adapted the new "trick photography" effect of the close-up and projected gigantic "severed heads" of actors upon the screen, cinema became a medium for our direct engagement with archetypes. A cinematic close-up is analogous to an aria in opera, a moment when a timeless dimension of human experience can be caught and contemplated (Balázs 1985). But once the archetypes are summoned, they take on their own life. The magical moment in *A Star is Born* where Garland (entertaining Mason) looks out at us and says, "Now here comes a big fat close-up!" framing her face with her own panning hands, is extraordinary not just because it reveals the role of the *anima* in creating the close-up, but because the *anima* wrests control of her own image away from the director. It is in the nature itself of the *anima* to use a medium to create images of herself and to concern herself with the style of these images. This relationship between the *anima* and the image of herself that she creates is corollary to the intense interaction between *anima* and persona.

Perhaps the most telling example of this dynamic comes as a silent monologue played out on Judy Garland's face, as the band singer is being readied for her first screen test. While the make-up men recite possibilities for dealing with the lack of statement in her visage, Garland, staring into a make-up mirror, tries on the arched look of "the Dietrich eyebrow" and puffs her lips to get the fullness of "the Crawford mouth." Then, for a fleeting moment, she stares in despair at her own trapped and suddenly shapeless face, the personification of an *anima* without an image, wondering if she will ever find one.

## Vertigo

That this anxiety lies at the core of the *anima* archetype is made even clearer by Alfred Hitchcock's *Vertigo*, where an unknown, and perhaps unknowable, woman, working to convince a detective that she really does not know who she is, becomes trapped by the fiction she has created. The movie turns on the slightly malicious question, "Who is Kim Novak?" – a question that becomes more frightening, and unanswerable, once the secret of her character's dual identity within the film is revealed.

The deluded detective is not really able to get to the heart of the conundrum, which deepens in accord with his self-deception. The initial sequences, for all their beauty in summoning up the enchantment of the *anima* archetype, belong to a familiar-enough theme in psychology and art – the man as victim of seduction. We even feel that the fall of James Stewart's character Scottie into "acute melancholia complicated by a guilt complex" is what he deserves from biting into this familiar apple. Indeed, the cumulative kitsch elements of the romance – the staginess of the exposition of the preposterous plot; the tourist's view of San Francisco in the long, languishing silent sequence; the poor quality of the "museum painting" of the nineteenth-century woman Kim Novak is supposed to be obsessed and perhaps possessed by; the monotonous unreality Novak brings to the reading of her lines; and James Stewart's ponderous earnestness as Scottie becomes her victim – all have a wearying effect, much like the depression of co-addiction.

But when the trickster beneath all this gnawing at the bone of hopeless love is exposed to us, and we see both characters know that it was all a trick, the film develops a wildness in which anything could happen. Stewart's solution – to precipitate the total loss of his object in the fever pitch of his disillusionment – is a truly shocking finale, forcing the audience to the conclusion that the premises of romantic love have themselves disappeared. If *Vertigo* has, as Royal S. Brown (1986) argues, the form of an Orphic tragedy, a story of the romantic artist's need to gaze murderously upon the illusion-based love at the center of his creative impulse, then the irretrievably lost Eurydice within this poet's film is the *anima* herself as we have known and used her to support the image of ideal romantic love. At the film's end, a bell tolls for the loss of the archetype.

The film's extraordinary poignancy turns upon Kim Novak's uncanny ability to make us care what happens to her, despite the palpable deceptiveness of her many guises. She is presented initially as Madeleine Elster, the impossibly elegant wife of a San Francisco shipbuilder. Later we learn that Novak is really Judy Barton, a San Francisco shop girl from Salina, Kansas, who had been coached to impersonate Madeleine by Madeleine's husband while he disposes of his actual wife. Novak's Madeleine is a classic 1950s woman, who confines her body within a gray tailored suit, her hair close around her head like a man's, except for the elegant feminine knot behind the head. Her image is the extreme of compliance to the demands patriarchy makes upon the feminine, to be voluptuous and pleasing within a masculine mold. Like a fourth-century BCE marble bust of Aphrodite, Novak-as-Madeleine is a personification of the goddess as patriarchal *anima*, asleep to her other feminine possibilities and almost Apollonian in the balance of her contours.

Later, when she appears, in shocking contrast, as Judy, Novak is painted in a hard Dionysian style, like a vulgar theater mask. She is incapable of getting Stewart's Scottie to find any taste for this more florid, and angry, assertion of femininity. Instead, Scottie forces her to recreate the Apollonian image for him by redoing her make-up, her hair, her clothes, and even her nails in the image of the former, illusory Madeleine. We realize to our horror that, for all the cruelty and male chauvinism of his project, this is the only style through which Novak's soft femininity can express itself. We pity her the more because we love her this way, recognizing that we, too, are fatally attracted by the patriarchal *anima* style. There can be no happy outcome, but the fall from grace of this presentation of the feminine at the end of the picture is nevertheless an occasion for pity and dread. The film that might have left us mourning for this unattainable *anima* image upsets us more at the end with the repulsed sense that, like Scottie, we have seen the end of any basis for all our illusions about love.

This cynicism is a sign of the emergence of the senex archetype once the *anima* disappears.[7] We can read *Vertigo* as the initiation of a vulnerable man into the psychological senescence produced when the *anima* is irretrievably lost. Jung has given this classic description:

> After the middle of life . . . permanent loss of the *anima* means a diminution of vitality, of flexibility, and of human kindness. The result, as a rule, is premature rigidity, crustiness, stereotypy, fanatical one-sidedness, obstinacy, pedantry, or else resignation, weariness, sloppiness, irresponsibility, and finally a childish *ramollissement* [softening of personality] with a tendency to alcohol.
>
> (Jung [1954] 1959: 147)

*Vertigo* defines the process by which the *anima* is sacrificed in a man destined to assume the senex character, making clear the role the *anima* plays in her own withdrawal from the psychological scene. The *anima* that seduces a man into permanent disillusionment with the feminine is under the spell of a malignant father complex, so that her energy is infected by the demands of the complex and ceases to serve the total personality. This is the shadow of the process that therapists more usually imagine the *anima* to be catalyzing for a man in midlife, which is normally the discovery of the value of his aliveness to him. In the dark variant depicted here, the *anima* is a tragic accomplice to a form of negative initiation, by which the man is denied an inner life in favor of a hollow victory over his emotions.

There are two sequences in this movie that are organized around the unexpected and uncanny experience of Madeleine/Judy staring directly into the camera.[8] In both cases, Novak's face is frozen with the unhappiness of her unfree condition, disclosing to us her tragic foreknowledge of the role she will be forced to play in Scottie's psychological demise. The first of these direct gazes occurs in the car just before she and Scottie reach the mission at San Juan Bautista where she will meet her accomplice, Gavin Elster. This gaze is transposed to the livery stable of the mission, where she sits in an old carriage rather than the car. She keeps staring for a long time, then begins to move to join Elster, who is set to throw his real wife's dead body from the top of the tower and make it look like a suicide.

The second of these direct gazes at the camera occurs when Judy sits in her hotel room, her face a mask of tragedy, and recalls what actually happened when she did reach the top of the bell tower ahead of Scottie. As before, the actress's gaze prefigures further actions that will lead to the completion of the project – which Elster set in motion and which Hitchcock, as director, will finally use her to complete – to destroy any basis Scottie, or the film watcher, may have for believing that a healthy connection to the feminine is possible.

Scottie's vulnerability to such control by a cynical complex is the vertigo of the film's title, visualized as an acrophobia that affects the way he sees the base of the bell tower's stairwell when he looks down.[9] Its square geometric shape is a Self-symbol that recedes further away from him as he contemplates its enlarging possibility: we are looking at a man's terror in the face of the depths of his own being. It is this terror that the father complex represented by Elster can successfully manipulate: since the *anima* promises connection to the Self, the complex moves the *anima* to convince the man that he must discard her for her own survival and mastery of his fear.

## Mask

If the *anima* in *A Star is Born* overtakes a failing persona, and is lost in *Vertigo* to a hollow persona, *Mask* suggests the healing of a wounded persona by an *anima* neither too strong nor too weak to do her real job of protecting the personality. Like *A Star is Born* and *Vertigo*, *Mask* is set in California, but twenty-five years later, in the matriarchal, counterculture California that had grown up to one side of the freeway, and the film is only superficially about a tragedy within patriarchy. Part of the fun of the film is to watch the resilience of a personality that could never get by if it played according to the patriarchal rules set for persona and *anima* behavior that the films from the 1950s delineate. The hero, Rocky Dennis, collects Brooklyn Dodgers cards from 1955, and some of his mother's biker friends tell him that that seems like yesterday, but clearly we have entered another system of values. His mother, Rusty Dennis, is a beautiful queen of the counterculture, permanently estranged from her critical Jewish father, and, as played with perfect ease and authority by Cher, who looks like a dark Aphrodite in this movie, she can oppose her own authority to anything that patriarchy can dish out to stand in her son's way. The film opens on a day when she has to take him to be enrolled in a new junior high school, and it will be a problem, because he was born with craniodiaphyseal dysplasia, a rare condition that causes him to deposit calcium in his skull at an abnormal rate. His face looks like a Halloween mask, or, more precisely, the long, bent facial shield of a Mycenaean warrior. His mother's defiance of doctors (who told her he would be retarded, blind, and deaf) and of school principals who don't think he can fit in (he gets along well with the other kids and is in the top 5 percent of his class) has become legendary, and her verve in defying their authority makes almost anything seem possible. When his head aches (they've been told that because of the pressure on his spinal cord he may have only a few months to live), Cher's Rusty can get him to talk himself out of it; when she puts her hands against his head, the pain goes away.

Rocky is, in turn, Rusty's conscience and her moral support, forcing her to look at her serious drug habit and urging her on to a stable relationship with one of the nicer bikers.

This is the naive condition of the mother complex in the junior high school period when it is most hopeful, humorous, and aspiring, when a son and mother living without a father can truly be two against the world. The boy, who is, in fact, hopelessly unadapted to the patriarchal world, gets by as a charming and poignant exception to the usual patriarchal expectations, and, for a time, it is possible for him to make a successful adaptation, as Rocky does. In a brilliant sequence that takes the movie down to the level of the myth involved, Rocky wins his class over with his retelling of the Trojan War. This choice is not accidental: like Achilles, who calls weeping to his mother for help when his girl is taken from him, Rocky is a mother's hero. He will not be able to outgrow fixation at the awkward developmental stage he epitomizes for everybody else.

Girls are a particular problem for Rocky: they admire him, but he cannot attract them. His mother brings a prostitute home for him, but that is no solution because Rocky needs to find out if he is lovable on his own. As this sequence makes clear, the *anima* is an archetype that the mother complex cannot deliver to a man; she must be found outside the mother's sphere of authority and as a consequence of his own initiative.

Pushing himself away from his mother with the excuse that she won't do anything about her excessive use of drugs, Rocky accepts a summer job as a counselor's aid at a camp for the blind, where he meets a beautiful blind girl his own age. Her name is Diana Adams, and, with his interest in mythology and the milky radiance Laura Dern brings to the part, Rocky is quick to associate her to the White Goddess whose name she bears.[10] When she asks him what he looks like, he tells her that he looks like the Greek god Adonis and then the truth about the condition deforming his face. She runs her hand over his features and tells him he "looks pretty good" to her. They fall in love, but she is a daughter of careful, protective, upper-middle-class parents from a southern California suburb, and when they come to pick her up her father takes a pained look at Rocky and whisks her away in the family station wagon. Rocky tries to telephone Diana but her mother intercepts his messages. It is evident that he will never be able to make a permanent connection with any patriarchal *anima* figure.

Bogdanovich appears to tell this true story naively, as if it were a docudrama enlivened only by the extraordinary naturalness of his direction, which gives the film the look of life. Yet everywhere, seamlessly introduced into the smooth cinematic narration, is his sense of the archetypal background of this strange but charming matriarchal constellation. In one scene, Rocky, teaching the blind girl how to associate to visual adjectives, gives her some cotton balls to feel and tells her, "This is billowy." The movie reverses this process, giving us images that bring us as close as a visual medium can to the texture of a mother complex, a secret sacred marriage between mother and son that finally excludes all other loves. Like Diana, we are given a first-hand grasp of the soft intractability of Rocky's mother complex.

In this set-up, the *anima's* contribution is an acceptance of the insolubility of the problem. Rocky goes to find Diana once more and learns that she is being sent away to school. His headaches are getting worse, and he will have to go back home to die. Caught between the feelings of her own parents and the powerful sway of Rocky's irresistible fate, Diana can only console Rocky with her acceptance of him and of his limited access to her. Beautiful as she is, she must return him to the still more beautiful goddess who is his mother and to the archetypal pattern of the son-lover who dies young. This brief connection with the *anima* is enough, however, to enable him to accept his fate. Rocky is able to move on within his myth and to objectify it for us, so that when he dies and his mother becomes the grieving goddess, we experience the completion of his pattern and the sense that there has been an individuation.

The film itself does not step outside the frame of reference of the mother complex; it is not afraid to be sentimental or defiant. Yet Bogdanovich somehow achieves objectivity by letting us see the entirety of Rocky's situation, in both its personal and its mythological aspects. I suspect that this rounding out is an effect of the *anima*. Within the mother complex that cannot be overcome, the *anima* can sometimes find opportunities lacking in a patriarchal pattern of development for establishing the wholeness of the arrested personality.

Both *A Star is Born* and *Vertigo* are patriarchal in their premises and narcissistic in their pathology. They can be understood by the nature of their affective tone, as well as through the archetypes they present. *A Star is Born* is hypomanic; *Vertigo* is depressed. *Mask*, although similarly concerned with persona wounding and *anima* vulnerability, is neither. Its even feeling-tone reveals a surprising resilience in the regulation of self-esteem, which seems a gift of the character's freedom from patriarchal expectations. In *Mask*, neither the persona nor the *anima* has very much to lose. Without a fantasy of patriarchal success, there is no expectation of ideal apotheosis for either pole of the adapting self and, therefore, no liability to titanic disappointment. Instead of tragedy, there is pathos in *anima* disappointment and a humorous humility in the face of the persona's shortcomings. Within this matriarchal pattern, the *anima* can play only a limited role in extending the range or the health of a personality, but she can satisfy other needs of the psyche: for self-acceptance, integrity, and love.

It remains for us to ask what it does for a cinema *auteur* to reflect his *anima* problem so directly on the screen. It is clear that these films concern themselves with fatal constellations and reject the hope of heroic healing. One likes, nevertheless, to imagine that these directors healed themselves, or at least resolved tensions in their creative personalities, with these films. I have observed, following Jung, that it is therapeutic simply to visualize the *anima* with such clarity. Jung often expressed the opinion that the way for a man to analyze his *anima* is to get to know her better. In this process, as these films make clear, a man will come to experience not only her style and her nature, but also her autonomy as a factor that stands behind his ego in shaping his destiny. This independence, which promises an endless creative capacity for self-renewal, is sharply restricted by the nature of the other personality complexes with which the *anima* must contend. The film medium allows the director to articulate the limits of his *anima*'s freedom in shaping his creative life.

We who are interested in psychological creativity may understand from the urgency with which these cinema masters have attended to the fate of the *anima* that the *anima*'s vicissitudes refer to an imagination struggling to keep alive its capacity for psychological connection to itself. It would not be wrong to infer that this desirable outcome is by no means a guaranteed inevitability.

## Notes

* This 1992 article, which originally appeared in *Gender and Soul in Psychotherapy*, edited by Nathan Schwartz-Salant and Murray Stein for Chiron Publications, Wilmette, Illinois, has been revised by the author for this publication.

1  The most succinct general description of the ways the *anima* manifests herself can be found in Hillman (1975: 42–44). A critical examination of the concept of the *anima* in analytical psychology is given in Hillman (1985).

2  I am indebted to the Jungian analyst Beverley Zabriskie for first making this distinction for me.

3  This is the basic principle, as well, of Jungian dream interpretation (see Jung [1906] 1973).

4  See my recorded seminar, "Film as Active Imagination," C.G. Jung Institute of San Francisco, October 10–11, 1981.

5　See Sarris (1968) for a discussion of rank and *auteur* in regard to Hollywood directors.

6　It is best to resist the temptation to draw conclusions about the personal psychology of a director from his films, but the notion of "personal filmmaking" – a term Pauline Kael ([1973] 1994: 505) coined for her *New Yorker* review of Martin Scorsese's *Mean Streets* in 1973 – does open up the psychology of the director's *creative* personality to critical inspection. See also Sarris ([1968] 1971).

7　Hitchcock supplies an exact personification of the senex archetype in the figure of the coroner who presides over the jury called to determine the cause of Madeleine's death after the first bell-tower episode. The coroner's tone in delivering the verdict of suicide insinuates that Scottie is at fault, which becomes the attitude Scottie assumes toward himself in his subsequent depression.

8　A particularly lucid account of the first of these moments can be found in Rothman (1988), who invokes Stanley Cavell's "melodrama of the unknown woman."

9　Lesley Brill, in his careful analysis of the camera's movement in *Vertigo* (1988: 202–206), points out that a geometric spiral is implied in this figure.

10　Robert Graves's use of this term for Diana/Artemis is well known (1960: 85–86). Peter Bogdanovich revealed to Barbara Grizzuti Harrison that he was reading Robert Graves's *The White Goddess* in 1981, just after his lover, Dorothy Stratten, was killed (Harrison 1990).

# References

Balázs, B. (1985) The close up. In *Film Theory and Criticism* (3rd edn), G. Mast and M. Cohen, eds. New York: Oxford University Press, pp. 255–264.

Brill, L. (1988) *The Hitchcock Romance: Love and Irony in Hitchcock's Films.* Princeton, N.J.: Princeton University Press.

Brown, R. S. (1986) *Vertigo* as Orphic tragedy. *Film/Literature Quarterly* 14(1): 32–43.

Graves, R. (1960) *The Greek Myths.* New York: Viking Penguin.

Harrison, B. G. (1990) Peter Bogdanovich comes back from the dead. *Esquire* 114(2): 146–156.

Hillman, J. (1975) *Re-Visioning Psychology.* New York: Harper & Row.

―― (1985) *Anima: An Anatomy of a Personified Notion.* Dallas: Spring Publications.

Jung, C. G. ([1906] 1973) Association, dream, and hysterical symptom. In *CW* 2: 353–407. Princeton, N.J.: Princeton University Press.

―― ([1954] 1959) Concerning the archetypes, with special reference to the anima concept. *CW* 9I: 54–72. Princeton, N.J.: Princeton University Press.

Kael, P. ([1973] 1994) Everyday inferno. In *For Keeps.* New York: Dutton, pp. 505–511.

Rothman, W. (1988) *Vertigo*: the unknown woman in Hitchcock. In *The "I" of the Camera*. Cambridge: Cambridge University Press, pp. 142–173.

Sarris, A. ([1968] 1971) Directors, how personal can you get? In *Confessions of a Cultist: On the Cinema, 1955/1969*. New York: Simon & Schuster, pp. 360–365.

Sarris, A. (1968) *The American Cinema*. New York: Dutton.

# Chapter 12

# "Gay sensibility," the hermaphrodite, and Pedro Almodóvar's films*

*James Wyly*

---

Films by Pedro Almodóvar
(All are available on videocassettes, in Spanish with English subtitles.)

*Pepi, Luci, Bom* (1980)
*Labyrinth of Passion* (1982)
*Dark Habits* (1984)
*What Have I Done to Deserve This?* (1985)
*Matador* (1986)
*Law of Desire* (1987)
*Women on the Verge of a Nervous Breakdown* (1988)
*Tie Me Up! Tie Me Down!* (1990)
*High Heels* (1991)
*Kika* (1993)
*The Flower of My Secret* (1996)
*Live Flesh* (1997)
*All About My Mother* (1999)

## Introduction

"[W]hen someone says, 'Well you are an openly gay director,' I say, 'Come on, stop. I'm a director.'" So Pedro Almodóvar, Spain's leading film-maker, commented upon the relationship of his homosexuality to his vocation in a recent interview (Marcus 1996: 68). Yet Almodóvar has always embraced his homosexuality publicly and many see it as a fundamentally determining influence on his films, the most recent of which, *All About My Mother*, was released in the United States in 1999. Indeed, Raymond Murray's remark, "His films . . . are always infused with a gay sensibility" (Murray 1994: 5) would seem only to state the obvious to most of those familiar with Almodóvar's work. Obvious, that is, until we ask the obvious question: what is a "gay sensibility" anyway? To be sure it is a phenomenon very much of our time, something many of us believe we recognize instantly when we encounter it. It is only when we attempt to describe it that we find ourselves in the midst of difficulties.

There are a number of reasons why Almodóvar's work can help with defining gay sensibility. First, Almodóvar is Spanish. He is a product of a culture which, due to the repressions of the Franco era, never experienced the cultural revolution of the late 1960s that swept through most western nations.This would at first seem a disadvantage, but in Spain after the death of Franco in 1975 there was also no establishment born of the 1960s to obstruct the full flowering of the culture of the 1980s and 1990s. Almodóvar's radicalism thus met no opposition in the form of an entrenched older generation of onetime innovators; so it could go farther and faster than its equivalents in other countries. In his work, therefore, we see the present especially clearly, relatively uncontaminated by the unrecognized conservatism of the immediate past.

Also, Almodóvar writes, sometimes outrageously, about his art. He thus gives us access to what a Jungian might call the ego's position in relation to the creative works.

And Almodóvar appears to be unconflicted about his gayness, at least superficially. Unlike a number of gay artists, he does not present, either in his films or in his writings about them, the cramped and defensive persona that so frequently results from living a homosexual life in the midst of a society that tries to deny such a life its validity. He gives us the impression that he *likes* being gay, without any necessity of self-justification, and this makes his creative works especially convincing as materials through which we can deepen our understanding of the sensibility involved.

Raymond Murray tells us Almodóvar

> left home at 17 and took a job as a telephone operator in Madrid where he became involved in the city's punked-out "hip" scene of the late '70's and early '80's – a bastion for gays, transvestites and drag queens. Upon Franco's death in 1975, he found himself in the center of the artistic community that would lead the country's cultural reawakening, a phenomenon known in Spain as "La Movida." He co-founded the cross-dressing punk rock band Almodóvar & McNamara as well as illustrated X-rated comic books. During this period he began making home-styled, 8mm films . . .

> (Murray 1994: 5)

This led to a very high-profile career, with thirteen of Almodóvar's films receiving international distribution. These range from *Pepi, Luci, Bom* of 1980 to the most recent, *The Flower of My Secret* (1996), *Live Flesh* (1997), and *All About My Mother* (1999), which in 2000 won a number of awards, including an Oscar (Best Foreign Language Film) and two awards from the British Academy (Best Film Not in the English Language and The David Lean Award for Direction). In addition there is a short book of essays, *Patty Diphusa and Other Writings*, which is available in English (Almodóvar 1992).

Wherever one enters into this *œuvre* one encounters in Almodóvar a noteworthy attitude toward his characters and stories. For example, the heroine of *The Flower of My Secret*, Leo (Marisa Paredes), is a highly successful writer of trashy romances. She is also a study in dependency and self-loathing. Though her novels have made her rich she has nothing but contempt for them, so she publishes them under a closely guarded pseudonym and even goes as far as to publish harshly critical reviews of them under another pseudonym. She tries maniacally to maintain the illusion that she is loved by her completely unloving husband, her selfish, demanding mother and her bitchy sister. As her life inevitably unravels under the strain of keeping all these balls in the air, she is drawn toward involvement with Angel (Juan Echanove), an editor who first publishes attacks on Leo's own attacks on her work (not knowing, of course, who wrote them) but who eventually also publishes a successful trashy romance under Leo's own trash-writer pseudonym. In the course of this flirtation Leo admits the failure of her disastrous marriage and rejects the near-irresistible temptation to have an affair with Antonio (Joaquín Cortes), her cleaning lady's incredibly sexy son. As she is drawn first into herself and then into involvement with the editor who is anonymously defending (while adopting!) her romance-writer persona, both of them change. Almodóvar has spoken about these changes. Of Leo, he says:

> this story really is how this woman [Leo] gets to be the owner of her solitude. So, the solution is not to fuck the first young boy that arrives [Antonio]. She needs more reciprocity, more than just to make love. I mean, for her to be free is not to be screwing all the time; it's just to be the owner of her decisions, without anxiety, without becoming nervous, quietly . . . it's just to do what you want without being completely crazy.
>
> (Marcus 1996: 68)

Thus she moves from dependency to solitude, the only position from which she is able to connect authentically with Angel. Meanwhile Angel, ostentatiously solitary in the beginning of the film, is in Almodóvar's words,

> really becoming a woman . . . When I talked to [the actor, Juan Echanove] he asked me, "Do you think he's like becoming gay or not?" and I said to him, "Not necessarily, perhaps. In any case, he's becoming lesbian, because he still likes very much women and he's becoming closer to [Leo] . . . he just gets closer to the female sensibility, and in his case, it's like a lesbian sensibility."
>
> (Marcus 1996: 72)

It is this development that enables him to begin an intimacy with Leo; and if we doubt its ongoing importance in Almodóvar's work we have only to remember the dedication he places just before the credits roll at the end of *All About My Mother*: "To Bette Davis, Gena Rowlands, Romy Schneider, to all actresses who have played actresses, to all women who act, to men who act and become women, to all the people who want to be mothers. To my mother."

We could discuss at some length the psychological and cultural constructions that lie behind Almodóvar's identifying certain changes in men and women and their behavior as becoming more "feminine" or "masculine," or "playing actresses" or "becoming women" or "wanting to be mothers"; but here I would like to concentrate instead upon the meaning of Almodóvar's willingness to describe what happens to his characters in just these terms, and the ease with which he accepts their fluid gender and relational boundaries. Clearly he is using the concepts of "masculine," "feminine," and "lesbian" in ways that have specific meanings for him which not everyone shares. For him they appear to be rather elastic and to have little, if anything, to do with the anatomical topography with which humans are born. This attitude, as we shall see, informs Almodóvar's stance toward all of his art, and if we can come to a psychological understanding of its meaning we shall arrive at a clearer sense of what constitutes Almodóvar's "gay sensibility."

## The hermaphroditic position

As a beginning, we may explore the hypothesis that Almodóvar's gay sensibility derives from a willingness to look at gender and sex from the premise suggested above, that neither masculine nor feminine qualities are necessarily established by anatomy. Because this position does not identify with one sex, the other is never foreign, never really "other." It would be logical to call this position "hermaphroditic" since it is equally informed by both masculinity and femininity in all their ramifications. Jung made the hermaphrodite essential to his conception of the child archetype (Jung, 1959, *CW* 9, i: para. 259ff.), and there is certainly something that may appear as childishly direct and simple in Almodóvar's act of ignoring the gender constructions that are basic to the conventional attitudes adults take toward one another. We can thus begin to think about the possibility of an archetypal foundation for Almodóvar's point of view by using Jung's notion of the child archetype as a point of departure.

But here I should pause for a moment to say that this word "hermaphrodite" needs to be read carefully. By "hermaphroditism" is meant the merging or combination of equal parts of masculinity and femininity, as is demonstrated in the original, mythic union of Hermes' and Aphrodite's son Hermaphroditos with the nymph Salmacis (Ovid 1955: 90ff.). The result is a third state of being, neither masculine nor feminine, which is fundamentally different from the current meaning of "androgyny," with which it can be confused. In the last thirty years or so we have come to use "androgyny" to mean either a man's awareness of an inner and opposite but discrete feminine sensibility (anima), or the reverse, a woman's discovery of masculine sensibility (animus). An androgynous sensibility is something a great many people can develop, as through a Jungian analysis. We might argue that Leo and Angel develop androgynous sensibilities in *The Flower of My Secret*. We should recognize, however, that Almodóvar's preexisting attitude toward their development is better called hermaphroditic. Hermaphroditic, yes, but childish in Jung's sense, no; for we shall see that Almodóvar's delight in his characters' situations is hardly the delight of Jung's child, stuck in immaturity even though pluripotential.

Its myth establishes that the stance of the hermaphrodite is from its inception separate from either the male or the female pole and encompasses both. This is different at the outset from Jung's concept of the hermaphrodite. For Jung, gender constructions evolve from the undifferentiated and therefore childish hermaphrodite. But in the myth as Ovid tells it the situation is reversed: the hermaphrodite evolves from polarized adult sexuality, and this "post-adult" manifestation is, as we shall see, closer to the hermaphroditism we find in Almodóvar's viewpoint.

## Law of desire and Patty Diphusa

If we are accustomed to seeing everything in terms of our culture's assumption of near-universal sexual dimorphism, a "hermaphroditic" stance toward the world can be disturbing. Almodóvar shocks sensibilities determined by the conventions of sexual polarity with characters and situations that can seem simultaneously outrageous, offensive, funny, and profound. Yet to watch his dizzy scenarios unfold is to be forced to adapt to Almodóvar's consciously pansexual viewpoint, which can be expressed by something like an actress playing a male-to-female transsexual – that is, a woman being a man being a woman. Almodóvar tells us how important such things are to him when he writes of Carmen Maura's role in *Law of Desire* (1987) – the plot of which involves two brothers, one of whom has had transsexual surgery in order to fulfill the fantasies of their father, with whom he had an incestuous relationship:

> This is a movie about guys; from now on nobody can accuse me of only directing women . . . I think in *Law* I got the best acting of my career. Carmen Maura did it. She's shocking in her rôle as Tina the transsexual. Beyond the circus-like aspect of looking like a man who has turned himself into a woman (Carmen's physical mimicry is incredible), Maura proves herself to be in possession of so many registers that her performance becomes an actual festival.
>
> This woman enlarges in front of the camera. She was so generous, intuitive, sincere, that for her sake alone I'm happy to have made the film. Fun, pathetic, well-muscled, the incarnation of ambiguity, rightly paranoid, etcetera, Tina Quintero [the character], thanks to Carmen Maura, is the most complete feminine portrait I have done to date.
>
> (Almodóvar 1992: 83)

In understanding this director's sensibility it is important that for Almodóvar his "most complete feminine portrait" is based on a character with biologically masculine origins. It is as though femininity apart from masculinity is an impossibility for him, and this separates his position clearly from the usual assumptions that dominate our culture about masculinity and femininity as a polarity. It clearly separates his ideas from the simple hermaphroditism Jung assigns to a child sensibility in his study of the child archetype, for this is not undifferentiated gender but a most sophisticated view of it.

Let us look more deeply, therefore, at a couple of examples of this hermaphroditic position from Almodóvar's works to see if they can't help us to elaborate what I am here calling his "gay sensibility."

We could do worse than to start with Patty Diphusa, the pseudonym Almodóvar adopted for the feminine persona whose "memoirs" he wrote in a series of columns for a Madrid magazine, *La Luna*, from 1983–84. (The Spanish word *patidifusa* can be roughly translated as "dumbfounded" or "flabbergasted," though linguistically it feels more contemporary than either.)

Patty is outrageous, to say the least. She introduces herself:

> I am PATTY DIPHUSA and I am one of those women who takes a leading rôle in her times. My profession? International sex symbol, or international porn star, whichever you prefer . . . And I'd like to add that not only do I have a body that drives men wild, but I've also got a brain. But I only show it off once in a while. It's not considered good taste among gentlemen to show them that behind your perfect Barbie Superstar bod, you're hiding a privileged mind.
>
> (Almodóvar 1992: 3–4)

And later: "as many intelligent people have said, there is only one INTERESTING person in Madrid. And that person is ME. PATTY DIPHUSA" (Almodóvar 1992: 53). This girl doesn't lack self-confidence, and the X-rated adventures she recounts are everything she has led us to expect they will be.

But there is more to her than that. The final installment of her memoirs is entitled, "I, Patty, Try to Get to Know Myself through my Author," and Patty begins this way:

> I've been wanting to expose my author for some time now. I don't know if he'll let me, but I'm gonna give it a try.
>
> PATTY – In the first place, I'd like to know if I'm a man, woman or transvestite.
>
> PEDRO – You're a woman, naturally. A woman who never sleeps, but when you get right down to it, a woman.
>
> PATTY – And why don't I sleep? . . .
>
> PEDRO – You don't need to; you're full of life. The sign of our times is vertigo, frenetic activity. And you're the typical girl of our time.
>
> (Almodóvar 1992: 73–74)

As the dialog proceeds we see what is going on. As Patty Diphusa, Almodóvar speaks as an aspect of himself which he calls "the typical girl of our time." She expresses him in a feminine persona, and he can give her voice and then stand back and consciously examine what he is doing. The interview shows that he is aware of further psychological manifestations:

> PATTY – So I'm just a reflection of you, that horrible thing called an "alter ego"?
> PEDRO – No. You're a fantasy of the readers. You're what the readers would like to be.
> PATTY – Did you read my memoirs?
> PEDRO – I read them once through to see how many printer's errors there are and got very upset.
> PATTY – So you're a reader too. That is, you also want to be like me.
> PEDRO – I'd like to have your spontaneity and your positive sense of life.
>
> (Almodóvar 1992: 74)

Patty is not a Jungian anima, for there is no evidence of Pedro-as-masculine-ego forging a relationship with a mysterious inner feminine. Rather, she is a fully known aspect of Pedro's ego, a fact that is made clear in their final exchange:

> PATTY – Pedro, the interview's over and I still don't know anything about you.
> PEDRO – Yeah, but I already knew everything about you.
>
> (Almodóvar 1992: 77)

What all this suggests to me is that for Almodóvar it is unthinkable to be a complete man without free, conscious expression of that which we habitually identify as feminine, here called Patty Diphusa; and it is similarly unthinkable to be a complete woman without free, conscious expression of that which we habitually identify as masculine, as the director indicates in his comments about Carmen Maura's portrayal of Tina Quintero. From Almodóvar's point of view, complete men and complete women become virtually indistinguishable. In *All About My Mother* this is carried to the extent that the main characters all function essentially as hermaphrodites: the story-line plays out among women and transsexuals, none of whom has any apparent need for an opposite-gendered partner in order to fulfill their destiny within the film's plot.

This conscious position on Almodóvar's part seems fundamentally different from the Jungian ideal of a gender-identified ego that develops a relationship with an originally unconscious anima or animus. With Almodóvar there is no difference in degree of consciousness between masculine and feminine for either sex, nor is there developmental movement toward a gendered opposite. The duality is fully present and conscious from the beginning. Through its expression comes the "spontaneity and positive sense of life" that Almodóvar's readers and viewers find in his works, a vitality that is as attractive to his straight audience as to his gay one. This joyfully hermaphroditic duality is essential to Almodovar's creative sensibility and contributes to our perception of it as "gay." It is not, however, childish.

## Matador

To review Almodóvar's films only to point out in each of them how his gay sensibility is fundamental would rapidly become tedious, and it would also undercut the many surprises that lie in wait for anyone who is moved to rent the videotapes and watch them first hand. Let me confine myself as a demonstration to a few remarks on *Matador* (1986), perhaps the most difficult and, at least in terms of its plot, the most wildly improbable of all these films. The interested reader should then be able to look for this quality in the others as s/he wishes.

The plot of *Matador* is more than quintessentially Almodóvarean; it must rank high among the loopiest and most unlikely stories ever developed in film. The suspension of disbelief it requires of its viewer is considerable. It is nonetheless brutally tragic and actually offers little of the ribald comic-relief for which Almodóvar has become famous. In it I believe we can find a statement about the evolution of the gay sensibility we have been discussing, as well as an important psychological observation about the nature of homosexuality as a mind-set.

Briefly, the plot is this. We are introduced to Angel Giménez (Antonio Banderas), a baby-faced young student of bullfighting who lives with his judgmental, sour, and fanatically religious mother. His bullfighting class is taught by Diego Montes (Nacho Martínez), an older, famous matador who had to retire from the ring after being gored. Though Angel blindly idealizes his teacher and everything he stands for, he is in every way the opposite of the macho type one associates with bullfighters. Of course this is noticed by Diego, who asks him why he's pursuing this vocation, tells him he's too young, says he's different from all the other students he's had and not the right type to become a matador, and finally inquires of his acolyte whether he likes men. We are led to assume that to this last the answer must be "yes," for Angel panics. Attempting to prove himself according to the code he has learned from Diego, he tries to rape Eva Soler (Eva Cobo), a young model who is his neighbor and also Diego's girlfriend. He bungles the job so completely that Eva refuses to take the assault seriously; when Eva, freeing herself, falls and cuts her face, Angel passes out at the sight of a few drops of blood. It is obvious that he will never make a successful bullfighter.

Meanwhile, there have been a number of sex-related murders in the city. Angel goes to the police and confesses to them, but the audience already knows that the murdered women were killed by Diego while the murdered men were killed by the beautiful woman whom the court has appointed as Angel's defense lawyer, María Cardenal (Assumpta Serna). Both Diego and María like to kill their sexual partners at the moment of orgasm, so they are predestined for each other. We further discover – and here suspension of disbelief gives way to stunned incredulity (the viewer is truly rendered "patidifusa") – that Angel has confessed because he had been experiencing the murders clairvoyantly and wanted to save Diego from facing prosecution. But through the efforts of Inspector del Valle (Eusebio Poncela), a tough, sympathetic and probably gay detective who becomes convinced both of Angel's innocence and his clairvoyant powers, the real criminals are identified. They, however, have by now met and realized their mutual obsession with the ultimate sexual experience. As the law closes in they are arranging a final assignation/ suicide pact. Angel even receives news of this clairvoyantly and he, del Valle, his doctor, and Eva (who, like Angel, remains devoted to Diego in spite of having been replaced in his affections by María) speed to the scene. This posse arrives too late. A solar eclipse catches their attention as they approach the house in which they will find the inter-twined bodies of Diego and María in a pool of blood. As they stand over the gore in the final scene Angel says of Diego, "I couldn't save him." Yet of the corpses Inspector del Valle says, "I never saw anyone so happy." As the film ends we observe that this time Angel hasn't fainted at the sight of blood.

This scenario is beyond ridiculous, of course; but I have to admit that when I watch the film I accept it. For me, this means that embedded in the superficial absurdities and the far-fetched plot there must be some kind of metaphoric or psychological truth to which the psyche responds. We need to discover what it is.

To do so, let us suppose that instead of going to the police with his confession, Angel goes to a Jungian analyst. We shall further suppose the analyst, following an instinct, does not believe Angel is really either a murderer or chronically psychotic. How might the analyst deal with the phenomena Angel is experiencing? The analyst would have to assume that Angel's fantasies, even if clairvoyant, are manifestations of his own unconscious process caused by some kind of intrapsychic turmoil. It would be significant that the turmoil expresses itself by selecting images of a powerful woman seducing men in order to kill them and vice versa, but from here on the analyst would take the position that these images have more to do with Angel's polarized psyche rather than with a bizarre situation among real people. The images would suggest to the analyst that each pole of this sexual opposition is obsessed with possessing and eliminating the other. Once we accept the archetypal elements in these manifestations, the two protagonists' killing each other at the moment of orgasm starts uncannily to resemble the symbolism Jung found in the plates of the *Rosarium Philosophorum* (1550) to illustrate the "Psychology of the Transference" (Jung, 1954, *CW* 16: para. 353ff.). In these alchemical woodcuts, Sol and Luna join in intercourse (Plate V) and die united (Plate VI).

With this clue, the absurd love-death of *Matador* starts to make sense. Angel's impotent despair, born of his inability to conform to the extreme masculinity his culture has caused him naïvely to idealize, evokes an intrapsychic *coniunctio* experience, an extreme compensation from the Self that is a *reductio ad absurdum* in which the masculine and feminine components, whose previously intractable opposition seems to have held Angel paralyzed, destroy each other with their desire for each other. As though to reinforce the point, Almodóvar's film puts the demise of the matador and the defense lawyer at the moment of a solar eclipse, an apparent conjunction between sun and moon.

Before we look further at the implications of this material we need to think about its relationship to Almodóvar's intent when he made the film. Did he intend to give us a "symbolic" film? Has he studied alchemy? Did he – God forbid – intend to make a "Jungian" movie or a send-up of one? I doubt it. Almodóvar has written a paragraph about *Matador* which is worth quoting in order to clarify his conscious stance regarding the film. He says:

> *Matador* . . . [is] the most abstract of my films about some-thing absolutely concrete – sexual pleasures. It's a very stylized and very hard film, a tragicomedy in which death is conceived as an element of sexual arousal. In the tone of a legend, *Matador* is the other face of *Law of Desire*, a much more naturalist film that

still deals with an abstraction: desire. They aren't moral movies, although in both, the protagonists have to pay a very high price to satisfy their passions.

(Almodóvar 1992: 126)

While this explanation doesn't completely make sense, it does tell us that although Almodóvar sees the film as about sexual pleasures, which I have to say I do not, he also sees it as "abstract," "stylized," "in the tone of a legend," and without a "moral." He appears to be dimly aware of a deeper, imaginal content, but not of that content's substance. This means that the Jungian viewers who are going to take our mythic reading of this film seriously will also have to take responsibility for it. It is we who are conceptualizing Almodóvar's film about sexual desire and its relation to death according to our psychological understanding of this motif.

Let us in this spirit think a bit more than Almodóvar may have done about this merged "death" of the masculine and feminine. Psychologically, it has substance, for as we know the psyche is in one sense a closed system: when things die they don't disappear, but instead their energy is transformed and appears in new imagery. Dying together thus, the *Rosarium*'s polarized "lights," Sol and Luna, become one consciousness, the hermaphrodite. And when Angel fails in his effort to build a life based on the masculine–feminine polarity, the very death of that polarity opens the possibility of a new stance to him, one that is in some new sense more ruggedly hermaphroditic. When, at the end of the film, he doesn't faint, we see him as finally fit for life, and we are entitled to imagine he has encountered an ego-position beyond the binary sexual opposition to which as a "feminine" boy he could not adapt himself. Is this nothing but a regression to the unchallenged hermaphroditism of the child, or is it a more progressive liberation from the stultifying power of one's parents' and culture's assumptions about gender? Is it not that Angel, the student matador, has arrived at the same self-awareness some gay men and women find when they accept that their erotic inclinations do not conform to the pattern of sexual opposition cultural expectations have laid out for them? An identity that is neither "masculine" nor "feminine" has no sexual opposite available for projection on another individual. Eros then becomes a matter of shared experience with likes, in which both partners own both sides of their masculine/feminine identity: neither masculine-seeking-feminine-for-completion nor its opposite, but both. It therefore does not need anything from either sex to complete itself. This suggests independence from the need for connection with the kind of discrete opposite that motivates much heterosexual desire. We are faced with an eros founded in wholeness and sameness, not in opposition and difference.

## Eros' sibling: a post-Jungian view of the hermaphrodite

To play homonymically with words, if we wish to imagine eros as mediating a "cure" for a "pathology" of excessive personal isolation, we may think about a "homeopathic" eros as being operative in gay people, as opposed to an "allopathic" one. Cicero maintained that Eros' parents were Hermes and Aphrodite (Kerényi 1951: 172), deities who, Ovid tells us, were the parents of Hermaphroditos as well. The classical associations have resonance with our thoughts about Hermaphroditos' place in homo-erotic relationships: names designating two aspects of the same child. We may perceive in these fragments of myth a more bisexual time when eros did not mediate exclusively between masculine and feminine.

The hermaphrodite that emerges here is different from the hermaphrodite Jung describes in "Psychology of the Transference" (Jung, 1954, CW 16: para. 353ff.) and "The Psychology of the Child Archetype" (Jung, 1959, CW 9, i: para. 259ff.). We ought to think briefly about why this is so.

A close reading of "The Psychology of the Child Archetype" reveals that though Jung employs the term "hermaphrodite" he is in fact writing about androgyny in its less mature form. He acknowledges the importance and complexity of the archetype of the hermaphrodite but forces the mythologem into a developmental schema that locates it in an original, undifferentiated union of opposites, which he relates to a "primitive state of mind" (Jung, 1959, CW 9, i: para. 292), which moves through increasing differentiation, to a developed awareness of an inner opposite or a "union of the conscious and the unconscious personality" within a mature fantasy of polarity. Then he speaks of a man's unconscious as feminine and a woman's as masculine, which implies a process of developing awareness of an unconscious, gender-determined opposite (Jung, 1959, CW 9, i: para. 294). For Jung here, the adult flowering of "androgyny," which he called "hermaphroditism," was a sophisticated *result* of psychological development over time, while we have noted that in Almodóvar's work it appears as the *given constant attitude* from which developments are contemplated.

The meaning of the hermaphrodite in "Psychology of the Transference" (Jung 1959) is more complicated, but again Jung uses the term "hermaphrodite," which he admits refers to an archetype, to designate a stage in development that is in fact specific to the argument about transference that Jung is trying to make. This can be seen in Jung's selectivity regarding the *Rosarium* plates themselves: there are in fact twenty plates, not ten, and the series does not end with a depiction of a hermaphrodite (Fabricius 1994: 230–233, and *passim*). Jung's designation of Plate X as terminal is arbitrary, so the idea of the hermaphrodite as a goal of a developmental process is Jung's even though he implies that purpose belongs to the archetype itself.

Furthermore, Jung does not deal satisfactorily with his own ambivalence toward the image, which comes through in his feeling-reaction to the hermaphrodite of *Rosarium* Plates VI ("Death") through X ("The New Birth"). First, he denies the male–female equality which is so evident in the image, for he cracks a couple of his usual jokes about the relatively primitive nature of masculine feeling and feminine thinking to establish the inferiority of the contrasexual aspects of the "soul" that the alchemical opus is supposedly liberating (Jung, 1954, *CW* 16: paras. 520–522). This is unsatisfactory amplification of the image, for there is no evidence of this inferiority in the plates themselves. Then he insults the hermaphrodite by calling the goal of the opus a "baffling paradox" (Jung, 1954, *CW* 16: Para. 532).

Jung further distances himself from consideration of the coequal sexual integration implied by the hermaphroditic symbol on arbitrary esthetic grounds and with surprising vehemence, by calling this image "monstrous," "horrific," a "hideous abortion" and a "perversion of nature" which he attributes to "the immaturity of the alchemists' minds" (Jung, 1954, *CW* 16: Para. 533). In spite of his distaste for the image, which he may be forcing, rhetorically, to break down some of his readers' prejudices toward it, he articulates some essential questions about the hermaphrodite (Jung, 1954, *CW* 16: paras. 534–535). But Jung's inability to look at it without loathing forces him to leave the image as he found it, relatively unconscious, as a symbol arbitrarily dissociated from its archetype and with no clear understanding of how it is to be experienced or what it could do for those who are able to withstand their encounter with what it represents. Elie Humbert has summed up Jung's understanding thus: the hermaphrodite is an image of "the symbolic function" (Humbert 1984: 81). That, of course it can be; but is that all?

Jung's rather astonishing revulsion toward the figure of the hermaphrodite needs to be taken into account whenever we consider what he said about it. Admittedly, the *Rosarium*'s hermaphrodite is far from beautiful, but then so are its cellulite-thighed Luna, tubercular-looking Sol, and the malnourished little Soul who belly-flops down from lowering clouds which have just bathed the hermaphrodite in "dew" the apparent consistency of barbecue sauce. If personal esthetics were the issue here we should dismiss not only the ungainly hermaphrodite, but the entire *Rosarium* out of hand.

By now it is sufficiently evident that Jung's attachment to contrasexual theory and his esthetic and personal reactions conditioned what he saw when he looked at the image of the hermaphrodite. He could not long sustain the idea of a truly hermaphroditic mythic being, but instead immediately converted it into an image of an abstract goal related to his own view of psychological development. I do not mean to question the importance of these ideas of Jung's, or even the value of his creative misreading of this image in their service. However, it is vital for us to remember what Jung fails to tell us: that he adopted the hermaphrodite to represent something in his theories which it did not represent innately.

All this demonstrates that Jung's discussions of the hermaphrodite are not so much discussions of the nature of this archetype, the importance of which he does acknowledge, as they are discussions of the creative elaborations Jung made of its symbol, the twin-sexed figure. The anonymous author of the *Rosarium* made a similar move when he adapted the dual-sexed figure as an image of a recurring, intermediary stage in the movement of the alchemical process. Against these adaptations, we need to bear in mind Ovid's statement of the hermaphrodite's origins. Ovid's version of the situation hardly begins uniquely, with a seductive nymph and a beautiful youth; but something about *this* nymph and *this* youth cause their attraction to lead not to a temporary, procreative union of masculine and feminine but to merger and a permanent reincarnation in a new form. We are reminded of Almodóvar's Angel, in whose experience, when the masculine and feminine opposites encounter each other, they do not procreate,but instead eliminate one another irreversibly.

From the works of Almodóvar we have extrapolated not a *goal* in Jung's sense but a *position* or a *viewpoint* or an *attitude*; and we have found in the film *Matador* a mythic statement about its origin which parallels Ovid's. In calling it "hermaphroditic" I believe we are brought closer than Jung in this instance to discussing an archetype as Jung himself defined it. We have been speaking of a psychological abstraction, represented by a symbol, that may in certain cases determine important aspects of consciousness, not a phase of a developmental process which, if fully embraced and wholeheartedly displayed, must be seen as a monstrous fixation.

## Conclusion: gay sensibility

All that remains, then, is to observe the parallels between the herma-phroditic image and the consciousness attributable to "gay sensibility" which is so evident in Almodóvar's work. There we find a psychological position that encompasses both ends of the continuum we identify as sexual, and that therefore needs nothing more from either pole to complete itself. That, surely, is the ultimate implication of the hermaphrodite. Its archetypal dominance of Almodóvar's perspective makes him equally at home with feminine and masculine psychological manifestations, and he shows us over and over again with a cheerful irony that is entirely serious that for him man is founded in woman and woman in man. His work as a gay artist strongly suggests that "gay sensibility" can be defined as a sensibility determined by activity of the archetype of the hermaphrodite. From such a perspective the two gender positions are equal and psycho-logically inseparable. Almodóvar gives us an extraordinarily sustained elaboration of the nature of the hermaphroditic archetype, and as the complexities of sex and gender become ever more urgent issues for reconsideration in our society we could do worse than inform ourselves by studying his *œuvre*.

## Note

* Original version published in *The San Francisco Jung Institute Library Journal*, Vol. 17, No. 4, 1999: 19–35.

## References

Almodóvar, P. (1992) *Patty Diphusa and Other Writings*. Trans. Kirk Anderson. Boston, Mass. and London: Faber & Faber.

Fabricius, J. (1994) *Alchemy: The Medieval Alchemists and Their Royal Art*. London: Diamond Books.

Humbert, E. (1984) *C.G. Jung: The Fundamentals of Theory and Practice*. Wilmette, Ill.: Chiron.

Jung, C.G. All references are by volume and paragraph number to the hardback edition of C.G. Jung, *The Collected Works* (*CW*), edited by Sir Herbert Read, Dr Michael Fordham and Dr Gerhard Adler, and translated in the main by R.F.C. Hull. London: Routledge.

Kerényi, C. (1951) *The Gods of the Greeks*. London: Thames & Hudson.

Marcus, L. (1996) "Man of La Mancha: An Interview with Filmmaker Pedro Almodóvar," in *Windy City Times*, June 27: 68–72.

Murray, R. (1994) *Images in the Dark: An Encyclopedia of Gay and Lesbian Film and Video*. Philadelphia, Pa.: TLA Publications.

Ovid, *Metamorphoses* (1955) Trans. Rolfe Humphries. Bloomington, Ind.: Indiana University Press.

*Rosarium Philosophorum*. Printed as second part of *De alchimia opuscula* (1550). Frankfort. Plates reproduced and quoted in J. Fabricius (1994) *Alchemy: The Medieval Alchemists and Their Royal Art*. London: Diamond Books.

# Glossary

**Active imagination**  A way of lowering the normal threshhold of consciousness so that a state similar to dreaming is achieved but one in which conscious ego-control is still present. As dream-type images come, the individual is able to engage more consciously with them and create a dialogue with them. These images also have a life of their own and unfold according to their own logic. Psychologically this creates a new situation as previously unconscious mental contents become more available to ego-consciousness.

**Alchemy**  Jung viewed the methods and symbols of the alchemists as revealing not so much chemical experimentation but psychological exploration similar to – and therefore a precursor of – Jung's own method of analytical psychology. The alchemists projected their internal processes onto the materials and the experiments they were engaged in and thus when working on their *materia* they were in fact working on their inner conscious–unconscious processes. In a similar way, Jung believed that analyst and patient were mutually involved in a transformative relationship with "the other" and that from such a joining together in the work – or *coniunctio* – transformation of the personality is able to occur. (As writers in the present volume often suggest, an analogy to this "alchemical" process is the relationship between the viewer and the numinous image on the cinema screen – which may involve a projection of an as yet unknown internal figure with whom a mutative relationship can be developed.)

**Amplification**  Association provides a way of developing meaning from spontaneous imagery and dreams motifs by allowing linked images and meaningful associations to the original stimulus to be found. By contrast, amplification does not require the individual to travel away from the image in a chain of links but instead to go further into the image in detail and thus make it fuller, richer and more detailed.

It is rather like turning up the volume on a stereo so that the full impact and dynamic range of the music (or image) *actually present* is available through such an amplification.

***Anima*** and ***animus***   The internal psychological feminine principle held by a man and the corresponding masculine principle at work in a woman's psyche. Both are psychic images arising from an inherent archetypal structure common to all human beings. As the fundamental forms which underlie the "feminine" aspects of man and the "masculine" aspects of woman, they are seen as opposites.

**Archetype**   Archetypes are the unconscious structuring principles of the psyche which make our experience, perception and behaviour distinctly human – although the expression of this may vary widely between cultures and across history. Archetypes are the parts of the psyche which are inherited, instinctual patterns which may be realised in the individual personality. The archetype is a psychosomatic concept, linking body and psyche, instinct and image. Jung did not regard psychology and imagery as correlates or reflections of biological drives as if the latter were primary, and so his assertion that images evoke the aim of the instincts implies that they are linked in a non-hierarchical way.

**Complex**   While the contents of the collective unconscious are the archetypes, complexes are the contents of the personal unconscious in Jung's psychology. A complex is a collection of images, ideas and behaviours which have a common emotional tone; it derives its force ultimately from a corresponding archetype. Complexes contribute to behavioural patterns and are marked by their powerful emotional tone. As Jung said, you do not have complexes but complexes have you!

Jung opposed "monolithic" ideas of personality, proposing that we have many selves or sub-personalities and that it is the complexes which constitute these minor personalities within us and which may, under certain circumstances, behave like independent beings and undermine the best intentions of our ego.

**Ego**   Jung saw the ego as the centre of consciousness, concerned with such matters as maintenance of personality, perception, cognition and mediation between conscious and unconscious. However, he also emphasised that the ego was far from the whole – or the most important part of – the personality and was in fact influenced by what he called the Self (often with a small "s"); thus it is important that the ego–self axis or relationship – which parallels the conscious–unconscious relationship – is fostered and attended to.

**Imaginal world** Analogous to the results and aims of active imagination, the *mundus imaginalis* is a state of psychological perception that is neither wholly rational or sense dependent nor wholly lost in the ego-less realm of dream imagery, but is a state midway between the two. From this state arises insights not normally available to consciousness.

**Individuation** While fostering individuation is the aim of analytical psychology treatment, Jung believed that there was an impetus towards individuation in every living thing. It refers to the tendency for an organism to continue to become itself, to fulfil its own unique potential to become wholly itself. Jung was at pains to emphasise that for humans this would not mean a self-centred *individualism* but, on the contrary, by becoming oneself one was able to be more deeply in touch with the collective and thus with the experience of other people.

*Lapis philosophorum* The philosophers' stone, the goal of the alchemist. The *lapis* is connected to individuation and self-realisation.

**Myth** Jung believed that the preconditions for the formation of myths must be present within the structure of the psyche itself, and that they are experienced by human beings rather than invented. Mythic tales and motifs illustrate what happens in the primitive areas of the mind when an archetype has free rein and there is little conscious intervention on the part of man.

**Numinous** A word first coined by Rudolf Otto in the anthropology of religious experience and used by Jung to describe powerful emotional or spiritual experiences encountered either in dreams or in waking consciousness. Although the power of the experience is archetypal, mysterious and enigmatic, an individual message is conveyed which remains deeply impressive. (Our contention is that some film imagery can have this effect.)

**Self** "The self" is Jung's term for the whole personality, including the ego which is the aspect of personality of which we are consciously aware. The self (spelt with a small "s" in the *Collected Works* to distinguish it from the eastern idea of Atman or the great Self) is so vast we cannot expect to know all of it during our lifetimes, but the task of individuation is to go as far as we can towards this. The self is also an archetypal image of man's fullest potential and the unity of the personality as a whole. The self has another shade of meaning as the unifying principle – the self archetype – within the human psyche, where it occupies the central position of authority in relation to psychological life and, therefore, the destiny of the individual.

**Shadow** The part of the personality that one does not identify with or wishes to disown; it usually refers to negative aspects, but may also include positive aspects that – due to family or social beliefs – have remained rejected and unavailable to the individual. It is an archetype whose powerful affects – obsessional, possessive, autonomous – are capable of startling and overwhelming the well-ordered ego, and it often takes the form of a projection onto others. It is one of the aspects of the unconscious that is encountered early on in a Jungian analysis.

**Symbol** For Jung, if an expression stands for a *known* thing, even if this expression is commonly called "symbolic", it is not a symbol but a *sign*. If an expression stands for an *unknown* something, which, therefore, by definition cannot be expressed or represented more clearly in any way, then such an expression is a *symbol*. For Jung, the *semiotic* refers to representations of *known* things, while the *symbolic* refers to representations of the *unknown*. He understood a symbol as an intuitive idea that cannot yet be formulated in any other or better way. (In the present book, Don Fredericksen goes into this matter in detail.)

*Syzygy* A term applied to any pair of opposites when spoken of as a pair, whether in conjunction or opposition, and most frequently used in relation to the linkage of the masculine and the feminine principles expressed as *anima* and *animus*.

*Temenos* A term borrowed by the alchemists to refer to the womb-like container which was used to combine matter in a closed space and to which heat may be applied. In psychotherapy, the rules or boundaries of the therapist–client relationship provide containment or a *frame* within which the healing may occur. Similarly, we may find film acting as a *temenos* or frame which makes transformative effects possible.

*Note*: For a fuller and more comprehensive collection of definitions we suggest you refer to Andrew Samuels, Bani Shorter and Fred Plaut, *A Critical Dictionary of Jungian Analysis* (London: Routledge, 1986).

# Index